GACE 004 Early Childhood Special Education Teacher Certification Exam

By: Sharon A. Wynne, M.S.

XAMonline, INC.
Boston

To obtain permission(s) to use the material from this work for any purpose including workshops or seminars, please submit a written request to:

XAMonline, Inc.
21 Orient Avenue
Melrose, MA 02176
Toll Free 1-800-301-4647
Email: info@xamonline.com
Web www.xamonline.com

Library of Congress Cataloging-in-Publication Data

Wynne, Sharon A.
GACE: Early Childhood Special Education 004 Teacher Certification / Sharon A. Wynne.
ISBN: 978-1-64239-024-7
1. Early Childhood Special Education 2. Study Guides 3. GACE
4. Teachers' Certification & Licensure 5. Careers

Disclaimer:
The opinions expressed in this publication are the sole works of XAMonline and were created independently from the National Education Association, Educational Testing Service, or any State Department of Education, National Evaluation Systems or other testing affiliates.

Between the time of publication and printing, state specific standards as well as testing formats and website information may change that is not included in part or in whole within this product. Sample test questions are developed by XAMonline and reflect content similar to that on real tests; however, they are not former tests. XAMonline assembles content that aligns with state standards but makes no claims nor guarantees teacher candidates a passing score. Numerical scores are determined by testing companies such as NES or ETS and then are compared with individual state standards. A passing score varies from state to state.

Printed in the United States of America **œ-1**

GACE: Early Childhood Special Education
ISBN: 978-1-64239-024-7

Table of Contents

Great Study and Testing Tips!

What to study in order to prepare for the subject assessments is the focus of this study guide, but equally important is *how* you study.

You can increase your chances of truly mastering the information by taking some simple but effective steps.

Study Tips:

1. **Some foods aid the learning process.** Foods such as milk, nuts, seeds, rice, and oats help your study efforts by releasing natural memory enhancers called CCKs (*cholecystokinin*) composed of *tryptophan*, *choline*, and *phenylalanine*. All of these chemicals enhance the neurotransmitters associated with memory. Before studying, try a light, protein-rich meal of eggs, turkey, and fish. All of these foods release the memory enhancing chemicals. The better the connections, the more you comprehend.

Likewise, before you take a test, stick to a light snack of energy-boosting and relaxing foods. A glass of milk, a piece of fruit, or some peanuts will release various memory-boosting chemicals and help you to relax and focus on the subject at hand.

2. **Learn to take great notes.** A by-product of our modern culture is that we have grown accustomed to getting our information in short doses (e.g., TV news sound bites or newspaper articles styled after USA Today).

Consequently, we've subconsciously trained ourselves to assimilate information in neat little packages. If your notes are scrawled all over the paper, it fragments the flow of the information. Strive for clarity. Newspapers use a standard format to achieve clarity. Your notes can be much clearer through the use of proper formatting. A very effective format is called the *"Cornell Method."*

Take a sheet of loose-leaf lined notebook paper and draw a line all the way down the paper about 1-2" from the left-hand edge.

Draw another line across the width of the paper about 1-2" up from the bottom. Repeat this process on the reverse side of the page.

Look at the highly effective result. You have ample room for notes, a left hand margin for special emphasis items or inserting supplementary data from the textbook, a large area at the bottom for a brief summary, and a little rectangular space for just about anything you want.

3. <u>Get the concept, then the details</u>. Too often we focus on the details and don't gather an understanding of the concept. However, if you simply memorize only dates, places, or names, you may well miss the whole point of the subject.

A key way to understand things is to put them in your own words. If you are working from a textbook, automatically summarize each paragraph in your mind. If you are outlining text, don't simply copy the author's words.

Rephrase them in your own words. You remember your own thoughts and words much better than someone else's, and subconsciously tend to associate the important details with the core concepts.

4. <u>Ask Why?</u> Pull apart written material paragraph by paragraph and don't forget the captions under the illustrations.

Example: If the heading is "Stream Erosion," flip it around to read "Why do streams erode?" Then answer the questions.

If you train your mind to think in a series of questions and answers, not only will you learn more, but it will also help to lessen test anxiety because you are used to answering questions.

5. <u>Read for reinforcement and future needs</u>. Even if you only have 10 minutes, put your notes or a book in your hand. Your mind is similar to a computer; you have to input data in order to have it processed. *By reading, you are creating the neural connections for future retrieval.* The more times you read something, the more you reinforce the learning of ideas.

Even if you don't fully understand something on the first pass, *your mind stores much of the material for later recall.*

6. <u>Relax to learn; go into exile</u>. Our bodies respond to an inner clock called biorhythms. Burning the midnight oil works well for some people, but not everyone.

If possible, set aside a particular place to study that is free of distractions. Shut off the television, cell phone, and pager, and exile your friends and family during your study period.

If you really are bothered by silence, try background music. Light classical music at a low volume has been shown to be particularly effective in aiding concentration. Music that evokes pleasant emotions without lyrics is highly recommended. Try just about anything by Mozart. It relaxes you.

7. Use arrows, not highlighters. At best, it's difficult to read a page full of yellow, pink, blue, and green streaks. Try staring at a neon sign for a while and you'll soon see that the horde of colors obscure the message.

A quick note, a brief dash of color, an underline, or an arrow pointing to a particular passage is much clearer than a horde of highlighted words.

8. Budget your study time. Although you shouldn't ignore any of the material, *allocate your available study time in the same ratio that topics may appear on the test.*

By setting your personal study topics in much the same way that the test will be patterned, you will be better equipped to answer all of the test questions.

Testing Tips:

1. **Get smart, play dumb.** *Don't read anything into the question.* Don't make an assumption that the test writer is looking for something other than what is asked. Stick to the question as written and don't read extra things into it.

2. **Read the question and all the choices *twice* before answering the question.** You may miss something by not carefully reading and re-reading both the question and the answers.

If you really don't have a clue as to the right answer, leave it blank on the first time through. Go on to the other questions, as they may provide a clue as to how to answer the skipped questions.

If, later on, you still can't answer the skipped ones . . . *Guess.* The only penalty for guessing is that you *might* get it wrong. Only one thing is certain; if you don't put anything down, you will get it wrong!

3. **Turn the question into a statement.** Look at the way the questions are worded. The syntax of the question usually provides a clue. Does it seem more familiar as a statement rather than as a question? Does it sound strange?

By turning a question into a statement, you may be able to spot if an answer sounds right, and it may also trigger memories of material you have read.

4. **Look for hidden clues.** It's actually very difficult to compose multiple-foil (choice) questions without giving away part of the answer in the options presented.

In most multiple-choice questions you can often readily eliminate one or two of the potential answers. This leaves you with only two real possibilities; automatically, your odds go to Fifty-Fifty for very little work.

5. **Trust your instincts.** For every fact that you have read, you subconsciously retain something of that knowledge. On questions that you aren't really certain about, go with your basic instincts. *Your first impression on how to answer a question is usually correct.*

6. **Mark your answers directly on the test booklet.** Don't bother trying to fill in the optical scan sheet on the first pass through the test.

Just be very careful not to mismark your answers when you eventually transcribe them to the scan sheet.

7. **Watch the clock!** You have a set amount of time to answer the questions. Don't get bogged down trying to answer a single question at the expense of ten questions you can more readily answer.

SUBAREA I. UNDERSTANDING AND ASSESSING STUDENTS WITH DISABILITIES

OBJECTIVE 1 UNDERSTAND HUMAN DEVELOPMENT

Skill 1.1 Demonstrating knowledge of typical and atypical human growth and development (e.g., cognitive, linguistic, physical, social, emotional)

SOCIAL EMOTIONAL

This topic pertains to children whose behavior or emotional development deviates from society's standards for normal behavior for certain ages and stages of development. Behavioral expectations vary from setting to setting—for example, it is acceptable to yell on the football field, but not as the teacher is explaining a lesson to the class. Different cultures have their own standards of behavior, further complicating the question of what constitutes a behavioral problem. People also have their personal opinions and standards for what is tolerable and what is not. Some behavioral problems are openly expressed; others are inwardly directed and not very obvious. As a result of these factors, the terms behavioral disorders and emotional disturbance have become almost interchangeable.

While almost all children will, at some time, exhibit behaviors that are aggressive, withdrawn, or otherwise inappropriate, the IDEA definition of serious emotional disturbance (SED) (see Objective 17.01) focuses on behaviors that persist over time, are intense, and impair a child's ability to function in society. The behaviors must not be caused by temporary stressful situations or other causes (e.g., depression over the death of a grandparent or anger over the parents' impending divorce). In order for a child to be considered seriously emotionally disturbed, he or she must exhibit one or more of the following characteristics over a **long period of time** and to a **marked degree** that **adversely affects** a child's educational performance**.**

- Inability to learn, which cannot be explained by intellectual, sensory, or health factors
- Inability to maintain satisfactory interpersonal relationships
- Inappropriate types of behaviors
- General pervasive mood of unhappiness or depression
- Physical symptoms or fears associated with personal or school problems
- Schizophrenic children are covered under this definition, and social maladjustment by itself does not satisfy this definition unless it is accompanied by one of the other conditions of SED

The diagnostic categories and definitions used to classify mental disorders come from the American Psychiatric Association's publication Diagnostic and Statistical Manual of Mental Disorders (DSM-IV), the handbook that is used by psychiatrists and psychologists. The DSM-IV is a multiaxial classification system consisting of dimensions (axes) coded along with the psychiatric diagnosis. The axes are:

- Axis I — Principal psychiatric diagnosis (e.g., overanxious disorder)
- Axis II — Developmental problems (e.g., developmental reading disorder)
- Axis III — Physical disorders (e.g., allergies)
- Axis IV — Psychosocial stressors (e.g., divorce)
- Axis V — Rating of the highest level of adaptive functioning (includes intellectual and social). Rating is called Global Assessment Functioning (GAF) score.

While the DSM-IV diagnosis is one way of diagnosing serious emotional disturbance, there are other ways of classifying the various forms that behavior disorders manifest themselves. The following tables summarize some of these classifications.

Externalizing Behaviors	**Internalizing Behaviors**
Aggressive behaviors expressed outwardly toward others	Withdrawing behaviors that are directed inward to oneself
Manifested as hyperactivity, persistent aggression, and irritating behaviors that are impulsive and distractible	Social withdrawal
Examples: hitting, cursing, stealing, arson, cruelty to animals, hyperactivity,	Depression, fears, phobias, elective mutism, withdrawal, anorexia and bulimia

Well-known instruments used to assess children's behavior have their own categories (scales) to classify behaviors. The following table illustrates the scales used in some of the widely used instruments.

Walker Problem Identification Checklist	**Burks' Behavior Rating Scales (BBRS)**	**Devereux Behavior Rating Scale** (adolescent)	**Revised Behavior Problem Checklist** (Quay & Peterson)
Acting out	Excessive self-blame	Unethical behavior	**Major scales**
Withdrawal	Excessive anxiety	Defiant-resistive	Conduct Disorder
Distractibility	Excessive withdrawal	Domineering-sadistic	Socialized aggression
Disturbed peer Relations	Excessive dependency	Heterosexual interest	Attention-problems-immaturity
Immaturity	Poor ego strength	Hyperactive expansive	Anxiety-withdrawal
	Poor physical strength	Poor emotional control	
	Poor coordination	Needs approval, dependency	**Minor scales**
	Poor intellectuality	Emotional disturbance	Psychotic behavior
	Poor academics	Physical inferiority-timidity	Motor excess
	Poor attention	Schizoid withdrawal	
	Poor impulse control	Bizarre speech and cognition	
	Poor reality contact	Bizarre actions	
	Poor sense of identity		
	Excessive suffering		
	Poor anger control		
	Excessive sense of persecution		
	Excessive aggressiveness		
	Excessive resistance		
	Poor social conformity		

Disturbance may also be categorized in degrees: mild, moderate, or severe. The degree of disturbance will affect the type and degree of interventions and services required by emotionally handicapped students. Degree of disturbance must also be considered when determining the least restrictive environment and appropriate education. One example of a set of criteria for determining the degree of disturbance is that developed by P.L. Newcomer:

CRITERIA	DEGREES OF DISTURBANCE		
	Mild	**Moderate**	**Severe**
Precipitating events	Highly stressful	Moderately stressful	Not stressful
Destructiveness	Not destructive	Occasionally destructive	Usually destructive
Maturational appropriateness	Behavior typical for age	Some behavior untypical for age	Behavior too young or too old
Personal functioning	Cares for own needs	Usually cares for own needs	Unable to care for own needs
Social functioning	Usually able to relate to others	Usually unable to relate to others	Unable to relate to others
Reality index	Usually sees events as they are	Occasionally sees events as they are	Little contact with reality
Insight index	Aware of behavior	Usually aware of behavior	Usually not aware of behavior
Conscious control	Usually can control behavior	Occasionally can control behavior	Little control over behavior
Social responsiveness	Usually acts appropriately	Occasionally acts appropriately	Rarely acts appropriately

Source: Understanding and Teaching Emotionally Disturbed Children and Adolescents, (2nd ed., p. 139), by P.L. Newcomer, 1993, Austin, TX: Pro-De. Copyright 1993. Reprinted with permission.

LANGUAGE DEVELOPMENT AND BEHAVIOR

Language is the means whereby people communicate their thoughts, make requests and respond to others. Communication Competence is an interaction of cognitive competence, social knowledge, and language competence. Communication problems may result from any or all of these areas, which directly impact the student's ability to interact with others. Language consists of several components, each of which follows a sequence of development.

Brown and colleagues were the first to describe language as a function of developmental stages rather than age (Reid, 1988 p. 44). Brown developed a formula to group the mean length of utterances (sentences) into stages. Counting the number of morphemes per 100 utterances, one can calculate a mean length of utterance, MLU. Total number of morphemes / 100 = MLU e.g. 180/100 = 1.8.

Summary of Brown's findings about MLU and language development:

Stage	MLU	Developmental Features
L	1.5-2.0	14 basic morphemes (e.g., in, on, articles, possessives)
LI	2.0-2.5	Beginning of pronoun use, auxiliary verbs
LII	2.5-3.0	Language forms approximate adult forms, beginning of questions and negative statements
Lv	3.0-3.5	Use of complex (embedded) sentences
V	3.5-4.0	Use of compound sentences

COMPONENTS OF LANGUAGE

Language learning is made up of five components. Children progress through developmental stages through each component.

Phonology

Phonology is the system of rules about sounds and sound combinations for a language. A phoneme is the smallest unit of sound that combines with other sounds to make words. A phoneme, by itself, may not have a meaning; it must be combined with other phonemes. Problems in phonology may be manifested as developmental delays in acquiring consonants or as reception problems, such as misinterpreting words because a different consonant was substituted.

Morphology

Morphemes are the smallest units of language that convey meaning. Morphemes are root words—free morphemes that can stand alone (e.g., walk) and affixes (e.g., ed, s, ing). Morphology refers to the system of rules for combining morphemes into words. Content words carry the meaning in a sentence, and functional words join phrases and sentences. Generally, students with problems in this area may not use inflectional endings in their words, may not be consistent in their use of certain morphemes, or may be delayed in learning morphemes such as irregular past tenses.

Syntax

Syntax rules, commonly known as grammar, govern how morphemes and words are correctly combined. Wood (1976) describes six stages of syntax acquisition (Mercer, p. 347):

> **Stages 1 and 2** - Birth to about 2 years: Child is learning the semantic system.
> **Stage 3** - Ages 2 to 3 years: Simple sentences contain subject and predicate.
> **Stage 4** - Ages 2 ½ to 4 years: Elements such as question words are added to basic sentences (e.g., where), and word order is changed to ask questions. The child begins to use "and" to combine simple sentences, and embeds words within the basic sentence.
> **Stage 5** - Ages 3 ½ to 7 years: The child uses complete sentences that include word classes of adult language. The child is becoming aware of appropriate semantic functions of words and differences within the same grammatical classes.
> **Stage 6** - Ages 5 to 20 years: The child begins to learn complex sentences and sentences that imply commands, requests, and promises.

Syntactic deficits are manifested when the child uses sentences that lack length or complexity for a child that age. The child may have problems understanding or creating complex sentences and embedded sentences.

Semantics
Semantics is language content: objects, actions, and relations between objects. As with syntax, Wood (1976) outlines stages of semantic development:

- **Stage 1** - Birth to about 2 years: The child is learning meaning while learning his or her first words. Sentences are one-word, but the meaning varies according to the context. Therefore, "doggie" may mean, "This is my dog," or "There is a dog," or "The dog is barking."
- **Stage 2** - About 2 to 8 years: The child progresses to two-word sentences about concrete actions. As more words are learned, the child forms longer sentences; until about age 7, things are defined in terms of visible actions. The child begins to respond to prompts (e.g., pretty/flower). At about age 8, the child can respond to a prompt with an opposite (e.g., pretty/ugly).
- **Stage 3** - Begins at about age 8: The child's word meanings relate directly to experiences, operations, and processes. Vocabulary is defined by the child's experiences, not the adult's. At about age 12, the child begins to give "dictionary" definitions, and the semantic level approaches that of adults.

Semantic problems take the form of:

- Limited vocabulary
- Inability to understand figurative language or idioms; interprets literally
- Failure to perceive multiple meanings of words and changes in word meaning from changes in context, resulting in incomplete understanding of what is read
- Difficulty understanding linguistic concepts (e.g., before/after), verbal analogies, and logical relationships such as possessives, spatial, and temporal
- Misuse of transitional words such as "although" and "regardless"

Pragmatics
Commonly known as the speaker's intent, pragmatics are used to influence or control the actions or attitudes of others. **Communicative competence** depends on how well one understands the rules of language, as well as the social rules of communication, such as taking turns and using the correct tone of voice.

Pragmatic deficits are manifested by failures to respond properly to indirect requests after age 8 (e.g., "Can't you turn down the TV?" elicits a response of "No" instead of "Yes" when the child turns down the volume). Children with these deficits have trouble reading cues that indicate the listener does not understand them. Whereas a person would usually notice this and adjust his or her speech to the listener's needs, the child with pragmatic problems does not do this.

Pragmatic deficits are also characterized by inappropriate social behaviors such as interrupting or monopolizing conversations. Children may use immature speech and have trouble sticking to a topic. These problems can persist into adulthood, affecting academic, vocational, and social interactions.

Problems in language development often require long-term interventions and can persist into adulthood. Certain problems are associated with different grade levels:

- **Preschool and Kindergarten**: The child's speech may sound immature, he/she may not be able to follow simple directions, and often cannot name things such as the days of the week and colors. The child may not be able to discriminate between sounds and the letters associated with the sounds. The child might substitute sounds and have trouble responding accurately to certain types of questions. The child may play less with his or her peers or participate in non-play or parallel play.

- **Elementary School**: Problems with sound discrimination persist, and the child may have problems with temporal and spatial concepts (e.g., before/after). As the child progresses through school, he or she may have problems making the transition from narrative to expository writing. Word retrieval problems may not be very evident because the child begins to devise strategies (such as talking around the word he or she cannot remember, or using fillers and descriptors). The child might speak more slowly, have problems sounding out words, and get confused with multiple-meaning words. Pragmatic problems show up in social situations, such as failure to correctly interpret social cues and adjust to appropriate language, inability to predict consequences, and inability to formulate requests to obtain new information.

- **Secondary School**: At this level, difficulties become more subtle. The child lacks the ability to use and understand higher-level syntax, semantics, and pragmatics. If the child has problems with auditory language, he or she may also have problems with short-term memory. Receptive and/or expressive language delays impair the child's ability to learn effectively. The child often lacks the ability to organize/categorize the information received in school. Problems associated with pragmatic deficiencies persist; because the child is aware of them, he or she becomes inattentive, withdrawn, or frustrated.

Cognitive Development
Children go through patterns of learning, beginning with pre-operational thought processes, and move to concrete operational thoughts. Eventually, they begin to acquire the mental ability to think about and solve problems in their heads because they can manipulate objects symbolically. Children of most ages can use symbols (such as words and numbers) to represent objects and relations, but they need concrete reference points. It is essential children be encouraged to use and develop the thinking skills they possess in solving problems that interest them. The content of the curriculum must be relevant, engaging, and meaningful to the students.

The teacher of special needs students must have a general knowledge of cognitive development. Although children with special needs have a cognitive development rate that may be different than other children, a teacher needs to be aware of some of the activities of each stage as part of the basis to determine what should be taught and when.

The following information about cognitive development was taken from the Cincinnati Children's Hospital Medical Center at www.cincinattichildrens.org.

Some common features indicating a progression from more simple to more complex cognitive development include:

Children (ages 6-12) begin to develop the ability to think in concrete ways. Concrete operations are operations performed in the presence of the object and events that are to be used. Examples: how to combine (addition), separate (subtract or divide), order (alphabetize and sort/categorize), and transform (25 pennies=1 quarter) objects and actions

Adolescents (ages 12-18) begin to develop more complex thinking skills, including abstract thinking, the ability to reason from known principles (form own new ideas or questions), the ability to consider many points of view according to varying criteria (compare or debate ideas or opinions), and the ability to think about the process of thinking.

What cognitive developmental changes occur during adolescence?
During adolescence, the developing teenager acquires the ability to think systematically about all logical relationships within a problem. The transition from concrete thinking to formal logical operations occurs over time. Every adolescent progresses at varying rates in developing his or her ability to think in more complex ways. Each adolescent develops his or her own view of the world. Some adolescents may be able to apply logical operations to school work long before they are able to apply them to personal dilemmas. When emotional issues arise, they often interfere with an adolescent's ability to think in more complex ways. The ability to consider possibilities as well as facts may influence decision making, in either positive or negative ways.

Some common features indicating a progression from more simple to more complex cognitive development:

Early Adolescence
During early adolescence, the use of more complex thinking is focused on personal decision making in school and home environments, including the following:

- Begins to demonstrate use of formal logical operations in school work
- Begins to question authority and society standards
- Begins to form and verbalize his or her own thoughts and views on a variety of topics, usually more related to his or her own life:
    - Which sports are better to play
    - Which groups are better to be included in
    - What personal appearances are desirable or attractive
    - What parental rules should be changed

Middle Adolescence
With some experience in using more complex thinking processes, the focus of middle adolescence often expands to include more philosophical and futuristic concerns, including the following:

- Often questions more extensively
- Often analyzes more extensively
- Thinks about and begins to form his or her own code of ethics
- Thinks about different possibilities and begins to develop his or her own identity
- Thinks about and begins to systematically consider possible future goals
- Thinks about and begins to make his or her own plans
- Begins to think long term
- Use of systematic thinking begins to influence relationships with others

Late Adolescence
During late adolescence, complex thinking processes are used to focus on less self-centered concepts as well as personal decision making, including the following:

- Develops idealistic views on specific topics or concerns
- Debates and develops intolerance of opposing views
- Begins to focus thinking on making career decisions
- Begins to focus thinking on emerging role in adult society
- Increased thoughts about more global concepts such as justice, history, politics, and patriotism

What encourages healthy cognitive development during adolescence?
The following suggestions will help to encourage positive and healthy cognitive development in the adolescent:

- Include adolescents in discussions about a variety of topics, issues, and current events.
- Encourage adolescents to share ideas and thoughts with adults.
- Encourage adolescents to think independently and develop their own ideas.
- Assist adolescents in setting their own goals.
- Stimulate adolescents to think about possibilities of the future.
- Compliment and praise adolescents for well-thought-out decisions.
- Assist adolescents in re-evaluating poorly made decisions for themselves.

Major Stages of Normal Motor and Language Development
The normal progression of learning demonstrated by a child is related to development growth in the areas of gross and fine motor abilities, as well as language development. This table (starting on the next page) presents a compilation of development milestones in motor and language skills that are normally achieved by children and youth of various ages.

Age in Yrs.	Motor (gross and fine)	Language (understood and spoken)
0-1	• Sits without support • Develops one- and two-arm control crawls • Stands • Walks with aid • Begins to indicate hand preference • Pincer grasp develops • Loses sight of object and searches • Transfers objects from one hand to another	• Responds to sound (loud noises, mother's voice) • Turns to sources of sound • Babbles vowel and consonant sounds • Responds with vocalization after adult speaks • Imitates sounds • Responds to words such as "up," "hello," "bye-bye," and "no" if adult gestures
1-2	• Begins scribbling in repetitive, circular motions • Holds pencil or crayon in fist • Walks unaided • Steps up onto or down from low objects • Seats self • Turns pages several at a time • Throws small objects • Turns doorknobs	• Begins to express self with one word and increases to 50 words • Uses several suggestive words to describe events • Understands "bring it here," "take this to Daddy" • Uses "me" or "mine"
2-3	• Begins a variety of scribbling patterns • Holds crayon or pencil with fingers and thumbs • Turns pages singly • Demonstrates stronger preference for one hand • Manipulates clay or dough • Runs forward well • Stands on one foot • Kicks • Walks on tiptoe	• Identifies pictures and objects when they are named • Joins words together in several phrases • Asks and answers questions • Enjoys listening to storybooks • Understands and uses "can't," "don't," "no" • Frustrated when spoken language is not understood • Refers to self by name

3-4	• Pounds nails or pegs successfully • Copies circles and attempts crosses such as "+" • Runs • Balances and hops on one foot • Pushes, pulls, steers toys • Pedals and steers tricycle • Throws balls overhead • Catches balls that are bounced • Jumps over, runs around objects	• Uses words in simple sentence form, such as "I see my book." • Adds "s" to indicate plural • Relates simple accounts of experiences • Carries out a sequence of simple directions • Beings to understand time concepts • Understands comparatives such as bigger, smaller, closer • Language (understood and spoken) • Understands relationships indicated by "because" or "if"
4-5	• Copies crossed lines or squares • Cuts on a line • Prints a few letters of alphabet • Walks backward • Jumps forward • Walks up and down stairs alternating feet • Draws human figures including head and "stick" arms and legs	• Follows several unrelated commands • Listens to longer stories but often confuses them when re-telling • Asks "why," "how," "what for" questions • Understands comparatives such as "fast," "faster," and "fastest" • Uses complex sentences such as "I like to play with my tricycle in and out of the house." • Uses relationship words such as "because" or "so" • General speech is intelligible but may be frequently mispronounced
5-6	• Runs on tiptoe • Walks on balance beam • Skips using alternate feet • Jumps rope • May ride two wheel bicycle • Roller skates • Copies triangles, name, numbers • Has firmly established handedness	• Generally communicates well with family and friends • Spoken language still has errors of subject-tense • Takes turns in conversation • Receives and gives information • With exceptions, use of grammar matches that of adults in family and neighborhood

	• Cuts and pastes large objects and designs • Includes more detail in drawing humans	
7-10	• Continued development and refinement of small muscles in writing, drawing, handling tools • Masters physical skills for game playing • Physical skills become important with peers and self-concept	• Develops ability to understand that words and pictures are representational of real objects • Understands most vocabulary used • Begins to use language aggressively • Verbalizes similarities and differences • Uses language to exchange ideas • Uses abstract words, slang, and often profanity
11-15.	• Adolescent growth spurts begin • May experience uneven growth resulting in awkwardness or clumsiness • Continued improvement in motor development and coordination	• Has good command of spoken and written language • Uses language extensively to discuss feelings and other more abstract ideas • Uses abstract words discriminately and selectively • Uses written language extensively

Source: B.R. Gearhart, Learning Disabilities: Educational strategies, 4th ed., Appendix B, pp. 371-373, 1985. Printed with permission of Charles E.

Skill 1.2 Demonstrating knowledge of the effects of various disabilities on physical, sensory, motor, cognitive, language, social, and/or emotional development and functioning

According to IDEA 2004, *student with a disability* means a student who has not attained the age of 21 prior to September 1st; who is entitled to attend public schools; and who, because of mental, physical, or emotional reasons, has been identified as having a disability that requires special services and programs approved by the department. The terms used in this definition are defined as follows:

The concern of the special educator is how a disability impacts a student's functioning in the education setting. Certainly, having a disability impacts a student socially as he or she learns to interact with others and react to outside responses. (Refer to Objective 29.04 for IDEA definitions and criteria for specific disabilities). General implications various disabilities are as follows.

- **Autism** impacts children to a great extent socially, as communication is difficult. Some autistic individuals report that even eye contact is painful. Because of the neurological component of autism, these children have sensory integration difficulties that may even cause an aversion to tags in clothing and a fixation on eating only a few foods. While some children on the Asperger's end of the autism spectrum have average or even above average intelligence, many other autistic children demonstrate below average intellectual functioning.
- **Deafness** creates a language deficit that impacts social interaction, written language, and reading skills. Because vocabulary and sentence structures are not heard with spontaneous repetition, these must be taught in isolation and sequence. Social language expressions must also be taught. Because of the isolation caused by deafness, these children often demonstrate social immaturity in comparison to their hearing peers.
- **Deaf-Blindness** influences the child with a disability as deafness does, but with additional implications. The deaf-blind child must be taught specialized mobility skills. Print material must be reformatted into large print or Braille according to the student's level of functional vision.
- **Emotional Disturbance** impacts the child's perception of the world and those around him or her. This can result in communication difficulty, inappropriate behavior/language, and possibly physical aggression.
- **Hearing Impairment**, although not as severe as deafness, can impact vocabulary and language development, reading skills, and written language. Again, due to limited exposure to social language, behavior can be immature for the chronological age, and communication is difficult.

- **Learning Disabilities** can impact the understanding of spoken and written language. The ability to attend to a speaker or a task may be compromised. In addition, children with specific learning disabilities may demonstrate inconsistent abilities across subject areas. For example, a student may have a learning disability that affects only math and not the other subject areas.
- **Mental Retardation** is represented by delayed cognitive functioning and social skills. Students who are mentally impaired may function as children of a much younger age.
- **Multiple Disabilities** are more prevalent with the advancing treatment of premature babies and other newborns with medical conditions. A child with multiple disabilities may display any combination of disabilities and associated educational concerns. For example, a child may have an orthopedic impairment and be deaf; the child's language and communication skills would be affected by the deafness, while, at the same time, the child would likely require physical therapy and appropriate orthopedic equipment.
- **Orthopedic Impairment** involves the physical and neurological functioning of the body. A child with an orthopedic impairment may have difficulty with speech articulation, gross motor movements (such as walking or running), and fine motor movements (such as writing or tying shoes). In the case of cerebral palsy, a child may also experience processing delays.
- **Other Health Impairment** means having limited strength, vitality, or alertness—including a heightened alertness to environmental stimuli—that results in limited alertness with respect to the educational environment, that: (i) is due to chronic or acute health problems such as asthma, attention deficit disorder, attention deficit hyperactivity disorder, diabetes, epilepsy, a heart condition, hemophilia, lead poisoning, leukemia, nephritis, rheumatic fever, sickle cell anemia, and Tourette's Syndrome; and (ii) adversely affects a child's educational performance.
- **Speech or Language Impairment** refers to difficulty with pronouncing words (articulation) or communicating through oral language. The language component may be in expressive or receptive language and may, for example, involve forming sentences with appropriate syntax, understanding questions, or being able to comprehend the inferred meaning of a phrase or passage.
- **Traumatic Brain Injury** refers to injury to the brain from an accident which results in physical impairment, speech and language difficulty, memory deficits, and/or physical disability.
- **Visual Impairment Including Blindness** impacts a student's mobility and the use of print text. A student may need to have print material formatted in a larger font or typed into Braille. Because of the inability to see themselves or others, instruction may be needed in personal care and physical appearance.

Skill 1.3 Recognizing the similarities and differences between individuals with and without disabilities in regard to growth and development.

Most children with disabilities will follow a *sequence* of development similar to that of children without disabilities. Depending upon the specific disability, however, the child with a disability will either move through this sequence of development *more slowly*, or *cease to move through this sequence* at some point in development. That is, the child's development will move at a significantly different rate, or become arrested at some point before reaching what would be considered adult level functioning.

This difference in rate or endpoint, however, may affect only one or a few aspects of the child's development. Other aspects of the child's development might very well proceed at what would be considered a normal pace and would proceed just as far as a child without a disability. For example, a child with a specific learning disability such as Dyslexia, might progress through most stages of development (e.g., physical, emotional, cognitive) in a manner similar to that of a child without Dyslexia, but development in one area (learning to read) would progress much more slowly. Similarly, a child with Cerebral Palsy might have serious developmental delays in motor skills, but "normal" progress in language and cognitive skills.

Other Skill sections (1.1, 2.1, and 3.2) discuss developmental difference in children with specific disabilities that affect only one or a few areas of development. Children with some disabilities, however, will experience more global developmental delays that affect most or all developmental areas. Today, these are referred to as Developmental Disabilities.

Common Characteristics of developmental Disabilities
Developmental Disability is a term used to describe lifelong disabilities caused by mental and/or physical impairments that are seen in childhood or infancy. These disabilities usually impact cognitive ability most heavily. The term usually refers to disabilities that affect at least three of the following areas of daily life:

- Learning
- Self-care
- Self-Direction
- Mobility
- Capacity for independent living and economic self-sufficiency
- Receptive and expressive language

Common developmental disabilities include mental retardation, autism, and genetic/chromosomal disorders such as Dow Syndrome and Fragile X Syndrome. These disabilities are discussed in greater detail in later Objective sections.

Skill 1.4 Recognizes the roles families and environment play in the development and learning of individuals with and without disabilities.

The Significance of Family Life and the Home Environment for Student Development and Learning

The student's capacity and potential for academic success within the overall educational experience are products of her or his total environment: classroom and school system, home and family, and neighborhood and community in general. All of these segments are interrelated and can either be supportive of or divisive against one another. As a matter of course, the teacher will become familiar with all aspects of the system, the school, and the classroom pertinent to the students' educational experiences. This includes not only processes and protocols, but also the availability of resources provided to meet the academic, health, and welfare needs of students. It is incumbent upon the teacher to look beyond the boundaries of the school system to identify additional resources as well as issues and situations which will affect (directly or indirectly) a student's ability to succeed in the classroom.

Examples of Resources

- Libraries, museums, zoos, planetariums, etc.
- Clubs, societies, and civic organizations; and community outreach programs of private businesses, corporations, and government agencies. These can provide a variety of materials and media, as well as possible speakers and presenters.
- Departments of social services operating within the local community. These can provide background and program information relevant to social issues that may be impacting individual students. These can also be resources for classroom instruction regarding life skills, at-risk behaviors, etc.
- Organizations devoted to support for specific disabilities. these can not only provide support to families; they are often an excellent source of information and materials for use in helping the student with a particular disability succeed in school.

Initial contacts for resources outside of the school system will usually come from within the system itself: from administration; teacher organizations; department heads; and other colleagues.

Family Contributions and Potential Issues

Family support and involvement is a powerful factor in any student's success in school, and this is even more true of students with disabilities. Much depends on the family's perception of the student. The student's self esteem and self image will depend in large part on the family's view of the student and his/her disability. If the student is a well loved, valued member of the family; if the disability is understood and accepted by the family; if the family recognizes and rewards the child's growth and progress regardless of how it compares to that of other students; if the family is proactive in getting the child's special needs met, this child will have a much better chance of success.

Unfortunately, it is rare to find a family that can meet all these requirements. It is not uncommon, for example, to find parents who cannot accept a child's disability and simply have the attitude that someone (usually the school or the teacher) should "fix" the child. Sometimes parents are unable to accept the fact that their child has a disability and may blame the school or feel that the child should be held to unrealistic standards. Some families feel that if they just hire enough tutors and if the child works hard enough they will "get better." Sometimes this works, but for some children it will not work. Other families might fear the stigma they feel will attach to the family and the child because of the disability. All of these things must be considered when trying to help the student and the family deal with the disability.

Students from multicultural backgrounds may face additional challenges: Curriculum objectives and instructional strategies may be inappropriate and unsuccessful when presented in a single format that relies on the student's understanding/acceptance of the values and common attributes of a specific culture which is not his or her own.

Parental/family influences: Attitude, resources, and encouragement available in the home environment may be attributes for success or failure.

Income: Families with higher incomes are able to provide increased opportunities for students. Students from lower income families will need to depend on the resources available from the school system and the community. This should be orchestrated by the classroom teacher in cooperation with school administrators and educational advocates in the community.

Educational level: Family members with higher levels of education often serve as models for students and have high expectations for academic success.

Additionally, families with specific aspirations for children (regardless of their own educational backgrounds) often encourage students to achieve academic success and are most active participants in the process.

Family crises or dysfunction: A family in crisis (caused by economic difficulties, divorce, substance abuse, physical abuse, etc.) creates a negative environment that may profoundly impact all aspects of a student's life, and particularly his or her ability to function academically. The situation may require professional intervention. It is often the classroom teacher who will recognize a family in crisis situation and instigate an intervention by reporting on this to school or civil authorities.

Regardless of the positive or negative impacts on the students' education from outside sources, it is the teacher's responsibility to ensure that all students in the classroom have an equal opportunity for academic success. This begins with the teacher's statement of high expectations for every student, and develops through planning, delivery, and evaluation of instruction. Such actions provide for inclusion and ensure that all students have equal access to the resources necessary for successful acquisition of the academic skills being taught and measured in the classroom.

OBJECTIVE 2 UNDERSTAND THE VARIOUS CHARACTERISTICS AND NEEDS OF STUDENTS WITH DISABILITIES

Skill 2.1 Demonstrating knowledge of types, prevalence, etiologies, and characteristics of high incidence disabilities

Please refer to Skill 14.4 for the official definitions of disabilities by IDEA and to Skill 2.3 for more on educational implications of disabilities.

The Causation and Prevention of a Disability
No one knows exactly what causes various disabilities. There is a wide range of possibilities that make it almost impossible to pinpoint the exact cause. Listed below are some factors that can attribute to the development of a disability.

Problems in Fetal Brain Development - During pregnancy, things can go wrong in the development of the brain, which alters how the neurons form or interconnect. Throughout pregnancy, brain development is vulnerable to disruptions. If the disruption occurs early, the fetus may die, or the infant may be born with widespread disabilities and possibly mental retardation. If the disruption occurs later, when the cells are becoming specialized and moving into place, it may leave errors in the cell makeup, location, or connections. Some scientists believe that these errors may later show up as learning disorders.

Genetic Factors - Learning disabilities can run in families, demonstrating that there may be a genetic link. For example, children who do not have certain reading skills—such as hearing separate sounds of words—are likely to have a parent with a similar problem. A parent's learning disability can take a slightly different form in the child. Due to this, it is unlikely that specific learning disorders are directly inherited.

Environment - Additional reasons for why disabilities appear to run in families stem from the family environment. Parents with expressive language disorders may talk less to their children, or their language may be muffled. In this case, the lack of a proper role model for acquiring good language skills causes the disability.

Tobacco, Alcohol, and Other Drug Use - Many drugs taken by the mother pass directly to the fetus during pregnancy. Research shows that a mother's usage of cigarettes, alcohol, or other drugs during pregnancy may have damaging effects on the unborn child. Mothers who smoke during pregnancy are more likely to have smaller birth weight babies. Newborns who weigh less than 5 pounds are more at risk for learning disorders.

Heavy alcohol use during pregnancy has been linked to Fetal Alcohol Syndrome (FAS), a condition resulting in low birth weight, intellectual impairment, hyper-activity, and certain physical defects.

Problems During Pregnancy or Delivery - Complications during pregnancy can also cause learning disabilities. The mother's immune system can react to the fetus and attack it as if it were an infection. This type of problem appears to cause newly-formed brain cells to settle in the wrong part of the brain. In addition, during delivery, the umbilical cord can become twisted and temporarily cut off oxygen to the fetus, resulting in impaired brain functions.

Toxins in the Environment - New brain cells and neural networks are produced for a year after the child is born. These cells are vulnerable to certain disruptions. There are certain environmental toxins that may lead to learning disabilities. Cadmium and lead are becoming a leading focus of neurological research. Cadmium is used in making some steel products. It can get into the soil and therefore into the foods we eat. Lead was once common in paint and gasoline, and is still present in some water pipes.

Children with cancer who have been treated with chemotherapy or radiation at an early age can also develop learning disabilities. This is very prevalent in children with brain tumors who received radiation to the skull.

Etiology of Visual Disabilities
Visual impairment can range in severity from minor problems correctable by glasses, to blindness. Blindness is legally defined as having "visual acuity of not greater than 20/200 in the better eye with correction or a field not subtending an angle greater than 20 degrees." Levels of impairment even within this definition may vary from total blindness to the ability to see images of light and dark, to very blurry vision, etc.

There are many causes of blindness in children, including genetic conditions, damage to the eye, prematurity, abnormal shape of the eye or its blood vessels, birth asphyxia, glaucoma, etc. Most of the causes of childhood blindness occur before the child is born and affect the child throughout life.
Etiology of Hearing Disabilities

There are also many levels and causes of hearing loss. Hearing loss can range from total deafness, with no auditory input at all, to minor loss of input, and it can affect the total range of sounds and frequencies or only certain specific frequencies. It can be *conductive,* related to middle ear pathology, or *sensorineural,* related to nerve damage.

Conductive hearing loss can be caused by chronic conditions such as fluid in the ear, frequent ear infections, poor eustachian tube function, tumors, or malformations in the ear. Causes of sensorineural impairments include perinatal infections (e.g., Rubella), heredity, asphyxia at birth, drug use, physical damage after birth or bacterial Meningitis.

In order to prevent disabilities from occurring, information on the causes of disabilities should be widely available so that parents can take the necessary steps to safeguard their children from conception up until the early years of life. While some of the causes of disability are unavoidable or incidental, there are many causes that can be prevented.

Characteristics of Children with Emotional Disabilities
Children with emotional disturbances or behavioral disorders are not always easy to identify. It is usually easy to identify the acting-out child who is constantly fighting, who cannot stay on task for more than a few minutes, or who shouts obscenities when angry. On the other hand, it is not always easy to identify the child who internalizes his or her problems, who may appear to be a "model" student, but suffers from depression, shyness, or fears. Unless the problem becomes severe enough to impact school performance, the internalizing child may go for long periods of time without being identified or served.

Studies of children with behavioral and emotional disorders show they may share some general characteristics:

Lower academic performance: While it is true that some emotionally disturbed children have above average IQ scores, the majority are behind their peers in measures of intelligence and school achievement. Most score in the "slow learner" or "mildly mentally retarded" range on IQ tests, averaging about 90. Many have learning problems that exacerbate their acting out or "giving-up" behavior. As the child enters secondary school, the gap between the child and his or her non-disabled peers widens, often until the child may be as many as 2 to 4 years behind in reading and/or math skills in high school. Children with severe degrees of impairment may be difficult to evaluate.

Social skills deficits: Students with social skills deficits may be uncooperative, selfish in dealing with others, unaware of what to do in social situations, or ignorant of the consequences of their actions. This may be a combination of lack of prior training, lack of opportunities to interact, and dysfunctional value systems and beliefs learned from the family.

Classroom behaviors: Often, emotionally disturbed children display behavior that is highly disruptive to the classroom setting. Outward directed emotionally disturbed children may get out of their seats and run around the room; hit, fight, or disturb their classmates; steal or destroy property; or be otherwise defiant, noncompliant, and/or verbally disruptive. They may not follow directions and often do not complete assignments.

Aggressive behaviors: Aggressive children often fight or instigate their peers to strike back at them. Aggressiveness may also take the form of vandalism or destruction of property. Aggressive children also engage in verbal abuse.

Delinquency: As emotionally disturbed, acting-out children enter adolescence, they may become involved in socialized aggression (e.g., gang membership) and delinquency. Delinquency is a legal term, rather than a medical one; it describes truancy and actions that would be criminal if they were committed by adults. Not every delinquent is classified as emotionally disturbed, but children with behavioral and emotional disorders are especially at risk for becoming delinquent because of their problems at school (the primary place for socializing with peers), deficits in social skills that may make them unpopular at school, and/or dysfunctional homes.

Withdrawn behaviors: Children who manifest withdrawn behaviors may consistently act in an immature fashion or prefer to play with younger children. They may daydream or complain of being sick in order to "escape." They may also cry often, cling to the teacher, ignore those who attempt to interact, or suffer from fears or depression.

Schizophrenia and psychotic behaviors: Children may have bizarre delusions, hallucinations, incoherent thoughts, and disconnected thinking. Schizophrenia typically manifests itself between the ages of 15 and 45: the younger the onset, the more severe the disorder. These behaviors usually require intensive treatment beyond the scope of the regular classroom setting.

Gender: Many more boys than girls are identified as having emotional and behavioral problems, especially hyperactivity and attention deficit disorder, autism, childhood psychosis, and problems with under-control (e.g., aggression, socialized aggression). Girls, on the other hand, have more problems with over-control (e.g., withdrawal and phobias). Boys are much more prevalent than girls in problems with mental retardation and language and learning disabilities.

Age characteristics: When they enter adolescence, girls tend to experience affective or emotional disorders such as anorexia, depression, bulimia, and anxiety at twice the rate of boys, which mirrors the adult prevalence pattern.

Family characteristics: Having a child with an emotional or behavioral disorder does not automatically mean that the family is dysfunctional. However, there are family factors that create or contribute to the development of behavior disorders and emotional disturbance.

- Abuse and neglect
- Lack of appropriate supervision
- Lax, punitive, and/or lack of discipline
- High rates of negative types of interaction among family members
- Lack of parental concern and interest
- Negative adult role models
- Lack of proper health care and/or nutrition
- Disruption in the family

Characteristics of individuals with autism:
This exceptionality appears very early in childhood. Six common features of autism are:

Apparent sensory deficit -The child may appear not to see, hear, or react to a stimulus, and may then react in an extreme fashion to a seemingly insignificant stimulus.

Severe affect isolation - The child does not respond to the usual signs of affection, such as smiles and hugs.

Self-stimulation - Stereotyped behavior takes the form of repeated or ritualistic actions that make no sense to others, such as hand flapping, rocking, staring at objects, or humming the same sounds for hours at a time.

Tantrums and self-injurious behavior (SIB) - Autistic children may bite themselves, pull their hair, bang their heads, or hit themselves. They can throw severe tantrums or direct aggression and destructive behavior toward others.

Echolalia - Also known as "parrot talk," the autistic child may repeat what is played on television or respond to others by repeating what was already said. Alternatively, he or she may simply not speak at all.

Severe deficits in behavior and self-care skills - Autistic children may behave like children much younger than themselves.

Skill 2.2 Demonstrating knowledge of causes and effects of common medical conditions and health impairments affecting students with disabilities (e.g., diabetes, asthma, seizure) affecting students with disabilities

In addition to having a disability that affects learning, students may also have medical conditions and other health impairments that effect the school day. Such medical complications must be considered when developing schedules and curricular plans. Students may miss school due to medical conditions that require extensive rest or hospital-based intervention. Cooperative programs with home and hospital teachers can decrease the impact of such absences.

Also of considerable concern is the tendency to overcompensate. Teachers should try not to focus too much on the medical implications of a student's handicap. Interruptions for suctioning, medication or other medical interventions should not be disruptive to the classroom and learning atmosphere. Focus should be on maximizing opportunities for educational success and social interaction, not on limitations and isolation. For example, class parties can include food treats that meet a student's dietary restrictions, or medical intervention can be completed during individual work times rather than during group learning activity periods.

Students with seizures will require considerable medical support. A seizure is an abnormal electrical discharge in the brain. Incidences and behaviors range from experiencing odd tastes or smells to jerking and spasms throughout the body. The individual may experience altered consciousness or the loss of consciousness, muscle control, or bladder control. Seizures may be triggered by repetitive sounds, flashing lights, video games, touching certain parts of the body, certain drugs, low sugar level, or low oxygen levels in the blood.

Asthma is another well-known condition found in students with and without disabilities. Asthma is a condition in which the person's airway becomes inflamed, often followed by airway constriction. The inflammation may cause coughing, wheezing, tightness of chest, and shortness of breath. The cause of asthma is not completely known, but research indicates that if children are exposed to tobacco smoke, infections, and some allergens early in life, it will increase their chances of developing asthma. Research also indicates there may be a family connection; in many cases, children who have asthma have other family members with this condition. Short-acting inhaled beta-agonists are the preferred quick-relief medicine. The most common side effects of beta-agonists inhalers are rapid heartbeat, headache, nervousness, and trembling. As with all medication, such treatment can be administered only by the nurse.

Juvenile diabetes is another condition that may affect students. It is a condition in which the pancreas cannot produce insulin, or insulin is produced in extremely small amounts. People with type 1 need to take insulin injections in order to live. A student with diabetes should have a plan worked out with the child's doctor and the school nurse. This plan may include such things as allowing the child to eat snacks during the day, monitor blood sugar level, and take insulin shots.

Some students may also require tube feeding. Tube feeding is a method of providing nutrition to people who cannot sufficiently obtain calories by eating or to those who cannot eat because they have difficulty swallowing. Tubes that transport nutritional formulas can be inserted into the stomach (G tubes), through the nose and into the stomach (NG tubes), or through the nose and into the small intestine (NJ tubes). The NG and NJ tubes are considered to be temporary; the G tube is considered more permanent, but it can be removed. Tube feeding is common among students with dysphagia, a condition that hampers swallowing. Other students may need to use catheters. A catheter is a thin, flexible, hollow plastic tube that can be used to perform various diagnostic and/or therapeutic procedures. They are designed to gain access to the body with as little trauma as possible.

Skill 2.3 Recognizing the educational implications of various types of disabilities (e.g., emotional/behavioral disorders, learning disabilities, physical disabilities mental retardation)

Please refer to Skill 1.1 and 14.4.

Learning and development depend upon a broad spectrum of innate, internal, and environmental factors. Children are born with certain mental and physical tools, which are further shaped by the environment. Damage or deficits in any of these myriad factors can produce disabilities. Some disabilities, such as mental retardation, affect the entire range of cognitive abilities. The majority of disabilities, however, directly affect one or more, but usually not all, areas of physical and mental functioning.

This means that often a child's disability will affect some aspects of learning more than others. For example, a child who is blind will not learn visually, but may have cognitive processes that operate the same way, and at the same level as sighted peers. One child may have an "average" or even high processing speed, but a low working memory. Another may have "normal" working memory but a slow processing speed. A child with some forms of Dyslexia may struggle to decode words, but comprehend at a high and abstract level. Another may read aloud well, decoding words efficiently, but without comprehension. This means that a child with a disability may learn in exactly the same way a child without disabilities learns *in some areas* and for learning in those areas, standard "good practice" instructional techniques will work for the child. In the area(s) impacted by the disability, however, the child may learn differently and need special accommodations or instructional techniques to address those special needs.

In order to address the different manner in which a child with a disability learns, it is necessary to understand the specific child's disability and how it is affected by the specific child's environment. Later Objective sections address methods for assessing a child's disability and designing instructional techniques appropriate for the child's needs. There are some *general* similarities, however, among children with disabilities, and the special education teacher should be aware of them and plan for instruction and accommodations to address them.

Characteristics of children with mild learning, intellectual, and behavioral disabilities:

- Lack of interest in schoolwork
- Prefer concrete rather than abstract lessons
- Possess weak listening skills
- Low achievement; limited verbal and/or writing skills
- Respond better to active rather than passive learning tasks
- Have areas of talent or ability often overlooked by teachers
- Prefer to receive special help in regular classroom
- Higher dropout rate than regular education students
- Achieve in accordance with teacher expectations
- Require modification in classroom instruction and are easily distracted
- Characteristics of students who have specific learning disabilities:
- Hyperactivity - a rate of motor activity higher than normal
- Perceptual difficulties - visual, auditory, and perceptual problems
- Perceptual-motor impairments - poor integration of visual and motor systems, often affecting fine motor coordination.
- Disorders of memory and thinking - memory deficits, trouble with problem-solving, poor concept formation and association, poor awareness of own metacognitive skills (learning strategies)
- Impulsiveness - acts before considering consequences and has poor impulse control, often followed by remorselessness.
- Academic problems in reading, math, writing or spelling, with significant discrepancies in ability levels

Mental Retardation" is the term historically applied to overall developmental delays and disabilities in all academic and cognitive abilities. Children with this condition generally display significantly below average intellectual functioning on all cognitive measures, as well as deficits in at least two adaptive skills. These problems typically impact all aspects of the educational experience. The degree of cognitive impairment will have a profound impact on the choice of educational programming. In addition, a child with these generalized disabilities will probably need life-long assistance in some form. Characteristics with regard to the degree of cognitive impairment fall into four categories.

Mild (IQ of 50-55 to 70) This level is sometimes referred to as " generalized learning disability" today, in order to avoid the stigma often associated with the term, "retardation."

- Delays in most areas (communication, motor, academic)
- Often not distinguished from normal children until of school age.
- Can acquire both academic and vocational skills; can become self-supporting

Moderate IQ of 35-40 to 50-55)
Only fair motor development; clumsy
Poor social awareness
Can be taught to communicate
Can profit from training in social and vocational skills; needs supervision, but can perform semiskilled labor as an adult

Severe (IQ of 20-25 to 35-40)
Poor motor development
Minimal speech and communication
Minimal ability to profit from training in health and self-help skills: may contribute to self-maintenance under constant supervision as an adult

Profound (IQ below 20-25)
Gross retardation, both mental and sensor-motor
Little or no development of basic communication skills
Dependency on others to maintain basic life functions
Lifetime of complete supervision (institution, home, nursing home)

Teachers of special education students should be aware of the similarities as well as the differences between areas of disabilities.

Students with disabilities (in all areas) may demonstrate difficulties with social skills. For a student with hearing impairment, social skills may be difficult because of not hearing social language. However, the emotionally disturbed student may have difficulty because of a special type of psychological disturbance. An autistic student, as a third example, would be unaware of the social cues given with voice, facial expression, and body language. Each of these students would need social skill instruction, but in a different way.

Students with disabilities (in all areas) may demonstrate difficulty in academic skills. A student with mental retardation will need special instruction across all areas of academics, while a student with a learning disability may need assistance in only one or two subject areas.

Students with disabilities may demonstrate difficulty with independence or self-help skills. A student with a visual impairment may need specific mobility training, while a student with a specific learning disability may need a checklist to help in managing materials and assignments.

Special education teachers should be aware that although students across disabilities may demonstrate difficulties in similar ways, the causes may be very different. For example, some disabilities are due to specific sensory impairments (hearing or vision), some to cognitive ability (mental retardation), and some to neurological impairment (autism or some learning disabilities). The reason for the difficulty should be a consideration when planning the program of special education intervention.

Additionally, special education teachers should be aware that each area of disability has a range of involvement. Some students may have minimal disability and require no services. Others may need only a few accommodations and have 504 Plans. Some may need an IEP (Individualized Education Program) that outlines a specific special education program to be implemented in an inclusion/resource program, self-contained program, or in a residential setting.

A student with ADD may be able to participate in the regular education program with a 504 Plan that outlines a checklist system to keep the student organized and additional communication between school and home. Other students with ADD may need instruction in a smaller group with fewer distractions and would be better served in a resource room.

When planning an appropriate special education program, special educators should be knowledgeable of the cause and severity of the disability as well as its manifestations in the specific student. Because of the unique needs of the child, such programs are documented in the child's IEP.

The special education teacher will need to be prepared to address these common areas of difficulty by assessing each child's specific needs and strengths and designing instruction accordingly.

Skill 2.4 Recognizing the uses and possible effects of various types of medications (e.g., stimulant, antidepressant, seizure) in relations to students' learning, development, and functioning

Many students with disabilities will be taking medication to help them cope with those disabilities. These medications may cause side effects, impacting behavior and educational development. Teachers should be knowledgeable of some of the possible side effects to ensure they don't misperceive the child's behavior. Some medications may impair concentration, which can lead to poor processing ability, lower alertness, and drowsiness and hyperactivity. Students who take several medications may have an increased risk of behavioral and cognitive side effects.

Students' parents should let the school know when they are beginning or changing medication so they can look out for possible side effects. If educators are aware of the types of medication that their students are taking, along with the possible side effects, they will be able to respond more positively when some of the side effects of the medication change their students' behaviors, response rates, and attention spans.

Antidepressants
There are three different classes of antidepressants that students might take.

- ***Selective serotonin-reuptake inhibitors (SSRIs):*** The SSRIs block certain receptors from absorbing serotonin. Over time, SSRIs may cause changes in brain chemistry. The side effects of SSRIs include dry mouth, insomnia or restless sleep, increased sweating, and nausea. They can also cause mood swings in people with bipolar disorders.

- **Tricyclic antidepressants:** These are considered good for treating depression and obsessive-compulsive behavior. They cause similar side effects to the SSRIs, such as sedation; tremor, seizures, dry mouth, light sensitivity, and mood swings in people with bipolar disorders.

- **Monoamine oxidase inhibitors (MAOIs):** These are not as widely used as the other two types, because many have unpleasant and life-threatening interactions with other drugs, including common over-the-counter medications. People taking MAOIs must also follow a special diet, because these medications interact with many foods. The list of foods to avoid includes chocolate, aged cheeses, and more.

Stimulants

Stimulants are often prescribed to help with Attention Deficit Disorder (ADD) and Attention Deficit Hyperactivity Disorder (ADHD). The drugs can have many side effects including agitation, restlessness, aggressive behavior, dizziness, insomnia, headache, or tremors.

In severe cases of anxiety, an anti-anxiety medication (tranquilizer) may be prescribed. Most tranquilizers have a potential for addiction and abuse. They tend to be sedating, and can cause a variety of unpleasant side effects, including blurred vision, confusion, sleepiness, and tremors.

OBJECTIVE 3 Understand factors affecting learning and development of students with disabilities

Skill 3.1 Demonstrating knowledge of the effects (e.g., on education, recreation) of various disabilities on learning and behavior

Sensory Disabilities
Sensory or perceptual disabilities are deficits in one or more of the five senses. The most common sensory disabilities relevant to education are visual and hearing disabilities. Although there are a number of types and levels of such disabilities, most of them affect a child's learning and education in one of two primary ways:

INPUT: Since we use our senses to acquire information (input), visual and hearing disabilities restrict children's **access** to and ability to interact with the environment around them. Whether in daily life or school, in order to learn the child receives information from the surrounding world and responds to it. Reducing this information flow or hindering interaction with it can cause delays in both development and learning. When *access* is the primary problem for learning, solutions will concentrate on accommodations, or assistive technology, alternative methods of gaining access (e.g., hearing aids, sign language, Braille books, books on tape, etc.). Even when alternative methods of gaining access are available, the teacher must often make up for past deprivation with remedial work. It is not uncommon for a sensory disability to accompany other, more cognitive disabilities and this combination will further impact learning.

PROCESSING: in some cases, the visual or hearing disability is not a problem of restricted input, but a problem in mental processing or integration of sensory input (e.g., Central Auditory Processing Deficits, Visual Integration deficits, Sensory Integration Disorders). These disabilities lie within the brain and affect a child's ability to *use and integrate* sensory information. These disabilities require specialized instructional methods, alteration in the speed and/or format in which information is presented, and occasionally, assistive technology.

OUTPUT: In both types of disabilities, alternative methods of output may also be required. In other words, the child may need to be allowed to demonstrate what he knows in a manner different from that of other students.

Deaf-Blindness
The loss of vision and hearing cause more challenges when combined than individually. Deaf-blindness impacts motor skills, such as the ability to walk and move. It also impacts communication skills, including the ability to request things and to let others know feelings or expressions of displeasure. It also affects general development, such as the possibility of low muscle tone and development.

Deaf-Blindness impacts sensory information access, as mentioned above. Since BOTH senses are impacted, it is not possible to use one sense to compensate for the lack of the other. For example, if a child is blind, access to textbooks can be through books on CD. This will not help the child who is also deaf.
The access to generalized information for learning can also be impacted, as information is not learned incidentally. Information is learned through direct one-on-one instruction. The information received through distance senses can vary; for some, vision and hearing are progressively lost, while for others, it is a life-long disability.

Motivation to interact with the environment can be reduced due to the effect of vision and hearing loss. This will impact the individual throughout his or her life and career choices, and may make the individual more solitary (although he or she will need help and support to function effectively in society).

Impaired vision and hearing interfere with the individual's ability to understand and respond to the communication and movement of others in the environment. The impact on recreation is also very high, as many sporting activities require the use of sight or sound to appreciate them. When choosing a career, individuals with deaf-blindness have a limited number of professions they can go into, as their disabilities impact their abilities to see and communicate.

Attention Deficit Disorders
A person with ADD or ADHD is at an increased risk of having brain malfunctions that can lead to lack of insight and foresight, lack of fear and remorse, impulsivity, poor abstract thinking and social skills, low anger threshold, an inability to realize the consequences of actions or to learn from experience, and a lack of empathy for animals and people.

ADD has a clear impact on the learning and behavior of individuals throughout life. In the school setting, ADD can render an individual unable to pay attention to details, or give him or her a tendency to make careless errors in school or other activities. The individual may also have difficulty sustaining attention in task or play activities. This will impact individuals in school and when they get jobs, as they may not be able to focus on tasks and complete them satisfactorily. They have problems following instructions and problems with organization. Individuals with ADD have a tendency to lose things like homework, keys, or work assignments. They are also distractible and can be very forgetful.

Attention Deficit Disorders can also affect *input and output* in much the same way sensory disabilities do (see above). If the student is unable to *attend* to the information the teacher is providing, the student will, in effect, lack *access* to that information. Since Attention Deficit Disorders typically have a negative impact on organization of information, such disabilities may also affect the student's ability to *process* the information once received.

About half of all children with ADHD also have a specific **learning disability**. The most common learning problems are reading dyslexia and difficulty with handwriting. Although ADHD isn't categorized as a learning disability, its interference with concentration and attention can make it even more difficult for a child to perform well in school.

Autism

Individuals with autism are affected by their symptoms every day; this sets them apart from unaffected students. Because of problems with receptive language, they can have problems understanding some classroom directions and instruction, along with subtle vocal and facial cues from teachers. This inability to fully decipher the world around them often makes education stressful. Teachers need to be aware of a student's disorder, and should ideally have specific training in autism education. This will enable them to better help the student get the best out of his or her classroom experiences.

Individuals with autism spectrum disorders sometimes have high levels of anxiety and stress, particularly in social environments like school and work. If an individual shows aggressive or explosive behavior, it is important for educational teams to recognize the impact of stress and anxiety.

Skill 3.2 Recognizing the impact of physical and health-related disabilities on individuals, their families, and society

Children with physical impairments possess a variety of disabling conditions. Although there are significant differences among these conditions, similarities also exist. Each condition usually affects one particular system of the body: the cardiopulmonary system (i.e., blood vessels, heart, and lungs), the neurological system (i.e., spinal cord, brain nerves), or the musculoskeletal system (i.e., muscles, bones). Some conditions develop during pregnancy, birth, or infancy. Other conditions occur later due to injury (trauma), disease, or factors not fully understood.

In addition to motor disorders, individuals with physical disabilities may have multi-disabling conditions such as concomitant hearing impairments, visual impairments, perceptual disorders, speech defects, behavior disorders, mental handicaps, or difficulties with performance and emotional responsiveness. Some characteristics of individuals with physical disabilities and other health impairments are:

- Lack of physical stamina; fatigue
- Chronic illness; poor endurance
- Deficient motor skills; normal movement may be prevented
- Physical limitations or impeded motor development; a prosthesis or an orthosis may be required.
- Limited mobility or inability to explore one's environment
- Limited self-care abilities
- Progressive weakening and degeneration of muscles
- Frequent speech and language defects; communication may be prevented; echolalia orthosis may be present
- May experience pain and discomfort throughout the body
- May display emotional (psychological) problems, which require treatment
- Social adjustments may be needed; may display maladaptive social behavior
- May necessitate long-term medical treatment, which can become a financial burden on the family
- May have embarrassing side effects from certain diseases or treatment
- May exhibit erratic or poor attendance patterns, which leads to the child missing many skills and the parent or caregiver to miss days of work

Related Technology
Technology has helped individuals with physical and health impairments to gain access to and control of the environments around them, to communicate with others, and to take advantage of health care. In addition to high-tech devices such as computers, there are low-tech devices like built-up spoons and crutches. Computers, spell checkers, and automated language boards provide means for communication to occur.

Mobility has been assisted by use of lightweight or electric specialized wheelchairs. These include motorized chairs, computerized chairs, chairs in which it is possible to rise, wilderness sports chairs, and racing chairs (Smith & Luckasson, 1992). Electronic switches allow persons with only partial movement (e.g., head, neck, fingers, toes) to be more mobile. Even driving a car is possible. Mobility is also enhanced by the use of artificial limbs, personalized equipped vans, and electrical walking machines.

Skill 3.3 Demonstrating knowledge of the effects of different learning environments, classroom management strategies, and intervention techniques on students' development and learning

(See also Skill 7.1 for placement options)

It may be determined at a student's IEP meeting that some time in the general education setting is appropriate. The activities and classes listed for inclusion may be field trips, lunch, recess, physical education, music, library, art, computers, math, science, social studies, spelling, reading, and/or English. The IEP will specify which classes and activities, as well as the amount of time that the student will spend with general education peers. The IEP will also list any modifications or accommodations that will be needed.

Modifications that may be considered for the general education classroom include the amount of work or type of task required. Modifications for a student with a learning disability might include a reduced number of spelling words or a task of writing the vocabulary word that goes with a given definition instead of writing the definition that goes with a given word.

Accommodations are changes made to the school environment or a student's use of necessary equipment to overcome a disability. For example, an accommodation for a student with a hearing impairment might include the use of an auditory trainer or another student to serve as a note-taker.

Prior to the student starting in a general education placement (regardless of the minutes on the IEP), the general education teacher and support staff (if any) should be trained on the student's disability and his or her needs according to the IEP. Sometimes this training happens as the student's IEP is developed. Other times it is done at a later date.

Student expectations in the inclusion setting:

The student with a disability should be well aware of his or her responsibilities in the general education setting ahead of time. These expectations should be a combination of behavior and task performance. Although students should be aware of needed accommodations and modifications, and should be self-advocates for such, they should not use their disabilities as excuses for not fulfilling the expectations.

Students may benefit from previewing material, using a checklist to keep track of materials and assignments, keeping an assignment notebook, reviewing materials after the lesson, and using study aids such as flashcards. Sometimes, a behavior tracking chart may also be used.

Monitoring student progress in the inclusion setting:

Once the student is in the general education setting for the time and activities listed on the IEP, the special education teacher will need to monitor student progress. This can be done through verbal follow-up with the general education teacher or by asking the teacher to complete a progress form periodically. Of course, grades and the student's ability to restate learned information or answer questions are also indicators.

Evaluation of the student's future placement in the inclusion setting:

If the student is successful in the general education activities and classes listed on the IEP, the special education teacher may consider easing back on modifications and accommodations on the next IEP. He or she may also consider adding minutes or classes for student's general education inclusion.

If the student has difficulty in the general education activities and classes, the special educator may consider adding more modifications or accommodations on the next IEP. If the student had significant difficulty, he or she may need to receive more services in the special education classroom.

Classroom Management Strategies

Effective classroom management strategies can impact the learning environment for students with disabilities. There are a number of strategies that can be used to foster an environment for learning.

Expect the best from all students in the classroom. The positive relationship between high teacher expectations and high student behavior has been demonstrated. Expecting students to succeed is an effective classroom management technique. Teachers who expect the best from students and are able to communicate these expectations will receive respect and cooperation from their students. This is the first step to reducing behavior problems.

Make the behavior expectations clear by spelling out exactly what the rules of the class are at the beginning of the school year in a positive manner. Give examples of a student following the rule and a student not following the rule, so that everyone is clear how the rule is to be carried out. It is a good practice to include the students in the rule-making process, as this will give them ownership of the rules and will make them more likely to follow them.

Have plenty of rewards in place with minimal punishments. Discipline problems can arise when educators overuse punishment. The use of rewards is a better system of ensuring good behavior, as a reward brings attention to good behaviors and provides models for all students.

Ensure that any punishment given fits the crime or rule that was broken. If several students were misbehaving, it would not be appropriate to punish the entire class. This approach will anger the students who are not misbehaving and may even cause additional problems. If there is no natural punishment to fit the student's misbehavior, an alternative would be to remove privileges, such as extra computer time, from the student who misbehaves.

Be consistent with rewards and punishments. If rules and consequences are not done consistently, discipline problems will occur. Teachers should also make sure they get to know each student well so they can modify the punishments and rewards based on the individual student's likes and dislikes. A punishment to one student may be a reward to another.

Skill 3.4 Demonstrating knowledge of the effects of cultural, linguistic, and socioeconomic differences on learning and development and strategies for addressing such differences

The United States is a pluralistic, multicultural society and the students in its educational institutions reflect the richness of this diversity in their ethnic, cultural, and language backgrounds. It is important, therefore, to understand the impact this diversity will have on learning.

Consideration for ELL (English Language Learner) Students
Since not only reading, but most school subjects involve language based skills, it is obvious that native language will have a profound impact on acquiring these skills. Even children who are not officially classified as ELL students may be from non-English speaking backgrounds that will impact their learning.

It is important to remember that ALL the components of language described in earlier skills are significantly different for ELL students. The phonology of their language will be different. English has a set of 44 phonemes. While there will be varying amounts of overlap with other languages, their phonemes will not be identical. English will have some that the other languages do not have and the child's language will have phonemes that may conflict with English phonemes. The morphology of their language, the rules for making words, will also differ. Units of meaning will differ. Some may *look or sound* the same but have very different meanings, thus interfering with learning to read in English.

The syntax, rules for making sentences, for order and placement of words, will also differ, often interfering with reading in English. Even pragmatics and body language will differ. Experience with print may also differ significantly. Some languages read from right to left or top to bottom. Others print only consonants and have complex rules for adding vowel sounds when speaking. Such differences will also impact learning to read in English.

Jim Cummins (1994 and 1999) describes the stages of second language learning and how they impact academics and learning to read in English. He describes two levels of English language acquisition: BICS and CALP.

BICS (Basic Interpersonal Communication Skills) are the conversational English skills that are learned first. Conversational English is highly contextualized; that is, it is supported by facial expressions, body language, gestures and other supports found in face to face communication. It is also relatively undemanding cognitively. BICS takes about 2 years to fully master.

CALP (Cognitive Academic Language Proficiency) refers to the language level needed to learn academic subjects taught in that language. This form of language proficiency depends heavily on linguistic cues alone, has very little context, and is far more formal and difficult to learn. This is the form of English that is used in classrooms and textbooks. Research shows that average time to proficiency varies with age of arrival in the US:

- Age 8-11 at arrival: 4-5 years to proficiency
- Age 5-7 at arrival: 5-8 years to proficiency
- Age 12+ at arrival: Longer...and probably will not reach this level by High School graduation

In teaching ELL students, it is important to remember that BICS fluency, fluency with everyday conversation, is NOT the same as CALP fluency, the fluency needed to learn to read and read to learn in English as a second language.
Reading and the ELL Learner

Research has shown that there is a positive and strong correlation between a child's literacy in his/her native language and his/her learning of English. This means that fostering progress in native language literacy is a perquisite for second language (English) reading progress. The degree of native language proficiency and literacy is a strong predictor of English language development. Children who are literate and engaged readers in their native languages can more easily transfer their skills to a second language (i.e., English).

What this means is that educators should not approach the needs of all ELL learners in reading in the same way. Those whose families are not from a focused oral literacy and reading culture in the native language will need additional oral language rhymes, read-alouds, and singing as supports for reading skills development in both their native and the English language.
Cultural and Ethnic Factors

Even without the language difference itself, cultural and ethnic differences will impact learning in all subject areas. As noted earlier, the child's background experiences are crucial to comprehending both what they read and classroom discussions. Some of the most important instructional strategies for comprehension involve "priming" or "activating" the child's prior experiences that are relevant to the material to be read. Children from different cultures come equipped with very different background experiences and the teacher may not know HOW to activate them because they are unfamiliar to the teacher.

Children in American culture will have experience with certain nursery rhymes, historical figures, even television shows and fictional characters. Students from other cultures may not share these experiences and may be confused by offhand references to them by teachers and in literature. For example, one child from a background that did not contain the Santa Claus figure was very confused by a holiday story that involved hanging stockings by the fire and finding them filled with candy the next morning. The only reason this child could imagine for hanging a stocking by the fire was to dry it out because it had gotten wet. The child, therefore, felt that the Santa figure was mean to put candy in a dirty, wet sock where it would get all mushy. Naturally enough, this child "failed" to identify the "main idea" in the story.

It is recommended that all teachers of reading, and particularly those who are working with ELL students, learn as much as they can about their students' background, and use meaningful, student-centered and culture- customized activities. These activities may include: language games, word walls and poems. Some of these activities might also, if possible, be initiated in the child's first language and then reiterated in English.

Cultural Perceptions of Students with Disabilities

Different cultures place varying values on education and the role of genders. As a result, different views may be taken regarding individuals with disabilities, as well as their appropriate education, career goals, and roles in society. Special educators must become familiar with the cultural origins of their students and the communities in which they teach. Educators who demonstrate respect for different students' cultures will build the rapport necessary to work with the student, family, and community to prepare him or her for future, productive work, independence, and possible post-secondary education or training (IDEA 2004).

While society has progressed, and many things are more acceptable today than they were years ago, having a disability still carries a stigma. Historically, people with disabilities have been ostracized from their communities. Up until the 1970s, a large number of people with special needs were institutionalized at birth because relatives either did not know what to do, felt embarrassed to admit they had a child with a disability, or gave in to the cultural peer pressure to put their "problem" away. Sometimes, this meant hiding a child's disability, which may even have meant locking a child in a room in the house. Perhaps the worst viewpoint of society, largely expressed up to the 1970s and still prevalent in some cultures today, is that the person with "special needs" is unable to contribute to society.

Today, American society has eliminated the "must institutionalize" method in favor of a "normalize" concept. Houses in local communities have been purchased for the purpose of providing supervision and/or nursing care that allows for people with severe disabilities to have "normal" social living arrangements. Congress passed laws that have allowed those with disabilities to access public facilities (See Skill 14.2). American society has widened doorways, added special bathrooms, and undergone other useful physical transformations. The regular education classroom teacher is now learning to accept and teach students with special needs. America's media today has provided education and frequent exposure of people with special needs. The concept of acceptance appears to be occurring for those with physically noticeable handicaps.

However, the appearance of those with special needs in media, (such as television and movies), are generally those who rise above their "label" as disabled because of an extraordinary skill. Most people in the community are portrayed as accepting the "disabled" person when that special skill is noted. In addition, those who continue to express revulsion or prejudice towards the person with a disability often express remorse when the special skill is noted or when peer pressure becomes too intense. This portrayal often ignores those who appear normal by appearance with learning and emotional disabilities, who often feel and suffer from the same prejudices.

The most significant group any individual faces is that of his or her peers. Pressure to appear normal and not "needy" in any area is still intense from early childhood to adulthood. During teen years, when young people are beginning to express their individuality, the very appearance of walking into a special education classroom can bring feelings of inadequacy, as well as labeling by peers that the student is "special." Being considered normal is the desire of almost all individuals with disabilities, regardless of the age or disability. People with disabilities today, as many years ago, still measure their successes by how their achievements mask or hide their disabilities.

The most difficult cultural/community outlook on those who are disabled comes in the adult work world, where disabilities of persons can become highly evident—often causing those with special needs to have difficulties in finding work and keeping their jobs. This is particularly difficult for those who have not learned to self advocate or accommodate for their area/s of special needs.

Skill 3.5 Recognizing the impact of language development and listening comprehension on students' learning

Please refer to the Language Development and Behavior section of Skill 1.1 for more information on the impact of deficits in overall language development.

Listening Comprehension

Listening comprehension is often referred to as *potential reading level* because it does not require reading skills. The assumption is that a child's listening comprehension will be higher than reading comprehension because the information does not require the additions skills needed for reading. When a child reaches complete automaticity in reading and decoding, reading comprehension should approach that of listening comprehension.

Since comprehension skills, as opposed to decoding skills, are similar to reading comprehension skills, it follows that a child's listening comprehension skills will affect the ultimate success in reading comprehension.

Reading Aloud to Children

Reading aloud to children helps build vocabulary and listening comprehension. It allows modeling of fluent reading and builds a love of reading.

During the preschool years, children acquire cognitive skills in oral language that they apply later on to reading comprehension. Reading aloud to young children is one of the most important things that an adult can do because they are teaching children how to monitor, question, predict, and confirm what they hear in the stories. In addition, reading to children provides vicarious experiences that can expand the cognitive context and schemata children can use to comprehend new material as they read. Research by Roe (1985, 1986) demonstrated that even a short (7 week) program of daily hour-long read alouds to kindergarten through second grade children significantly improved vocabulary skills.

Other Strategies to Enhance Oral Language Skills and Listening Comprehension
In addition to reading aloud to children, several other classroom strategies can improve listening comprehension as a prelude to reading comprehension.

Wordless picture books can be used to allow children to practice oral story telling skills, as well as to provide oral descriptions of pictures. This can be done by individual students, or the class as a group can make a sequential story in which each child's contribution is in part determined by the previous child's addition. This enhances both oral and listening skills, as well as cognitive concepts of making events match and follow a logical sequence.

Visualizing and describing what you see or visualize to other students so they can draw or describe it also promotes oral language skills. A variety of games and activities can use this format. These skills will contribute to eventual comprehension and writing tasks.

Oral Sharing and Questioning of all sorts can be helpful in developing language and listening skills. Whether it is "show and tell" time, book report time, or "news of the day" time, such oral sharing and queries help language development.

Listening for specific information in stories or articles read aloud to students is also helpful. If students are told to raise a hand when they hear a certain word or piece of information, (or, for more inferential tasks, a *clue* of some sort), they will listen with more purpose. In addition, the resulting experience is very close to what they will need to do later when they must refer to something they have read to find specific information.

Listening to classmates is another skill that can improve language development. In any classroom discussion, the teacher can periodically ask a student what a classmate just said. This forces them to listen to one another and not only to attend, but to process the meaning of one another's comments

Skill 3.6 Recognizing the impact of various disabilities on information-processing skills and on expressive/receptive language skills

Language development begins from the moment of birth. Children develop receptive language (their ability to understand language) skills first. Students can typically understand things well above their age level. When something interferes with that naturally developing skill, many different things are impacted beyond the language skill itself. Children often become frustrated because they misunderstood someone, or they may complete an activity inappropriately. This may then lead to a correction, which the student does not understand. Imagine being told to go close your closet door, and when you do, someone corrects you and tells you it was wrong. All you know is that you were told to close your closet door: that's what you understood. It becomes a very frustrating experience for both the child and adult.

Additionally, receptive language skills develop to include the ability to process and follow more than one direction at a time. Some students with deficits are unable to do this task. They need directions broken down into one step at a time in order to be successful. In some cases they need visual demonstration to accompany the verbal instructions, etc. Sometimes these misunderstandings lead to behavioral issues, which can be usually be solved through improving the receptive language skills of the child, by using different vocabulary, or by supplementing the oral language when communicating with the student.

After receptive language develops, expressive language (oral language) begins. Difficulties here can be just as frustrating for the student. These students are trying their best to communicate and get their points across, but no one seems able to understand what they are saying. Sometimes this is due to an articulation issue—a problem in the way words are pronounced (see below). Other times it is due to the fact that they are unable to put their feelings or thoughts into the appropriate words.

We have all been at the loss to recall a word. Phrases like "it's on the tip of my tongue" have become clichés because it is an occurrence that afflicts everyone once in awhile. For children with expressive language difficulties, it happens much more frequently. Behaviorally, they can become irritated and angry simply because no one understands what they are trying to communicate.

Both expressive and receptive language are integral parts of the learning process. Numerous research studies have been completed indicating that lecture is still the most used method of delivering information in classrooms. If a child struggles with language, this method is not going to work well for them. In fact, it will probably be one of the least effective methods. Furthermore, in the continuum of learning any skill—from reading to math or science to social studies—the basis for all learning begins with language.

Speech and Language Disorders
As a group, youngsters with speech and language impairments generally score below normal children on measures of intelligence, achievement, and adaptive social skills. However, this is in part attributable to the fact that a large percentage of children with mental, physical, behavioral, and learning disabilities exhibit speech and language disorders secondary to their major disability. Children with markedly deviant or delayed speech and language generally have concurrent difficulties with severe intellectual disabilities, chronic emotional/behavioral disturbances, or acute hearing problems, and function at a delayed developmental level. Some of it is due to the distortion in assessment that occurs when language disabilities interfere with comprehension of instructions, demonstration of knowledge, or both (see assessment issues in the next Objective).

Children with speech impairments who have no observable organic defects perform slightly lower than average on tests of motor proficiency. Problems are most likely to occur in the areas of coordination, application of strength, and rhythm. Children with communication disorders tend to demonstrate less interaction with peers.

In addition to these general characteristics, children with cleft palates tend to be underachieving and to show more personality problems (e.g., shyness, inhibition, and social withdrawal) than normal children. Children who stutter severely exhibit much anxiety and have low self-esteem.

Speech Disorders
Children with speech disorders are characterized by one or more of the following: Unintelligible speech, or speech that is difficult to understand, and articulation disorders (distortions, omissions, substitutions).

- Speech-flow disorders (sequence, duration, rate, rhythm, fluency).
- Unusual voice quality (nasality, breathiness, hoarseness, pitch, intensity, quality disorders.
- Peculiar physical mannerisms when speaking.
- Obvious emotional discomfort when trying to communicate (particularly stutterers and clutterers).
- Damage to nerves or brain centers which control muscles used in speech (dysarthria).

Language Disorders

Language disorders are often considered just one category of speech disorders, but the problem is really a separate one with different origins and causes. Language-disordered children exhibit one or more of the following characteristics.

- Difficulty in comprehending questions, commands, or statements (receptive language problems).
- Inability to adequately express their own thoughts (expressive language problems).
- Language that is below the level expected for the child's chronological age (delayed language).
- Interrupted language development (dysphasia).
- Qualitatively different language.
- Total absence of language (aphasia).

OBJECTIVE 4 UNDERSTAND TYPES AND CHARACTERISTICS OF VARIOUS ASSESSMENTS

Skill 4.1 Recognizing basic concepts and terminology used in assessment (e.g., reliability, validity, basal, ceiling)

Types of Assessment
Assessment types can be categorized in a number of ways, most commonly in terms of what is being assessed, how the assessment is constructed, or how it is to be used. It is important to understand these differences so as to be able to correctly interpret assessment results.

Formal vs. Informal: This variable focuses on how the assessment is constructed or scored. *Formal* assessments are assessments such as standardized tests or textbook quizzes; objective tests that include primarily questions for which there is only one correct, easily identifiable answer. These can be commercial or teacher made assessments, given to either groups or individuals. *Informal* assessments have less objective measures, and may include anecdotes or observations that may or may not be quantified, interviews, informal questioning during a task, etc. An example might be watching a student sort objects to see what attribute is most important to the student, or questioning a student to see what he or she found confusing about a task.

Standardized Tests are formal tests that are administered to either groups or individuals in a specifically prescribed manner, with strict rules to keep procedures, scoring, and interpretation of results uniform in all cases. Such tests allow comparisons to be made across populations, ages, or grades, or over time for a particular student. Intelligence tests and most diagnostic tests are standardized tests.

Norm Referenced vs. Criterion Referenced: This distinction is based on the standard to which the student's performance is being compared. ***Norm referenced*** tests establish a ranking and compare the student's performance to an established norm, usually for age or grade peers. What the student knows is of less importance than how similar the student's performance is to a specific group. *Norm* Referenced tests are, by definition, standardized. Examples include intelligence tests and many achievement tests. Norm referenced tests are often used in determining eligibility for special needs services. ***Criterion Referenced*** tests measure a student's knowledge of specific content (criteria), usually related to classroom instruction or individual learning objectives. The student's performance is compared to a set of criteria or a pre-established standard of information the student is expected to know. On these tests, what the student knows is more important than how he or she compares to other students. Examples include math quizzes at the end of a chapter, or some state mandated tests of specific content. Criterion referenced tests are used to determine whether a student has mastered required skills.

Curriculum-Based Assessment is a type of *criterion referenced* test in which the criteria are specific curriculum based skills. Examples would be quizzes assessing the student's mastery of math skills for a unit or year. The individual's performance is measured in terms of what objectives were mastered.

Group vs. Individual Assessments: This variable simply refers to the manner of presentation, whether given to a group of students or on a one to one basis. Group assessments can be formal or informal, standardized or not, criterion or norm referenced. Individual assessments can be found in all these types as well.

Authentic Assessments are designed to be as close to real life as possible so they are relevant and meaningful to the student's life. They can be formal or informal, depending upon how they are constructed. An example of an authentic test item would be calculating a 20 percent sales discount on a popular clothing item after the student has studied math percentages.

Rating Scales and Checklists are generally self-appraisal instruments completed by the student or observation-based instruments completed by teacher or parents. The focus is frequently on behavior or affective areas such as interest, motivation, attention or depression. These tests can be formal or informal and some can be standardized and norm referenced. Examples of norm referenced tests of this type would be ADHD rating scales or the Behavior Assessment System for Children.

Assessment Terminology
The following terms are frequently used in academic testing and assessment. They represent basic terminology and not more advanced statistical concepts.

Reliability - The consistency (stability) of a test over time to measure what it is supposed to measure. Reliability is commonly measured in four ways:

- Test-retest method - The test is administered to the same group or individual after a short period of time and the results are compared. A reliable test should produce very similar results.
- Alternate form (equivalent form) - Measures reliability by using alternative forms to measure the same skills. If both forms are administered to the same group within a relatively short period of time, there should be a high correlation between the two sets of scores if the test has a high degree of reliability.
- Interrater - This refers to the degree of agreement between two or more individuals observing the same behaviors or observing the same tests. This is particularly useful when using rating scales or checklists (above).
- Internal reliability - This is determined by statistical procedures or by correlating half of the test with the other half of the test.

Validity - The degree to which a test measures what it claims to measure, such as reading readiness, self-concept, or math achievement. A test may be highly reliable but it will be useless if it is not valid. There are several types of validity to examine when selecting or constructing an assessment instrument.

- Content - This type of validity examines the question of whether the types of tasks in the test measure the skill or construct the test claims to measure. That is, a test that claims to measure mastery in algebra, would probably not be valid if the majority of the items involved basic operations with fractions and decimals.
- Criterion-Referenced Validity – This involves comparing the test results with a valid criterion. For example, a doctoral student preparing a test to measure reading and spelling skills may check the test against an established test or another valid criterion such as school grades.
- Predictive Validity - Refers to how well a test will relate to a future criterion level, such as the ability of a reading test administered to a first-grader to predict that student's performance at third or fifth grade.
- Concurrent Validity - Refers to how well the test relates to a criterion measure given at the same time. For example, a new test that measures reading achievement may be given to a group, which will then also take a test that has established validity. The test results are compared using statistical measures. The recommended coefficient is 80 or better.
- Construct Validity - Refers to the ability of the test to measure a theoretical construct, such as intelligence, self-concept, and other non-observable behaviors. Factor analysis and correlation studies with other instruments that measure the same construct are ways to determine construct validity.

Ceiling -The ceiling is the point at which it can be predicted that the student will be unable to answer any more of the items. Specific tests have explicit rules for establishing a ceiling.

Skill 4.2 Recognizing the uses and limitations of various formal and informal assessments

Formal assessments include standardized criterion, norm-referenced instruments, and commercially prepared inventories, which are developmentally appropriate for students across the spectrum of disabilities. Criterion-referenced tests compare a student's performance to a previously established criterion rather than to other students from a normative sample. Norm-referenced tests use normative data, including performance norms by age, gender, or ethnic group, for scoring.

Informal assessment strategies include less objective measures such as observations, error analysis, interviews, teacher reports, and performance-based assessments that are developmentally appropriate for students across disabilities. Informal evaluation strategies rely upon the knowledge and judgment of the professional and are an integral part of the evaluation. Advantages of using informal assessments are the ease of design and administration, as well as the usefulness of information the teacher can gain about the student's strength and weaknesses.

Some elements can be either formal or informal tools. For example, observation may incorporate structured observation instruments as well as other informal observation procedures, including professional judgment. When evaluating a child's developmental level, a professional may use a formal adaptive rating scale while simultaneously using professional judgment to assess the child's motivation and behavior during the evaluation process.

Uses and Limitations of Assessments

One of the most important limitations of any test is simply the manner in which it is used and whether it is used and interpreted in a manner consistent with its purpose. When educators choose to use a particular test, whether norm or criterions referenced, standardized or not, they must consider the purpose for which the test was designed. Results of a test designed for one purpose or for use on a particular group, would not be valid for use on another group or for a different purpose. It is up to teachers to familiarize themselves with the purpose and audience for which any given test is intended.

Achievement tests are instruments that directly assess students' skill development in academic content areas. This type of test measures the extent to which a student has profited from educational and/or life experiences compared to others of like ages or grade levels. Emphasis needs to be placed upon the kinds of behaviors each test samples, the adequacy of its norms, the test reliability, and its validity.

An achievement test may be classified as a diagnostic test if strengths and weaknesses in skill development can be delineated. Typically, when used as a diagnostic tool, an achievement test measures one basic skill and its related components. For example, a reading test may measure word recognition, reading comprehension, reading fluency, decoding skills, and sound discrimination. Each skill measured is reported in sub-classifications.

In order to render pertinent information, achievement tests must reflect the content of the curriculum. Some achievement tests assess skill development in many subject areas, while others focus upon single content areas. Within similar content areas, the particular skills assessed and how they are measured differ from test to test. The more prominent areas assessed by achievement tests include math, reading, and spelling.

Achievement test usages include screening, placement, progress evaluation, and curricula effectiveness. As screening tests, these instruments provide a wide index of academic skill development, and may be used to pinpoint students for whom educational interventions may be necessary for purposes of remediation or enrichment. They offer a general idea of where to begin additional diagnostic assessment.

Placement decisions in special education include significant progress, or lack thereof, in academic achievement. It is essential that data from individually administered achievement tests allow the examiner to observe quantitative (i.e., scores) performance as well as to denote specific strengths and weaknesses inherent in qualitative (e.g., attitude, motivation, problem-solving) performance. Knowing how an individual reacts or produces answers during a testing situation is equally relevant to measured skill levels when making placement decisions. Achievement tests are routinely given in school districts across the nation as a means of evaluating progress. Scores of students can be compared locally, statewide, and with national norms. Accountability and quality controls can be kept in check through the reporting of scores.

Achievement tests may be norm-referenced or criterion-referenced, and administered individually or within groups. Results of norm-referenced achievements tests (e.g., Wechsler Individual Achievement Test (WIAT), or WJ III Achievement) considered important in making comparisons, may not provide information needed for individual program planning. Such tests may not provide information on types of behavior tests, sub-skill data, or types of scores reported. Criterion-referenced achievement tests (e.g., KeyMath Diagnostic Arithmetic Test, Brigance Diagnostic Inventories) contain items that correspond with stated objectives, thus enabling identification of cognitive deficiencies. Knowledge of specific skill deficits is needed for developing individualized education plans. For this reason, norm referenced tests are more likely to be used to determine eligibility for services, while criterion referenced tests are more useful for developing IEPs.

Teachers can be provided with measures showing the effectiveness of their instruction. Progress reflected by student scores should be used to review, and often revise, instructional techniques and content. Alternative methods of delivery (e.g., presentations, worksheets, tests) can be devised to enhance the instruction provided to students.

Skill 4.3 Demonstrating knowledge of assessment instruments used to evaluate students with disabilities

All children enrolled in our educational system will experience testing throughout their schooling, whether it is preschool sensory screenings, teacher-made quizzes, or annual standardized assessments. Many special needs students are initially identified using these tests and subsequently referred for further assessment. Testing provides new parameters of information from the time that a student is first suspected of having an educational disability, through placement, intervention, and monitoring of progress.

The Individuals with Disabilities Education Act (Public Law 101-476) and its revisions make definite statements about appropriate evaluation of students for identification, placement, and program purposes. The full, individualized assessment procedure, using instruments validated to test disability areas by those serving on the multidisciplinary team, must be fully understood in order to operate within the mandates of the law and to ultimately make important decisions about a child. Assessment in special education is continuous and occurs on a regular basis. It is part of the diagnostic treatment process through which teachers continually asses the student, plan instruction, implement the planned instruction, and then reassess so that instruction might be modified.

Assessment plays a vital role in the initial diagnosis, the decision to place, the planning of program goals and objectives, and the ongoing diagnostic evaluation of the exceptional student. The limitations of assessment are also addressed, especially as they relate to test bias, cultural, and linguistic concerns, and student identification. Evaluation by a multidisciplinary team is the means by which eligibility for special education services in determined. Public Law 94-142 is very explicit about the manner in which evaluations may be done by local school districts, and due process safeguards exist to protect against bias and discrimination.

Assessment is the gathering of information in order to make decisions. In exceptional student education, assessment is used to make decisions about:

- Screening and initial identification of children who may need services
- Diagnosis of specific learning disabilities
- Selection and evaluation of teaching strategies and programs
- Determination of the child's present level of performance
- Classification and program placement
- Development of goals, objectives, and evaluation for the IEP
- Eligibility for a program
- Monitoring of progress and continuation of a program
- Effectiveness of instructional programs and strategies
- Effectiveness of behavioral interventions

Accommodations needed for mandated or classroom testing
IDEA legislation requires that assessment and evaluation be both individualized and nondiscriminatory. While there are many assessment resources available for individualizing assessment, it can be difficult to find nondiscriminatory assessments when the student is from a cultural or language background other than that of mainstream America where typical standardized tests were normed. Many intelligence and achievement tests have been found to biased against certain racial and ethnic cultures.

Bias in testing occurs when the information within the test or the information required to respond to a multiple choice question or constructed response (essay question) on the test is information that is not available to test takers who come from a different cultural, ethnic, linguistic, or socio-economic background than do the majority of the test takers. Since they have not had the same prior linguistic, social, or cultural experiences as those of the majority of test takers, these test takers are at a disadvantage in taking the test. No matter what their actual mastery of the material taught by the teacher, they cannot address the "biased" questions. Generally, other "non-biased" questions are given to them, and eventually the biased questions are removed from the examination.

An example of such bias would be reading comprehension questions about the well-known fairy tale of the gingerbread boy. These questions may be simple and accessible for most American children. However, children who are recent arrivals from a different culture (e.g., the Dominican Republic) in which the story of the gingerbread boy was not known would be at a serious disadvantage. In that situation alternative questions consistent with the students' background would need to be constructed. Teachers and administrators are required by law to assure that the tests and assessments used are nondiscriminatory.

Assessing students with disabilities presents additional issues of possible bias that may not be immediately obvious. Bias also occurs if the test purports to measure one skill, but the manner in which it measures that skill depends on another skill that is limited in children with certain disabilities. For example, an open response question requiring written output to demonstrate comprehension of an inference about cause and effect is biased against students with writing disabilities. These students might fully understand the inferential cause and effect relationship, but be unable to write well enough to demonstrate that comprehension. This test question would also, therefore, be discriminatory and invalid for that population. In order to make appropriate decisions about assessment, the teacher or team must be very clear on exactly what they want to assess and whether the instrument or method they choose actually assesses that variable.

IDEA legislation also requires that no single assessment or measurement tool may be used to determine eligibility or placement. This is a critical assessment principle and one that is often overlooked. It is easy to look at the results of one assessment and jump to conclusions about a student's ability or needs. To get an accurate picture of a child's needs, however, it is necessary to use a variety of measures, and the law requires that educators do so.

IDEA legislation requires that assessment be in a language and a form that will give the most accurate picture of a child's abilities or disabilities. Clearly this principle has implications for ESL students, and IDEA does require that testing be in the child's preferred language. However, the requirement that it be in the most appropriate form is also significant. Since students with disabilities are often limited on one or another mode of expression or reception of information, a form of response that is fully accessible to the child must also be found.

The requirement of nondiscriminatory assessment also means that the assessments used must be validated for the specific purpose for which they will be used. (See above.)

Finally, as in all educational endeavors, confidentiality is a critical requirement. The Family Educational Rights and Privacy Act of 1974 states that all assessment and discussion of assessment is to be considered strictly confidential and shared only with those immediately involved in decision making and delivery of services to students. Parents have the right to review any and all assessments and their written approval is needed before assessment information can be shared with anyone else (e.g., counselors, outside medical or treatment sources, etc.).

Georgia Assessment Program

Georgia requires specific criterion-referenced assessments customized for the state of Georgia at the elementary, middle, and high school levels: the National Assessment of Educational Progress (NAEP) in grades 4, 8, and 12, and an optional norm-referenced test.

The required state assessments include:

- Criterion-Referenced Competency Tests (CRCT)
- End-of-Course Tests (EOCT)
- Georgia High School Graduation Tests (GHSGT)
- Georgia Writing Assessments
- Additional assessments include:
- Georgia Alternate Assessment (GAA)
- Georgia Kindergarten Inventory of Developing Skills (GKIDS)
- Norm-referenced test (Iowa Tests of Basic Skills)
- ACCESS for ELLS
- Lexile Framework for Reading

Students with significant cognitive disabilities may be assessed with alternate assessments based on alternate achievement standards. The expectations for alternate assessment may be different than those for the regular assessments and may address a narrower range of content, but must be clearly linked to the content standards for the grade in which the student is enrolled. The content may be reduced in complexity or reflect pre-requisite skills.

The Georgia Alternate Assessment (GAA) is a portfolio based assessment. The GAA was developed in accordance with the No Child Left Behind Act (NCLB) of 2001 and the Individuals with Disabilities Education Act (IDEA) of 2004, both of which require all students, including those with significant cognitive disabilities, to have access to a general curriculum. Both NCLB and IDEA require states to assess all students for progress toward meeting academic standards.

For students taking a GAA, the teacher determines the alternate achievement standard (e.g., expectation) for each student, based on the individual learning characteristics and needs of the student. The teacher designs instructional tasks that provide the student access to selected state curriculum standards based on an achievement expectation that is appropriately challenging and purposeful for the student.

Skill 4.4 Demonstrating knowledge of how to collaborate with parents/guardians, classroom teachers, related service providers, and others to gather background information on students' academic, medical, and family history

The assessment process is an essential part of developing an individualized program for students. The needs of the whole child must be considered in order to address all the needs of each child. Therefore, information should be gathered by using various sources of information.

Besides the general education teacher, a vital person or persons in the assessment process should be the parent. The parent can provide needed background information on the child, such as a brief medical, physical, and developmental history. Paraprofessionals, doctors, and other professionals are also very helpful in providing necessary information about the child.

Ways of gathering information:

- **Interview:** Interviews can be in person or on paper. The related parties can be invited to a meeting to conduct the interview; if the parent does not respond after several attempts, the paper interview may be sent or mailed home.

- **Questionnaires:** Questionnaires are also a good way of gathering information.

Some questionnaires may have open-ended questions, and some may have several questions that are to be answered using a rating scale. Questionnaires must, of course, be in the primary language of the person being queried.

- **Conference/ Meeting:** With parents' permission, it may be useful to conduct a meeting—either one-on-one or in a group setting—to gather information about the child. Everyone who may be able to offer any information about the child and his or her academic progress, physical development, social skills, behavior, medical history, and/or needs should be invited to attend.

Relevant background information regarding the student's academic, medical, and family history should be used to identify students with disabilities and evaluate their progress.

An evaluation report should include the summary of a comprehensive diagnostic interview by a qualified evaluator. A combination of candidate self-report interviews—with families and others—and historical documentation, such as transcripts and standardized test scores, is recommended.

The evaluator should use professional judgment as to which areas are relevant in determining a student's eligibility for accommodations due to disabilities. In order to properly identify students with disabilities and evaluate their progress, the evaluator should include background information regarding academic, medical, cultural, and family history. The evaluation should include a developmental history; relevant medical history, including the absence of a medical basis for the present symptoms; academic history, including results of prior standardized testing; reports of classroom performance; relevant family history, including primary language of the home and the candidate's current level of fluency in English; relevant psychosocial history; a discussion of dual diagnoses, alternative or co-existing mood, behavioral, neurological, and/or personality disorders along with any history of relevant medication use that may affect the individual's learning; and exploration of possible alternatives that may mimic a learning disability.

By utilizing all possible background information in the assessment, the evaluator can rule out alternative explanations for academic problems (such as poor education, poor motivation and study skills, emotional problems, or cultural and language differences). If the student's entire background and history is not taken into account, it is not always possible to institute the most appropriate educational program for the student with disabilities.

OBJECTIVE 5 UNDERSTAND PROCEDURES FOR CONDUCTING ASSESSMENT ACTIVITIES TO ADDRESS THE INDIVIDUAL NEEDS OF STUDENTS WITH DISABILITIES

Skill 5.1 Demonstrating knowledge of screening, pre referral, (e.g., pyramids of intervention, response-to-intervention), referral, and eligibility determination, including procedures for early identification of young children who may be at risk for disabilities

The following information may be helpful to familiarize a new educator with common procedures. State specific information about these procedures can be found at http://public.doe.k12.ga.us/index.aspx

Referral

Referral is the process through which a teacher, parent, or some other person formally requests an evaluation of a student to determine eligibility for special education services. The decision to refer a student may be influenced by: (1) student characteristics, such as the abilities, behaviors, or skills that students exhibit (or lack of them); (2) individual differences among teachers in their beliefs, expectations, or skill in dealing with specific kinds of problems; (3) expectations for assistance with a student who is exhibiting academic or behavioral learning problems; (4) availability of specific kinds of strategies and materials; (5) parents' demand for referral or opposition to referral; and (6) institutional factors that may facilitate or constrain teachers in making referral decisions.

It is important that referral procedures be clearly understood and coordinated among all school personnel. All educators need to be able to identify characteristics typically exhibited by special needs students.

The student suspected of having a disability is referred to a multidisciplinary team. This multidisciplinary committee is charged with determining if a student is in need of any special education services. Members of this team generally include all school members involved in the education of the student; the school psychologist, a special educator, parents, or outside agencies that may be involved with the student; and sometimes the students themselves. This committee also, if appropriate, develops and reviews the Individual Education Program (IEP). From the initial referral, schools districts have sixty calendar days to complete an individual evaluation and then an additional thirty calendar days to complete an eligibility meeting. Reevaluations occur every three years, with annual updates to the IEP occurring in between, as well.

Evaluation

The evaluation is comprehensive and includes norm- and criterion-referenced tests (e.g., IQ and diagnostic tests), curriculum-based assessment, systematic teacher observation (e.g., behavior frequency checklist), samples of student work, and parent interviews. The results of the evaluation are twofold: to determined eligibility for special education services, and to identify a student's strengths and weaknesses in order to plan an individual education program.

The wording in federal law is very explicit about the manner in which evaluations must be conducted, and about the existence of due process procedures that protect against bias and discrimination. Provisions in the law include the following:

- The testing of children in their native or primary language unless it is clearly not feasible to do so.
- The use of evaluation procedures selected and administered to prevent cultural or ethnic discrimination.
- The use of assessment tools validated for the purpose for which they are being used (e.g., achievement levels, IQ scores, adaptive skills).

Assessment by a multidisciplinary team utilizing several pieces of information to formulate a placement decision.

Eligibility

The state of Georgia requires the following to be considered in determining eligibility for special education:

- Student Information: general information such as school attending, parent/guardian, primary language spoken in the home.
- Case History: background review such as attendance history, retentions, academic concerns, etc.
- Summary of Interventions and Data Prior to Referral: the interventions attempted with the student prior to referral and the results of those interventions.
- Summary of Progress Monitoring Toward Achieving Standards: results of supplementary instruction provided.
- Results of Relevant District, State, and Benchmark Assessments: scores from individual assessments and state and school district required grade level assessments.
- Individual Student Data: Quantitative and qualitative data that address the areas of concern. Data must be presented on all areas of suspected delay. Specific strengths and weaknesses should be identified as well as the educational impact associated with the delay.

- Exclusionary Factors: Available information must be reviewed to determine whether the student has any unresolved issues that could be addressed through general education supports.
- Decision Making on Educational Impact: Documentation must support the decision on whether or not the student needs special education classification to reach grade level benchmarks.
- Summary of Considerations: Each area of delay must be addressed, as well as the impact of the delay on the eight broad areas of cognition.
- Eligibility Determination: After reviewing all available data, a determination of specific area(s) of eligibility (or lack of eligibility) is made.
- Evaluation Team Information: All required members must sign and indicate agreement or disagreement. If a member disagrees, he/she must attach a written statement indicating the reason for the disagreement.

Criteria for Specific Eligibility Categories

Autism Spectrum Disorder:

- Delay, arrests, or inconsistencies in developmental rates and sequences in motor, sensory, social, cognitive, or communication skills.
- Difficulties in social interaction and participation.
- Deficit in the use of verbal/nonverbal language, particularly for social communication.
- Unconventional, unusual, or repetitive responses to sensory stimuli.
- Displays stress over changes and/or engagement in repetitive activities.

Deafblind: Hearing and Visual impairments that, together, cause severe communication and educational needs that cannot be accommodated in programs solely for children with deafness or blindness.

Deaf/Hard of Hearing:

- Absence of measurable hearing such that primary sensory input for communication is other than auditory or
- Absence of enough measurable hearing that the ability to communicate is adversely affected but child usually relies on auditory channel for sensory input for communication.
- Adverse impact on education documented.

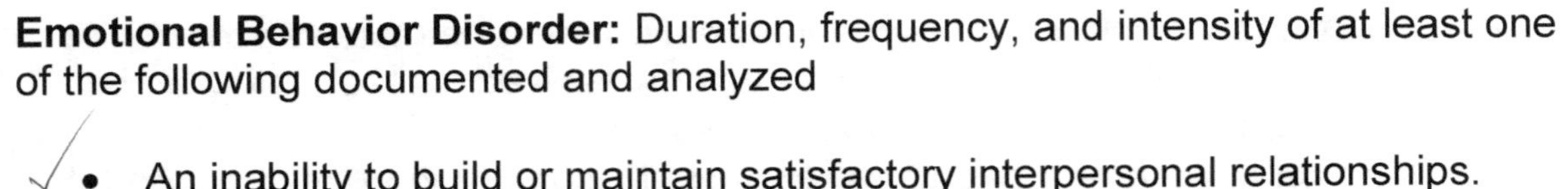

Emotional Behavior Disorder: Duration, frequency, and intensity of at least one of the following documented and analyzed

- An inability to build or maintain satisfactory interpersonal relationships.
- An inability to learn that is not explained by intellectual, sensory, or health factors.
- Consistent or chronic inappropriate behavior or feelings under normal circumstances.
- Displaying pervasive mood of unhappiness or depression.
- Displaying tendency to develop physical symptoms, pains, or unreasonable fears associated with personal or school problems.

Intellectual Disability

- Intellectual functioning based on multiple sources of information documenting IQ scores below 70.
- Significant limitations in child's effectiveness in meeting standards of maturation, learning, personal care, independence, or social responsibility.
- Adaptive behavior in school and home that is at least two standard deviations below the mean in one of three areas: conceptual, social, or practical OR composite score that is two standard deviations below the mean.
- Deficits in intellectual functioning and adaptive behavior existed prior to age 18.

Orthopedic Impairment

- Medical report indicating the diagnosis and prognosis.
- Deficits in academic functioning, emotional development, adaptive behavior, motor or communication skills
- Other Health Impaired
- Chronic or acute health problems documented with medical report that indicates limits in strength, vitality, or alertness.
- Deficits in pre-academic or academic functioning, adaptive behavior, social/emotional development, motor or communication skills as a result of the health impairment.

Significant Developmental Delay

- A child that scores two standard deviations below the mean in one of the areas: adaptive development, cognition, communication, motor skills, or emotional development.
- A child that scores 1.5 standard deviations below the mean in at least two of the areas: adaptive development, cognition, communication, motor skills, or emotional development.

Specific Learning Disability

- Primary deficit in basic psychological processes identified.
- Underachievement in one or more of the following areas: oral expression, listening comprehension, written expression, basic reading skills, reading comprehension, reading fluency, mathematical calculation, or mathematical problem solving.
- Progress monitoring over a minimum of twelve weeks that indicates the child is not expected to make progress toward the benchmark.

Speech/Language Impairment

- An impairment in the areas of articulation, fluency, voice, or language that adversely affects educational performance.

Traumatic Brain Injury

- Deficits in cognitive, social, or motor skills due to acquired injury that adversely impact educational performance in cognition, language, memory, attention, reasoning, abstract thinking, judgment, problem solving, sensory, perceptual and motor abilities, physical functions, communication and information processing.
- Medical report or other that documents a traumatic brain injury has occurred.

Visual Impairment

- After correction, a vision impairment that adversely affects educational performance.

Levels or Tiers of Intervention

There are a number of models of intervention (e.g., Response to Intervention {RTI}, pyramids of intervention, Three Tier Intervention) designed to provide graduated levels of intervention designed to meet a range of needs in students with disabilities. Generally, these have three tiers designed to organize and deliver needed instruction and accommodation. The purpose is to organize staff and resources so students with the greatest needs can the most help before being identified for special education services."

The first tier is usually a "Core" program that serves as the basic foundation for instruction in general education classes. It is usually a commercially published program chosen by the school system. Such a program is designed to meet the instructional needs of *most of the students.* This program is provided during the first "tier" of instruction, in which all students participate. An effective core program should include:

- Research-based instructional strategies that explicitly teach strategies and skills;
- Systematic and sequential instruction that moves children from simple to more complex skills and strategies;
- Ample practice opportunities that allow children to practice skills and strategies in reading and writing text;
- A specified minimum block of time for the relevant instruction per day;
- Assessment tools for diagnosing children's needs and monitoring progress; and
- Provide professional development that will ensure teachers have the skills necessary to implement the program effectively and meet the needs of their children.

Even the most effective core program will not reach all students. Some students will need additional help, and the next tier supplemental intervention programs, are designed to provide that additional or more specialized help. The intent is that these programs can be used to differentiate instruction in a general education setting, either through small group or individual work with the teacher or through additional staff assistance. This assistance is provided in a second "tier" through which extra assistance is provided daily.

The third tier is an Intensive Intervention Program designed for students with more severe learning difficulties in broad ranges of skills. This is usually a much smaller group of students who have been diagnosed as typically two years or more behind grade level. These programs provide intensive instruction, often of a specialized nature, for an additional half hour of instruction for children in "tier 3." These programs are designed to be more intensive, more explicit, more systematic, and more motivating

Skill 5.2 Demonstrating knowledge of how to develop, select, adapt, and modify assessment instruments and strategies for students with diverse characteristics and needs (e.g., related to culture, communication, response modes, and language)

The term "multicultural" incorporates the idea that all students—regardless of gender, social class, and ethnic, racial, or cultural characteristics—should have an equal opportunity (Banks & Banks, 1993). This is as true in the evaluation of students as it is in assuring fairness at the work site.

The issue of fair assessment for individuals from minority groups has a long history in law, philosophy, and education. Slavia and Ysseldyke (1995) point out three aspects of this issue which are particularly relevant to the assessment of students:

Representation
Individuals from diverse backgrounds need to be represented in assessment materials. It is essential that persons from different cultures be represented fairly. Of equal importance is the presentation of individuals from differing genders in non-stereotypical roles and situations.

Acculturation
It is important that individuals from different backgrounds receive opportunities to acquire the tested skills, information, and values. When students are tested with standardization instruments, they are compared to a set of norms in order to gain an index of their relative standing, and to make comparisons. We assume that the students we test are similar to those on whom the test was standardized. That is, we assume that their acculturation is comparable. Acculturation is a matter of educational, socioeconomic, and experiential background rather than gender, skin color, race, or ethnic background. When it is said that a child's acculturation differs from that of the group used as a norm, what is really meant is that the experiential background differed, not simply that the child is of a different ethnic origin (Slavia & Ysseldyke, 1991). Differences in experiential background should therefore be accounted for when administering tests. Please refer to Objective 18.04 for more details on acculturation.

Language
The language and concepts that comprise test items should be unbiased. Students should be familiar with terminology and references when they are administered tests, especially when the results of the tests are going to be used for decision-making purposes. Many tests given in regular grades relate to decisions about promotion and grouping of students for instructional purposes. Tests and other assessment instruments that relate to special education are generally concerned with two types of decisions: eligibility and program planning for individualized education.

When selecting a test, many factors are considered; perhaps the most important consideration is the purpose for testing. The teacher may be screening a large group of students to determine which students would benefit from further assessment of skills; performing a progress check; diagnosing capabilities or deficiencies; evaluating special placement qualifications or benefits from special programs following a pre-determined period; or determining mastery on criterion objectives. The decision to use a criterion-referenced rather than a norm-referenced test, an informal versus a formal type of test, or an individual rather than a group administered test may be based upon one's reason for testing. Scope and content, as well as the form in which scores are reported, are related to purpose and should be given primary consideration.

Additional evaluative criteria might include:

- **Limitations.** Are there special limitations (e.g., hearing, sight, and physical) present? Are there test norms covering these limitations, or will special adaptations or accommodations be necessary? If norm-referenced measures are used, are the student's characteristics and acculturation similar to those with whom the test was normed? Is the test age or grade appropriate?
- **Number.** Is individual testing required, or will an entire class or small group of students be tested at one time?
- **Training.** Has the teacher been fully trained to administer the test, or does the test require administration, scoring, and interpretation of results by a person trained in another specialty area (e.g., speech pathologist, school psychologist)?
- **Presentation-Response Modes.** How are the test items presented to the student (e.g., attending to figures, watching demonstrations, reading)? Likewise, what method of response is required of the student? Will enough information be provided by student responses (e.g., pointing to the correct answer, writing the answer on a form) to determine capability versus chance factors?
- **Format.** Depending on the types of questions-responses selected, what format does the teacher want to use? For example, if written answers are desired for written queries, will true-false, multiple choice, or essay type questions be used?
- **Time.** Are there specific and required time constraints, or can testing be flexible and open-ended?
- **Cost.** Is the cost of the test and supplementary materials reasonable in relation to desired results? Are the test items current and sufficiently matched to the curriculum to be worth the investment? How expensive will it be to replace consumable items (e.g., test booklets, answer forms)? Can items be copied legally?
- **Physical Facility.** Are the physical attributes of the room, such as lighting, ventilation, sound reduction, and well-fitting, comfortable furniture, conducive to good testing?

- **Space Considerations.** Is there adequate space for administering the test to a group of students? Does the amount of available room allow for proper spacing of test takers? If one student is to be tested, can suitable provisions be made for any other students for whom the teacher is responsible during that period? (Teachers should never be required to administer an individual test for program or placement purposes while attempting to supervise other students. This invalidates the test results.)
- **Professional Resources.** A teacher may use descriptive materials provided by publishing companies (e.g., test manuals, catalogues) in his or her selection process. However, prior to making final decisions, the teacher should investigate professional reference sources for specific information about potential tests. Has the test user reviewed the *Standards for Educational and Psychological Tests*, a resource cooperatively prepared by The American Psychological Association, the American Educational Research Association, and the National Council on Measurement in Education? Is the teacher familiar with the data compiled by the Buros Institute of Mental Measurements in their publications *Tests in Print* and *Mental Measurement Yearbooks*? Is he or she aware of the computerized data-based serviced offered by this institute?

Individualizing informal assessments

Although standardized testing will often be used for program placement and eligibility issues, informal, individually administered tests can be very useful in providing detailed qualitative information for diagnosis and instructional design. When administering an informal individual test, the tester has the opportunity to observe the individual's responses and to determine how such things as problem solving are accomplished. Within limits, the tester is able to control the pace and tempo of the testing session and to rephrase and probe responses in order to elicit the individual's best performance. If the child becomes tired, the examiner can break between sub tests or end the test; if he loses his place on the test, the tester can help him to regain it; if he dawdles or loses interest, the tester can encourage or redirect him. If the child lacks self-confidence, the examiner can reinforce his efforts. In short, such informal individual tests allow the examiner to encourage best efforts and to observe how a student uses his skills to answer questions. Thus, informal individual tests provide for the gathering of both quantitative and qualitative information. Standardized tests, whether administered individually or to a group, do not allow such flexibility. The examiner cannot rephrase questions or probe or prompt responses.

IDEA requires that a variety of assessment tools and strategies be utilized when conducting assessments. Before utilizing a formal or informal tool, the practitioner should make sure that the tool is the most appropriate one that can be used for that particular student. If it is norm-referenced, it should be scored on a group to which the student belongs. Many assessment tools can be used across disabilities. Dependent upon the disability in question, such as blindness, autism, or hearing impairment, some assessment tools will give more information than others or will need modifications.

The choice between standardized and informal testing should be primarily determined by purpose and efficiency. When testing for program evaluation, screening, and some types of program planning (such as tracking), standardized tests are appropriate.

When planning individual programs and specific lesson plans and instructional interventions, more informal, individually administered tests can be useful. When a student is being evaluated for placement in a special education program, all areas related to the suspected disability must be assessed. Individual tests should be administered when there is a reason to question the validity of results of group tests or when an in-depth evaluation of the test taker's performance is needed.

Special consideration may need to be given to a particular student who possesses limitations that require accommodations to make a test or assessment accessible to the student. If a student cannot read the instructions or content (e.g., math reasoning test), or is unable to perform the type of response required, the test results are then reflecting measured inability to read or write rather than skill or ability in the area of the test content. Children with learning disabilities or physical impediments may know the answers but be unable to deliver them orally.

Modifications of Tests and Assessment

Test taking is not a pleasant experience for many students with behavioral and/or learning problems. They may lack study skills, may experience anxiety before or during a test, or may have problems understanding and differentiating the task requirements for different tests. The skills necessary to be successful vary with the type of test. Certain students have difficulty with writing answers, but they may be able to express their knowledge of subject matter verbally. Therefore, modifications of content area material may be extended to methods and modifications for evaluation and assessment of student progress.

Teachers of students with special needs will frequently find it necessary to modify their assessment techniques and procedures in order to accurately assess the students' knowledge and skills. Because certain disabilities can interfere with performance on an assessment, it is often necessary for the teacher to break down the task or skill and test each part separately. Many of the common accommodations and modifications in testing are designed to separate the specific skill or knowledge being tested from some other ability or skill impacted by a disability. For example, when testing a student with Dyslexia on retention of a concept in science, it would be inappropriate to use a reading/writing assessment. The student's response to a written test would be confounded by the inability to read the test or to compose readable written responses. In such cases an oral exam might more accurately assess the student's science knowledge.

- Some of the ways that teachers can modify assessment for individual needs include:
- Help students to get used to timed tests with timed practice tests.
- Provide study guides before tests.
- Make tests easier to read by leaving ample space between the questions.
- Modify multiple choice tests by reducing the number of choices, reforming questions to yes-no, or using matching items.
- Modify short-answer tests with cloze (fill-in) statements, or provide a list of facts or choices that the student can choose from.
- Essay tests can be modified by using partial outlines for the student to complete, allowing additional time, or including test items that do not require extensive writing.

Students with visual/spatial issues may need assessments with questions or problems presented one at a time either singly on a piece of paper or enclosed in large boxes with plenty of white space around them.
In general, Accommodations or modifications in assessment usually fall into the following categories:

- **Setting:** Changes in the location of the testing, such as separate seating or room, special lighting of noise buffers, adaptive furniture, small group or one to one testing.
- **Timing and Scheduling**: Changes in the duration or time of the test such as allowing extra time or an absence of time limits, frequent breaks, or scheduling the test at a time of day when a student functions best—has had specific medication, etc.
- **Presentation of Test**: Changes in how the test is given to a student, such as oral testing, large print or Braille, sign language, colored overlays or special paper, etc. This would also include allowing the teacher to clarify directions or read the test to the student.

- **Student Responses**: Changes in how the student is allowed to respond to the test, such as allowing oral responses, multiple choice rather than essay, dictating open responses, use of assistive devices such as computer keyboards, spell checkers, writing software, etc.

Formal Assessments or Standardized Tests

Review the student's IEP for accommodations and modifications for testing before giving any standardized tests to a student with disabilities. Accommodations and modifications listed on the IEP should be consistently used throughout the school year. (e.g., if a standardized test is to be read to a student, then all tests should be read to the student during the year). You cannot give an accommodation or modification to a student just for standardized tests. The Georgia State Department of Education has a listing of accommodations and modifications that do not violate standardization of specific tests.

Skill 5.3 Demonstrating knowledge of how to administer nonbiased formal and informal assessments, including assessments of students from culturally and linguistically diverse backgrounds

Students from culturally and linguistically diverse backgrounds are over-represented in special education programs. Research has been conducted that suggests that the reasons for this over-representation are due to a bias against children from different backgrounds as well as a bias against students who come from low-income families. The style and emphasis of the school may be different from those found in the cultures of some students.. Because culture and language affect learning and behavior, the school system may misinterpret what students know, how they behave, and how they learn. Students from diverse backgrounds may also appear less competent than they actually are due to language difficulties.

When assessing students from diverse backgrounds, educators must make sure they test the student in their native language and use culturally sensitive assessment material.

Before performing any formal testing of a student who is a non-native speaker of English, it is important to determine the student's preferred language and to conduct a comprehensive language assessment in both English and the native language. It is highly inappropriate to evaluate students in English when that is not their dominant language unless the reason for the testing is to assess the student's English language proficiency. The IDEA states that tests and other evaluation materials must be provided and administered in the child's primary language or mode of communication unless it is clearly not feasible to do so. If possible, the evaluator in any testing situation or interview should be familiar to the child and speak the child's language.

When tests or evaluation materials are not available in the student's native language, examiners may find it necessary to use English-language instruments. Because this is a practice fraught with the possibility of misinterpretation, examiners need to be cautious how they administer the test and interpret results. Alterations may need to be made to the standardized procedures used to administer tests; these can include paraphrasing instructions, providing a demonstration of how test tasks are to be performed, reading test items to the student rather than having him or her read them, allowing the student to respond verbally rather than in writing, or allowing the student to use a dictionary.

IDEA requires that a variety of assessment tools and strategies be utilized when conducting assessments. Before utilizing a formal or informal tool, the practitioner should make sure that the tool is the most appropriate one that can be used for that particular population group. Many assessment tools can be used across disabilities. Dependent upon the disability in question (such as blindness, autism, or hearing impaired), some assessment tools will give more information than others.

When planning individual programs, individual tests should be used. When a student is being evaluated for placement in a special education program, all areas related to the suspected disability must be assessed. Individual tests should be administered when there is a reason to question the validity of results of group tests, or when an in-depth evaluation of the test taker's performance is needed.

Special consideration may need to be given a particular student who possesses limitations that make a group test inappropriate. Most group tests require that test takers be able to read and select graphic responses (e.g., marking or writing). If a student cannot read the instructions or content (e.g., a math reasoning test), or is unable to perform the type of response required, the test results are then reflecting measured inability to read or write rather than skill or ability in the area of the test content. Children with learning disabilities or physical impediments may know the answers, but be unable to deliver them orally.

Skill 5.4 Demonstrating knowledge of environmental factors (e.g., lighting, noise) that can affect the assessment of students with disabilities

The use of appropriate furniture when taking the test can impact the student with disabilities. Dependent upon the nature of the disability, the size of the desk, the shape of the desk and/or chair, and the heights and slopes of the chair/desk can impact the student's ability to concentrate, sit comfortably, or focus on the exam. Some students may perform better if allowed to take a position other than sitting (e.g., standing at an appropriately high counter or table, lying down working on a clipboard, etc).

Another environmental factor deals with having adequate space for equipment and specific personnel to assist the student. Students in wheelchairs or who require specialized equipment need to have adequate space in the testing area to accommodate their equipment and any additional staff.

Noise can also be a factor that impacts assessments. Noise created when using equipment such as computers, audio devices, and other assistive technology; could distract the students in the testing area. A separate examination venue may have to be set aside to ensure that students have sufficient quiet to concentrate. Additional steps may need to be taken to ensure that the least distractive assistive technology is utilized during testing situations to eliminate noise distractions. Flexible time arrangements can be set to prevent overloading the student.

Lighting is another environmental factor that can impact students with disabilities. This is especially important for students with low vision and vision difficulties. The elimination of glare can be very important to students with low vision. Students with visual impairments that are normally print users may need special equipment and materials. The student's vision may fluctuate or may be influenced by factors such as inappropriate lighting, light glare, or fatigue. These factors must be addressed in the testing environment.

Skill 5.5 Demonstrating knowledge of how to use ecological assessments, portfolio assessments, individualized inventories, task analyses, and functional assessments (e.g., behavioral, communication) to accommodate the unique strengths and needs of students with disabilities

Ecological Assessments

Ecological assessments entail assessing students in real-life contexts. This involves assessing the degree to which a student can meet the demands of a task in a realistic situation as close as possible to the one in which the student will eventually be performing the task. They usually involve making a detailed analysis of the steps and skills involved in a task and breaking it down into discrete steps to be learned. Such assessments can assist teachers in identifying the student's needs. Teachers can use the discrepancies between the skills needed and those the student has mastered for identifying potential instruction and support strategies.

There are numerous types of ecological assessments. These include the following:

- **Authentic Assessment -** A demonstration of a skill or behavior in a real-life context.
- **Curriculum-Based Assessment -** A broad approach of linking assessment to instruction.
- **Dynamic Assessment -** A technique in which the assessor actively engages the student in learning. Interactions between the evaluator and the student reflect upon the world of the student by focusing and feeding back environmental experiences in a manner that produces appropriate learning habits.
- **Performance Assessment -** A demonstration of the behavior that has been outlined by the assessor.
- **Product Assessment -** An analysis of the product of the student's performance.
- **Portfolio Assessment -** A collection of the product of a student's play and work that showcases the student's efforts, progress, and achievements.

Portfolio Assessment

The use of student portfolios for some aspect of assessment has become quite common. The purpose, nature, and policies of portfolio assessment vary greatly from one setting to another. In general, a student's portfolio contains samples of work collected over an extended period of time. The nature of the subject, age of the student, and scope of the portfolio all contribute to the specific mechanics of analyzing, synthesizing, and otherwise evaluating the portfolio contents.

In most cases, the student and teacher make joint decisions as to which work samples go into student portfolios. A collection of work compiled over an extended time period allows teachers, students, and parents to view the student's progress from a unique perspective. Qualitative changes over time can be readily apparent from work samples. Such changes are difficult to establish with strictly quantitative records typical of the scores recorded in the teacher's grade book.

Task Analysis

A teacher can use the set of behavioral specifications that are required for a task as an analysis to prepare tests to measure the student's ability to meet those specifications. If task analysis identifies which skills will be needed to perform a task successfully, then the criterion measurements will further identify whether the student possesses the necessary skills or knowledge for that task. The level of performance that is acceptable is the "criterion level."

- Criterion measurements must be developed along certain guidelines if they are to accurately measure a task and its sub-skills. Johnson and Morasky (1977) give the following guidelines for establishing criterion measurement:
- Criterion measurement must directly evaluate a student's ability to perform a task.
- Criterion measurements should cover the range of possible situations in order to be considered an adequate measure.
- Criterion measurements should measure whether or not a student can perform the task without additional or outside assistance. They should not give any information that the student is expected to possess.
- Criterion measurement requires that all responses should be relevant to the task being measured.

Behavioral objectives offer descriptive statements defining the task that the student will perform, state the conditions under which the task will occur, and show the criterion measurement required for mastery. The criterion measurement is the process for evaluating what the student can do. For the instruction to be meaningful, there must be a precise correspondence between the capabilities determined in a criterion measurement and the behavioral demands of the objective.

Functional Behavioral Assessments

A functional behavioral assessment is a procedure that identifies the problem behaviors a student may show in school, to determine the function or purpose of the behaviors, and to develop interventions to teach satisfactory alternatives to the behaviors. The first step in carrying out a functional behavioral assessment is for the school team to identify and agree upon the primary behavior that needs to be changed. The next step is to gather data on the occurrence of the target behavior, identifying frequency, intensity, and where, when, and how the behavior takes place. The third step is to develop a hypothesis about the function or purpose of the student's behavior and to develop an intervention. The last step is to evaluate the effectiveness of the proposed intervention.

Functional behavioral assessments have been utilized for students with severe disabilities, to help parents and teachers understand the function of inappropriate behavior, and to plan effective interventions. Functional Behavioral assessments are also a helpful approach to evaluating the reason for inappropriate behaviors for students who have milder disabilities, especially when their behaviors do not improve with the use of typical school interventions.

OBJECTIVE 6 UNDERSTAND HOW TO INTERPRET AND COMMUNICATE ASSESSMENT RESULTS

Skill 6.1 Applying knowledge of how to interpret the results of formal and informal assessments (e.g., standard score, percentiles)

Formal and Informal Assessments
Results of formal assessments are given in derived scores, which compare the student's raw score to the performance of a specified group of subjects. Criteria for the selection of the group may be based on characteristics such as age, sex, or geographic area. The test results of formal assessments must always be interpreted in light of what type of tasks the individual was required to perform.

Age and Grade Equivalents
The most commonly used derived scores are Age and Grade Equivalents. These scores are considered developmental scores because they attempt to convert the student's raw score into an average performance of a particular age or grade group.

Age equivalents are expressed in years and months (e.g., 7-3). In the standardization procedure, a mean is calculated for all individuals of the particular age who took the test. If the mean or median number of correct responses for children 7 years and 3 months was 80, then an individual whose raw score was 80 would be assigned an age-equivalent of 7 years and 3 months. *Grade equivalents* are written as years and tenths of years (e.g., 6.2 would read sixth grade, second month). Grade equivalents are calculated on the average performance of the group. They have been criticized for their use to measure gains in academic achievement and to identify exceptional students.

However, these scores are so often misinterpreted by parents and teachers alike that the International Reading Association (IRA) has issued a statement (1981) strongly urging teachers and schools NOT to use them. If they are used, the teacher must be *very* careful to explain what they do and **do not** mean. If, for example, 3rd grade Johnny's parents are told his grade equivalency on a reading test was 6.4, they are likely to think he is reading on a 6th grade level. The teacher will need to explain that the results mean Johnny got a score similar to the score a typical 6th grader would get on this (**3rd grade)** material. However, since the test material was NOT 6th grade material, this does not mean Johnny could read 6th grade material. It was 3rd grade material and Johnny did very well on it, as well as a 6th grader would. This sort of confusion on the part of parents (and even some teachers) is why the IRA prefers the score not be used.

In addition, Venn (2004) points out additional difficulties. Research shows that the accuracy and reliability of age and grade equivalencies decrease as students age. Finally, age and grade equivalencies are not expressed in equal units and equivalencies from *different tests are not comparable*, so a child's grade equivalency on one test cannot be compared to his or her grade score on another. Venn also notes that the American Psychological Association, in 1999, advocated the elimination of age and grade scores completely for all these reasons.

Quartiles, Deciles, and Percentiles
Quartiles, deciles, and percentiles indicate the percentage of scores that fall below the individual's raw score. Quartiles divide the score into four equal parts; the first quartile is the point at which 25 percent of the scores fall below the full score. Deciles divide the distribution into ten equal parts; the seventh decile would mark the point below which 70 percent of the scores fall. Percentiles are the most frequently used. A percentile rank of 45 would indicate that the person's raw score was at the point below which 45 percent of the other scores fell.

Standard Scores
These are raw scores with the same mean (average) and standard deviation (measure of variability or average distance from the mean). In the standardization of a test, about 68 percent of the scores will fall above or below 1 standard deviation of the mean of 100. About 96 percent of the scores will fall within the range of 2 standard deviations above or below the mean. A standard deviation of 20, for example, will mean that 68 percent of the scores will fall between 80 and 120, with 100 as the mean. The most common are T scores, Z scores, stanines, and scaled scores. Standard scores are useful because they allow for direct comparison of raw scores from different individuals. In interpreting scores, it is important to note what type of standard score is being used.

Skill 6.2 Demonstrating knowledge of how to use formal and informal assessments to evaluate the effectiveness of instruction and monitor students' ongoing progress

Assessment skills should be an integral part of teacher training, where teachers are able to monitor student learning using pre- and post-assessments of content areas; analyzing assessment data in terms of individualized support for students and instructional practice for teachers; and designing lesson plans that have measurable outcomes and definitive learning standards. Assessment information should be used to provide performance-based criteria and academic expectations for all students in evaluating whether students have learned the expected skills and content of the subject area.

For example, in an Algebra I class, teachers can use assessments to see whether students have learned the knowledge necessary to engage in the subject area. If the teacher provides students with a pre-assessment on algebraic expression and ascertains whether the lesson plan should be modified to include a pre-algebraic expression lesson unit to refresh student understanding of the content area, then the teacher can create, if needed, quantifiable data to support the need for additional resources to support student learning. Once the teacher has taught the unit on algebraic expression, a post assessment test can be used to test student learning and a mastery exam can be used to test how well students understand and can apply the knowledge to the next unit of math content learning.

Teachers can use assessment data to inform and impact instructional practices by making inferences on teaching methods and gathering clues for student performance. By analyzing the various types of assessments, teachers can gather more definitive information on projected student academic performance. Instructional strategies for teachers provide learning targets for student behavior, cognitive thinking skills, and processing skills that can be employed to diversify student learning opportunities.

The assessment information gathered from various sources is critical for identifying the strengths and the weaknesses of the student. Each test and each person will have something to offer about the child, therefore increasing the possibility of creating a well-developed plan to assist in the success of the student. The special education and general education teacher, along with other professionals, will use the assessment data to make appropriate instructional decisions and to modify the learning environment so that it is conducive to learning.

The information gathered can be used to make some of the following instructional decisions:

I **Classroom Organization:** The teacher can vary grouping arrangements (e.g., large group, small group, peer tutoring, or learning centers) and methods of instruction (teacher directed, student directed)

II **Classroom Management:** The teacher can vary grading systems, vary reinforcement systems, and vary the rules (differentiated for some students).

III **Methods of Presentation/Variation of Methods Included:**
A. Content - amount to be learned, time to learn, and concept level
B. General Structure - advance organizers, immediate feedback, memory devices, and active involvement of students.
C. Type of Presentation - verbal or written, transparencies, audiovisual

IV **Methods of Practice:**
A. General Structure - amount to be practiced, time to finish, group, individual or teacher-directed, and varied level of difficulty
B. Level of Response - copying, recognition, or recall with and without cues
C. Types of Materials - worksheets, audiovisual, texts

V **Methods of Testing:**
A. Type - verbal, written, or demonstration
B. General Structure - time to complete, amount to complete, group or
C. individual testing
D. Level of response - multiple choice, essay, recall of facts

Instructional Decisions
Subject matter should be presented in a fashion that helps students organize, understand, and remember important information. Advance organizers and other instructional devices can help students:

- Connect information to what is already known
- Make abstract ideas more concrete
- Capture students' interest in the material
- Help students to organize the information and visualize the relationships

Organizers can be visual aids like diagrams, tables, charts, guides, or verbal cues that alert students to the nature and content of the lesson. Organizers may be used:

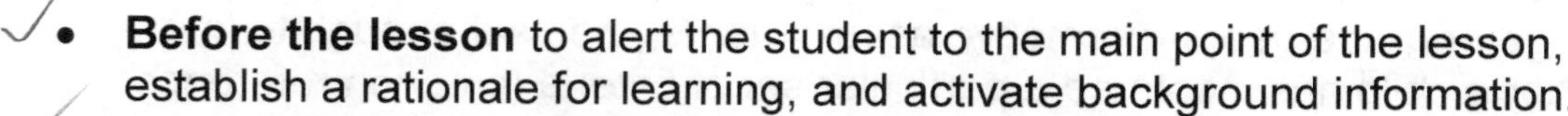

- **Before the lesson** to alert the student to the main point of the lesson, establish a rationale for learning, and activate background information.
- **During the lesson** to help students organize information, keep focused on important points, and aid comprehension.
- **At the close of the lesson** to summarize and remember important points.

Examples of organizers include:

- Question- and graphic-oriented study guides.
- Concept diagramming: students brainstorm a concept and organize information into three lists (always present, sometimes present, and never present).
- Semantic feature analysis: students construct a table with examples of the concept in one column and important features or characteristics in the opposite column.
- Semantic webbing: the concept is placed in the middle of the chart or chalkboard, and relevant information is placed around it. Lines show the relationships.
- Memory (mnemonic) devices such as diagrams, charts, and tables.

Applying test results to curriculum and instruction decisions
Assessment is critical to providing differentiated and appropriate instruction to all students, and monitoring progress toward objectives. These are the areas in which teachers will most often use assessment. Teachers should use a variety of assessment techniques to determine the existing knowledge, skills, and needs of each student. Depending on the age of the student and the subject matter under consideration, diagnosis of readiness may be accomplished through pre-test, checklists, teacher observation, or student self-report. Diagnosis serves two related purposes—to identify those students who are not ready for the new instruction and to identify for each student what prerequisite knowledge is lacking.

In order to effectively use assessment to drive instruction, a teacher must be able to use assessments to diagnose both problems and progress in student ability. Interpretation of test results for purposes of diagnosis goes beyond normative and criterion assessments. It is not enough to know how a student compares with age or grade peers (normative assessments), nor is it enough to know whether a child has mastered a particular set of criteria (criterion referenced assessment). In the field of Special Education, the teacher already knows the student doesn't, for example, read at grade level and hasn't met grade level criteria; that's why the student has been referred for special education help. What the teacher needs to know is ***why*** the student has these problems, and ***what to do about it.*** The teacher needs to be able to *interpret* assessment results to determine as closely as possible the exact nature of the student's problem and the best strategy for helping the student to overcome the problem.

Generally, this means the teacher will be using a *combination* of assessment sources, including standardized testing done by the school or outside agencies, classroom quizzes and assessments, informal observations and works samples, even parental input. Some of this information will already be available in the student's IEP or, possibly, 504 documents. The teacher will need to be able to interpret and apply this information, as well as her/his own observations.

Standardized intelligence testing can provide clues to the locus of, say, a reading problem. For the teacher, the overall composite intelligence measures are less useful than the subtests. A student might have an overall intelligence rating that is well within normal ranges, or even above normal, but have serious lacks in one or more subtests. It is these specific subtests that the teacher needs for diagnosis and design of instructional methods. For example, testing may show a student has adequate processing speed, but a very limited working memory. Such a combination may lead to problems that mirror attention difficulties, but have their roots elsewhere. This child is processing information quickly, but can't hold enough pieces of information in working memory long enough to make correct decisions. She/he needs to be taught strategies for expanding working memory, for "chunking" information so more will fit in the limited working memory, and strategies for carrying the pieces along the way to a decision. This might include note taking and graphic organizers or other mnemonic devices.

Testing may show another child to have adequate working memory, logic, and long term memory, and a very slow processing speed. This child needs a very different set of strategies to learn well. Extra time for assignments, avoiding the repetition of verbal instructions (which interrupts his processing), and *written* or *visually* based instructions may be more efficient learning strategies for this child. Standardized educational testing done by the school can also provide diagnostic clues to problems and possible treatments in the classroom. Educational testing will often have subtests of individual skills, such as word recognition, fluency, literal or inferential comprehension, writing composition and mechanics, etc.

Closely examining these areas can help a teacher diagnose problems and design remedies. For example, if the educational testing shows a child has adequate sight word recognition skills in isolation, but cannot read connected text fluently, it might be a good idea to go back and look at the student's phoneme and phonic blending skills. Does the student have a basic problem blending at the phoneme level? Combined with the text reading problem this may indicate more than just a phoneme awareness issue, more of an overall problem putting pieces of information together. Further diagnostic information might be found by looking at the student's ability to handle simple physical puzzles and recognize a whole from parts of a picture. A student with a disability based here will need instruction that helps him/her learn how to put information together. This might start at the most basic physical level with puzzles and progress to the use of word prediction software to help the child generalize this skill to a reading context.

Informal classroom assessments and simply looking at very specific areas of problems can also help the teacher with diagnosis. For example, a student who can answer multiple choice questions correctly, but cannot put that information into writing, may have encoding problems or even a form of Dysgraphia. Examination of what the child *can* do is as important as what he cannot do, because it helps pinpoint the locus of a problem or disability **and** points to methods of instruction the teacher can use to help the student. A child who can correctly compute an entire math worksheet quickly, but cannot do a simple word problem does not have *math* problem; he has a *language or reading* problem. The student needs strategies for relating the vocabulary and language of math to the concrete facts he already knows.

Skill 6.3 Applies knowledge of strategies for communicating assessment results to all stakeholders (e.g., students with disabilities, their parents/guardians, general education teachers, administrators).

Interpreting Test Results

The special educator must be able to communicate assessment results in understandable language for a variety of individuals. These individuals may include parents or guardians, paraprofessionals, professionals in general education, administration, and (in the case of older students) even the student him or herself.

A review of assessment and evaluation results may be done during an IEP meeting in which the formal test lingo is used but paired with an interpretation in layman's terms. Results may also be presented in the form of a written report.

Representing Test Results and Educational Implications in Written Format

Although the school psychologist often completes student evaluations and writes a report, this may be the task of the special educator when assessment is done in the classroom in preparation for the student's annual review. In this case, the special education teacher will be asked to write a report summarizing assessment findings and educational implications. The teacher should be able to organize the data in a concise, readable format. Some components of such a report include:

- Identifying information (student name, age, date of birth, address, gender)
- Reason for assessment
- Test administration information (date, time, duration of test, response of student)
- Test results
- Summary of educational recommendations

Communicating with families

Parents and family members will have many questions about their child's testing and diagnosis, but they may not have the specialized educational and psychological background to understand the implications of testing and diagnoses without help. Just as each child is an individual, different from all others in significant ways, each child's family is also different from other families. The teacher must tailor communication strategies to the needs of each individual family, just as she must tailor instruction to each individual child. It is important to define terms and explain procedures that might be confusing to parents without talking down to them or appearing condescending or patronizing.

Interpreting tests and diagnostic results to parents can present special challenges. Parents often see numbers and percentages without understanding their significance. They hear diagnostic terms and labels without understanding what they mean. When reporting test results, it is important to briefly define each test or subtest in terms the parent will understand. Telling parents that their child did well or poorly on the WRAML would not be helpful unless the teacher explains the relevant subtests briefly and outlines the implications for instruction. It is best to be as specific as possible and to give concrete examples of how test results predict learning problems. For instance, if the testing shows a child has poor auditory working memory, the teacher can point out that this may hamper the child's ability to remember lectured facts long enough to relate facts *together* to draw conclusions. This has implications for both instruction (maybe use graphic organizers to outline relationships visually) and for testing accommodations (e.g., allow the use of graphic organizers during a test).

Numbers can also be confusing to parents. They may have no idea what a Stanine is or what it means, so the term must be defined for them. There are two kinds of numbers that can be particularly confusing to parents: percentiles and grade equivalents. Percentiles can be confusing because parents are accustomed to looking at percentage correct for grading purposes. They may look at a score showing their child is at the 50th percentile and think the child is failing, because 50% correct would be a failing grade. They need to be assured that a score at the 50th percentile is, in fact, a fine score and indicates that their child is solidly in the middle, having performed better than 50 percent of those taking the test. In addition, they may not understand how wide the range of "normal" percentiles is and this too must be explained to them.

Another problem area when discussing test scores with parents can be grade equivalent scores. Many reading diagnostic tests yield a variety of scaled scores, including a grade equivalency. As noted above, these scores are particularly confusing to parents and should be avoided. If the teacher uses them care must be taken to see that they are not misinterpreted.

Finally, parents often want to know when their child will be "fixed," or "cured," or "at grade level." This is a very difficult question and most testing and diagnostic assessment simply will not answer it. The teacher needs to help the parents focus on what the results mean for instruction and accommodation. Of course, there will be implications for future planning, but it is unwise to try and make testing results into predictors of how long the child will need support.

Communicating with general education teachers and other staff
Interpreting results for general education teachers should center on specifics of the student's disability and implications for instructional objectives and methods, as well as accommodations necessary for the student to be successful when in the general education classroom. The special education teacher and general education teacher should consult on the development of lesson plans for any student who spends time in the general education class. This might mean helping the general education teacher modify or differentiate her lesson plans so the student can access the lesson in spite of the disability It would also mean familiarizing the general education teacher with the accommodations listed in the student's IEP. The teacher is legally bound to provide these instructional and testing accommodations in the general education setting.

When communicating with content area teachers it is important to address the issue of presenting the material to the student in a manner that allows him/her to access and learn it in spite of the child's disability. This often means selecting alternative texts that present the same grade level material written at a simpler reading level. The special education teacher can help the general education teacher select materials appropriate to the child's reading level. It might also be necessary to modify existing content materials to make the reading level more accessible to the child.

Skill 6.4 Applying strategies for recommending modifications and accommodations to curriculum, based upon assessment results

Instructional modifications should be tried in an attempt to accommodate the student in the regular classroom. Effective instruction is geared toward individual needs and recognizes differences in how students learn. Modifications are tailored to individual student needs. Some strategies for modifying regular classroom instruction shown in the following table are effective with at-risk students with disabilities and students without learning or behavior problems.

Strategies for Modifying Classroom Instruction

Strategy 1 Provide active learning experiences to teach concepts. Student motivation is increased when students can manipulate, weigh, measure, read, or write using materials and skills that relate to their daily lives.

Strategy 2 Provide ample opportunities for guided practice of new skills. Frequent feedback on performance is essential to overcome student feelings of inadequacy. Peer tutoring and cooperative projects provide non-threatening practice opportunities. Individual student conferences, curriculum-based tests, and small group discussions are three useful methods for checking progress.

Strategy 3 Provide multisensory learning experiences. Students with learning problems sometimes have sensory processing difficulties; for instance, an auditory discrimination problem may cause misunderstanding about teacher expectations. Lessons and directions that include visual, auditory, tactile, and kinesthetic modes are preferable to a single sensory approach.

Strategy 4 Present information in a manner that is relevant to the student. Particular attention to this strategy is needed when there is a cultural or economic gap between the lives of teachers and students. Relate instruction to a youngster's daily experience and interests.

Strategy 5 Provide students with concrete illustrations of their progress. Students with learning problems need frequent reinforcement for their efforts. Charts, graphs, and check sheets provide tangible markers of student achievement.

SUBAREA II. DEVELOPING PROGRAMS AND PROMOTING LEARNING FOR STUDENTS WITH DISABILITIES

OBJECTIVE 7 UNDERSTAND PROCEDURES FOR DEVELOPING, IMPLEMENTING, AND AMENDING INDIVIDUALIZED EDUCATION PROGRAMS (IEPS).

Skill 7.1 Demonstrating knowledge of the continuum of placement and services available for students with disabilities.

Least Restrictive Environment
One of the major components of IDEA is the provision of education for students with disabilities in the least restrictive environment (LRE). LRE can be legally defined as the place where: "to the maximum extent appropriate, children with disabilities, including children in public or private institutions or other care facilities, are educated with children who are not disabled, and that special classes, separate schooling, or other removal of children with disabilities from the regular educational environment occurs only when the nature or severity of the disability is such that education in regular classes with the use of supplementary aids and services cannot be achieved satisfactorily." In other words, students with disabilities are to be educated in the same settings and are to be members of the same classes as their nondisabled peers to the maximum extent possible, based on the learning characteristics and needs of the individual child. LRE means that the student is placed in an environment that is not dangerous or overly controlling or intrusive. The student should be given opportunities to experience what other peers of similar mental or chronological age are doing. Finally, LRE should be the environment that is the most integrated and normalized for the student's strengths and weaknesses.

There are many benefits of inclusive settings for student with disabilities.

- The student with a disability is a member of the same school community as his/her neighbors and siblings.
- The student with a disability is placed in age-appropriate grades and classes.
- The student with a disability is provided support, as needed, in school and community environments.
- The student with a disability is actively engaged in learning within the context of the classroom activities.
- The student with disabilities is able to learn age appropriate social and interpersonal relations behavior.

Considerations When Determining LRE

- **Accommodations:** Changes to instruction, materials, activities, or environment that do not dilute performance standards unless necessary.
- **Modifications:** Changes to materials, assessments, or products that require the student the produces less than the minimum of performance standards.
- **Location:** Consideration of where the student will receive instruction (e.g. special education setting or general education setting) as well as physical considerations for accessibility.
- **Personnel Supports:** Personnel required to provide support or instruction in the LRE.
- **Personnel Supports**
- **General Education:** Student receives all instruction in the general education setting with no personnel support.
- **Consultation:** Student receives at least one segment per month of direct service from a special education teacher. Service can be provided in either a general education or special education setting.
- **Supportive Instruction:** Student receives service in the general education classroom from personnel other than a special education teacher, such as an interpreter, paraprofessional, or job coach.
- **Collaboration:** The special education teacher shares teaching responsibilities with more than one general education teacher within the general education setting.
- **Co-Teaching:** The special education teacher and general education teacher equally share teaching responsibilities in the general education setting.
- **Special Education:** The special education teacher provides instruction in a special education setting.
- Current IDEA regulations recognize that the least restrictive environment is not the same for all children. There is no simple definition of LRE. LRE differs with each child's needs. LRE for one child may be a regular classroom with support services, while LRE for another may be a self-contained classroom in a special school. Schools are required to offer a continuum of services that will meet the needs of all children regardless of what constitutes LRE for each child.
- **Continuum of services:** A continuum of educational services must be made available by the LEA. Children must be placed in their least restrictive environment and, insofar as possible, with regular classmates. Deno (1970) describes a seven tier cascade system for such services.

Cascade System of Special Education Services

Level 1	Regular classroom, including students with disabilities able to learn with regular class accommodations, with or without medical and counseling services
Level 2	Regular classroom with supportive services (i.e. consultation, inclusion)
Level 3	Regular class with part-time special class (i.e. itinerant services, resource room)
Level 4	Full-time special class (i.e. self-contained)
Level 5	Special stations (i.e. special schools)
Level 6	Homebound
Level 7	Residential (i.e. hospital, institution)

Placement decisions must be made based upon the student's IEP, and the stipulated goals and objectives must be reviewed and rewritten on an annual basis. Thus, progress revisions may suggest the need for a change in placement to a less (or more) restrictive environment.

All individuals with disabilities should participate in academic and non-academic (i.e., extracurricular) services to the maximum extent appropriate, considering the individual needs of the child. If skills (e.g., self-help, social, physical education) need to be acquired by a child with disabilities in order to participate successfully in these services or activities, then the skills should be included as goals or objectives in the student's IEP.

The three tier RTI system described in Objective 20.01 is another approach to providing a continuum of services based upon the individual needs of each student.

Skill 7.2 Applies knowledge of how to use assessment information to make appropriate eligibility, program, and placement recommendations for students with disabilities, including those from culturally and linguistically diverse backgrounds.

In order to make appropriate decisions regarding the programming and placement for the student with a disability, the IEP committee must review the learning characteristics and instructional needs of the student as well as any specialized services needed (e.g. interpreter, physical access issues, and assistive technology).

Considerations for the IEP Committee:

- What is the student's current level of performance?
- Based on the information gathered, what goals and objectives are needed to address the student's academic and behavioral needs?
- Which objectives can be taught in general education settings? For each objective, the following must be considered:
- What age-appropriate and content appropriate settings are available at what times during the school day?
- What modifications to activities, materials, instruction, and/or environments are necessary in each setting?
- What are the needs in terms of personnel support(s) for the student, teacher, and/or class? Are specialized forms of instruction needed that cannot be provided in the general education class?
- If an objective cannot be addressed in a general education setting, which special education setting would be the most appropriate to teach the skill?
- What settings or activities can be provided to assure additional opportunities for interaction with nondisabled peers?
- How is the appropriateness of the LRE decision(s) going to be assessed?

Language Considerations
A child with a disability may come from a culturally diverse background. Although special education placement is not made because of a delay due to cultural diversity, if both a disability and a language difference exist, both should be considered when making placement and planning programming. In some instances, an ESL or ELL teacher may be a part of the IEP team and may provide consultation or direct instruction to the special education teacher.

If the special education student does not speak English as his or her native language, or if English is not used primarily by the family, language consideration will be important in the classroom. Key words and concepts will need to be presented in a parallel fashion (in both languages, first explaining in the student's native tongue and then in English).

Classroom Assessments

Not only will the student's needs regarding his or her disability be considered when making assignments and giving tests, his or her language will need to be considered, as well. It is important that the student be tested on his or her knowledge of the subject and not the ability to communicate in English. For example, assessment of a child's understanding of the water cycle may be evaluated by asking the student to draw the sequence and verbally explain it instead of writing a paragraph on the same.

Skill 7.3 Recognizing strategies for collaborating with students and their families in developing and monitoring progress toward instructional, behavioral, and social goals

Involving the special education student (when appropriate) and his or her family in setting instructional goals is necessary to develop a well-rounded IEP. When families help set goals for things that are important to the special education student, subsequent increased family cooperation and involvement are usually evident. Typically, the parent of the child knows the child best, so meshing the school goals and those of the family will provide a program that is most thorough in meeting the student's needs.

Please refer to Skills 12.1, 12.2, and 12.3 for details on collaborating with students and family.

Monitoring progress
Once a set of mutually accepted goals has been established with the help of teachers, parents and others, progress on these mutually accepted goals—as well as those initiated by the school—can be charted or measured in a variety of ways. The method used to track the goals should be those indicated in the goals and objectives section of the IEP.

Charting is a formal tracking method of student behavior and progress. Often based on a functional behavioral assessment portion of the IEP, the chart will include behaviors (positive or negative), the time covered, and frequency of the behavior (which is often shown with tally marks).

Anecdotal records are a journaling of behaviors observed in the home or classroom. Such records may be notes kept by the classroom teacher or therapist, or notes from the parent (often literally in the form of paper notes, passbook entries, or emails) regarding student success and challenges.

Observations are a more focused form of anecdotal records. They occur when a specific activity, class, or time period is observed and the behaviors and skills of the individual student are recorded. A comparison of student behavior in various settings often gives information needed to write appropriate IEP goals. Standard Classroom quizzes and assessments will also provide useful information on student progress.

Skill 7.4 Demonstrating knowledge of how to develop and implement comprehensive, longitudinal individualized programs (e.g., IEPs) in collaboration with students with disabilities, their parents/guardians, general education teachers, and other professionals

Please refer to Skills 12.1, 12.2, and 12.3 for more details.

No Child Left Behind (NCLB) was signed on January 8, 2002. It addresses accountability of school personnel for student achievement with the expectation that every child will demonstrate proficiency in reading, math, and science. For example, all students should know how to read by grade three.

General education curriculum should reflect state learning standards. Because special educators are responsible for teaching students to a level of comparable proficiency as their non-disabled peers, this curriculum should also be followed closely in the special education program.

Naturally, certain modifications and accommodations will be necessary to help students with disabilities meet learning standards. IEP goals and objectives are based on the unique needs of the child with a disability in meeting the curriculum expectations of the school (and the state/nation). Consider some of the following hypothetical cases:

Teachers in grades K-3 are mandated to teach reading to all students using scientifically-based methods with measurable outcomes. Some students (including some with disabilities) will not learn to read successfully unless taught with a phonics approach. It is the responsibility of the general education teacher and special education teacher to incorporate phonics into the reading program.

Students are expected to learn mathematics. While some students will quickly grasp the mathematical concept of groupings of tens (and further skills of adding and subtracting large numbers), others will need additional practice. Research shows that many students with disabilities need a hands-on approach. Perhaps those students will need additional instruction and practice using snap-together cubes to grasp the grouping-by-tens concept.

School districts, individual general education classrooms, and special education classrooms are no longer functioning independently. Learning standards set forth by the government now apply to all students and teachers, and these standards must be evidenced in curriculum and related IEP goals and objectives.

Developing an Appropriate IEP

An IEP is the document that forms the basis for special services and instruction in the educational setting. An IEP is developed when someone (e.g., parent, teacher, and specialist) asks for a meeting to consider the child's needs. Typical "team" members at a meeting include parents (and sometimes parent advocates), a general education teacher familiar with state standards, any special education teachers involved, specialists who can test or interpret tests for the team, a representative of the school district. The child may also be present, especially in secondary education.

If the team determines that the child is eligible for special education services, an IEP is written. According to IDEA, each IEP must contain the following:

- A statement of the present levels of educational performance of the child;
- A statement of annual goals, including short-term instructional objectives;
- A statement of the specific educational services to be provided to the child, and the extent to which the child will be able to participate in regular educational programs;
- The projected date for initiation and anticipated duration of such services; and
- Appropriate objective criteria and evaluation procedures and schedules for determining, on at least an annual basis, whether instructional objectives are being achieved.
- Instructional and program accommodations and supports that must be provided throughout the educational settings and, specifically, in state and district mandated testing.
- A clear rationale for any placement that involves nonparticipation in any part of the general education classroom
- Transition services, as appropriate and needed.

All teachers and staff who interact with a child on an IEP are required to follow the dictates of the IEP. In addition to goals and objectives, the IEP will specify what accommodations or instructional modifications are to be provided to the child. *Accommodations* usually concern *access* to the curriculum. A child with accommodations to access the curriculum will follow the same grade level standards and goals as general education students, and be graded on the same scale. *Modifications* usually refer to changes that significantly alter the standards, content, instructional level, or performance level required of the student. This means the student will be graded differently than grade peers. Whatever terminology is used, these distinctions are important, and it is the teacher's responsibility to be familiar with all aspects of the IEP, so as to ensure compliance with it.

Special education teachers must not only help their students understand and overcome their learning disabilities, they must also help the students' families and other teachers understand them and develop strategies to overcome them within the framework of instructional goals. Teachers need to take the information from assessments and understand how to transfer that into instructional objectives and teachable points. This can be a confusing process. It is important that you be able to help teachers, other specialists and parents work through this process. Taking the time to explain the process and how you arrived at specified instructional objectives will help more than one student.

Skill 7.5 Demonstrating knowledge of how to prioritize goals and objectives within areas of the general curriculum for students with disabilities based on their present level of performance

As a special educator, it is imperative to look to the general education curriculum as a means for developing appropriate goals and objectives for Individual Education Plans (IEPs). Since many students with disabilities are unable to complete the general education curriculum at the same level and at the same pace as students without disabilities, it is necessary to develop appropriate strategies and skills to prioritize the curriculum areas into attainable goals and objectives for these students.

The first step in prioritizing curriculum areas is to look for high stakes areas or those areas that are most easily able to be generalized to others. In this way, the teacher can target these skills with the students and provide the most intense instruction possible in the shortest amount of time. Choosing these types of skills provides the necessary foundation knowledge students need to be successful. There is always more to learn, but providing students with a solid foundation allows them the opportunity to achieve success in the future.

This is not always an easy process and may require the input of regular education teachers, curriculum specialists, or other district level personnel. It is also helpful to have specific data on the skills and curricular areas students have already mastered. This information, at the beginning, may allow teachers to eliminate portions of the curriculum at the onset. Using the information a student has already mastered is an excellent strategy for determining which curriculum can be eliminated, enhanced, or started at the most basic levels. It is for this reason that IDEA requires a *Current Levels of Performance* section prior to each long term goal written on an IEP.

Once the curriculum has been prioritized into meaningful areas, a gradation of success can be planned. In this way, students can tackle the skills in smaller, more manageable chunks of information to ensure mastery and success. Just as a car does not go directly from zero to sixty without seeing all the numbers in between, students do not go from a lack of knowledge to complete mastery in one giant step. It is necessary to analyze long term goals and break them down into steps, beginning with entry level objectives and working up to the final goal of mastery. Taking the time to build in smaller steps, even if they are only on those steps for short periods of time, provides a more realistic path. These paths may be measured in weeks, months, or even years depending on the abilities of the students, but should always be making forward progress toward the end goal of mastery of a specific objective.

The teacher and team must be very skilled at writing academic objectives that fall within the guidelines of the state and local expectations. In addition, these objectives must be measurable so that, when the unit or semester is complete, he or she can know for sure whether or not goals have been met. Once long range goals have been identified and established, the team must ensure that all goals and objectives are in conjunction with student ability and needs. Some objectives may be too basic for a higher level student, while others cannot be met with a student's current level of knowledge. Assessments discussed in previous sections can help identify a student's current level of performance for the first part of each goal of an IEP, and these assessments should provide information about needed accommodations and instructional modifications.

Sometimes, the curriculum itself is not the issue, but rather the manner in which the curriculum is taught. Modification and adaptation to the regular education curriculum and instruction is one of the cornerstones of special education services; it needs to be considered an integral part of this process. When prioritizing and planning appropriate instruction for goals and objectives, it is imperative to keep in mind which areas can be taught with simple modifications or adaptations and still yield student success. This balancing act is ongoing throughout special education.

Skill 7.6 Demonstrating knowledge of national, state, and local content and performance standards (e.g., Georgia Performance Standards).

Please refer to the Georgia department of education website http://public.doe.k12.ga.us/index.aspx for detailed information and specific standards for each grade level and subject area.

The Georgia Performance Standards (GPS) were developed in response to the Quality Basic Education Act of 1985, which mandated that Georgia must provide a curriculum that specifies what students are expected to know in each subject and grade. Georgia's standardized assessments (e.g., CRCT, GHSGT) must be in alignment with the curriculum.

GPS serves as a framework for instruction that helps teachers, students, and parents understand the concepts that should be taught at each grade level and for each course. GPS provides minimum standards of acceptance and does not prohibit teachers and schools from adding additional information, but does specify that schools must address each of the state required standards.
The standards outline clear expectations for instruction, assessment, and student work. The standards outline the criteria that constitute achievement of the standards, enabling the teacher to determine whether or not a student has mastered a skill or concept.

Skill 7.7 Demonstrating knowledge of how to sequence, implement, and evaluate long-term individualized learning goals.

In order to use the Georgia standards outlined in Skill 7.6 for writing goals and objectives for students with disabilities, it will be necessary to make modifications. Although the specific modifications will depend on each individual child's needs, when organizing and sequencing objectives, remember that skills are building blocks. A taxonomy of educational objectives, such as that provided by Bloom (1956), can be helpful in constructing and organizing both goals and objectives. Simple, factual knowledge of material is low on this cognitive taxonomy, and should be worked with early in the sequence. For example, matching, or memorizing definitions or memorizing famous quotes. Eventually, objectives should be developed to include higher level thinking such as comprehension (i.e., being able to use a definition); application (i.e., being able to apply the definition to other situations); synthesis (i.e., being able to add other information); and evaluation (i.e., being able to judge the value of something). Such a taxonomy can be used with the Differentiated Instructional practices discussed in Objective 26.07 to find entry points for each standard and align the goal not only with the standard, but with the child's current level of performance (As IDEA requires in an IEP).

For example, the Georgia Performance Standard (GPS), ELA3R2e for grade 3 states: "The student identifies and infers meaning from common root words, common prefixes (e.g., un-, re-, dis-, in-) and common suffixes (e.g., -tion, -ous, -ly)." Using the Differentiated Instruction approach discussed in Objective 26.07, a sample of differently leveled objectives for this standard might read:

- **Basic level:** (Student) will differentiate root words and common affixes by circling or highlighting the root word.
- **Moderate level:** (Student) will differentiate root words from affixes, then select the correct meaning for the affix from a group of 4 possible meanings.
- **Mastery level:** (Student) will differentiate root words from common affixes, state the meaning of the root word, and state how each affix changes the meaning of the root word.

Another example might be designing writing objectives for GPS Writing standard, ELA4W2 (The student demonstrates competence in a variety of genres) a, c, and d: "Critical Component: The student produces a narrative that: a. Engages the reader by establishing a context, creating a speaker's voice, and c. Creates an organizing structure, and d. Includes sensory details and concrete language to develop plot and character." Again, depending upon each student's level of performance, objectives might look like this:

- **Basic level:** Using a Cloze template for a personal narrative, (Student) will dictate responses for the blanks and select descriptive words from a list supplied by the teacher.
- **Moderate level:** Given a story template for beginning, middle and end, (Student) will fill in or dictate ideas for a short personal narrative, add at least one descriptive word in each part, then use this graphic organizer to dictate a short personal narrative.
- **Mastery level:** (Student) will write a short personal narrative that stays on topic, has a beginning, middle, and end, and uses descriptive words for people, places, things, or events.

The specific goals and objectives appropriate for any given child will require integration of the Georgia standards with the child's current level of performance and special needs.

OBJECTIVE 8 UNDERSTAND STRATEGIES AND TECHNIQUES FOR PROMOTING THE DEVELOPMENT OF COMMUNICATION, SOCIAL, AND LIFE SKILLS OF STUDENTS WITH DISABILITIES AND THE USES OF INSTRUCTIONAL AND ASSISTIVE TECHNOLOGIES TO SUPPORT STUDENTS' COMMUNICATION AND LEARNING.

SKILL 8.1 Demonstrating knowledge of how to support and enhance communication skills (e.g., developing vocabulary, self-monitoring oral language) of students with disabilities

Please refer to Skill 1.1 for oral language development.

Depending upon the nature and severity of the disability, the activities for communicative skills may need to be repeated in many contexts. When working with students with disabilities, however, it will be necessary to take the specific disability of each child into consideration.

A child with a Central Auditory Processing disorder, for example, may process speech more slowly than classmates without this disorder. This will usually also be true of students with Down's syndrome. For such students, it may be necessary for the teacher to speak more slowly and give the child additional time to respond. it may also be necessary for the teacher to slowly restate whatever a classmate says so that the student can understand it.

Some students will struggle with word finding and recall of key words when they talk. For these students, it can be helpful to discuss the subject ahead of time and provide a short list of key words the student may need. For example, if the topic is to be a sharing of what students did on vacation, the teacher can sit with the student and brainstorm a list of words about their vacation. These can be written clearly on a card and the student can use these to help "find" the words needed to express the ideas.

Some students need to learn to monitor what they are saying. For these students, it can be helpful to have them talk into a tape recorder; speaking as they normally would in class. Then have them listen to themselves to see if they said what they meant to say.

Skill 8.2 Demonstrating knowledge of the social skills needed for educational and other environments (e.g., giving and receiving meaningful feedback, engaging in conversations) and how to design instructional programs that enhance social participation across environments

Social skills training is an essential part of working with students who exhibit academic and social problems. Often these two problem areas, academic and social deficits, appear together. This issue presents a "chicken-and-egg" situation: Does the learning problem cause the behavior problem, or does the behavior problem cause the learning problem?

Social skills and adaptive behaviors can be learned in several ways. Most children learn through *Incidental Learning or Teaching.* That is, they learn through everyday experiences, observing those around them and seeing the consequences of their own and others' behavior. Children with disabilities, such as Autism Spectrum Disorders, ADHD, etc., may not learn appropriate social skills in this manner. Some children can learn through *Peer tutoring or Peer Interaction,* where the student is paired on a daily basis with a socially competent peer who serves as a model. The student is instructed to watch and imitate the model. In some cases this can be a successful approach to improving a child's social skills. However, many students with disabilities will need *Direct Skills Instruction* in order to learn appropriate social skills and adaptive behaviors. *Direct Skills Instruction* involves a systematic curriculum with objectives, exercises, and assessments that must be implemented by a teacher or counselor.

Peer

Direct

There are many such curricula available. The choice of curriculum will, of course, depend on the age, setting, and specific skills needed, and the specific disabilities in the student population. Whatever curriculum is chosen, however, it should be a *Validated Social Skills Curriculum*, that is, one that has been research tested for effectiveness. Such curricula will have certain key features. Typically, such a curriculum will include the following general topics or areas of behavior:

- Interpersonal or Peer relationships
- Conflict Management
- Self awareness of feelings and words to describe feelings
- Coping strategies for strong feelings
- Classroom behavior expectations
- Conversational rules of give and take
- Problem solving strategies when things go wrong
- Interpretation of body language and nonverbal cues
- Community or group dynamics and behavior
- Older students may also need job related social skills

- Methods used should include:
- Modeling of appropriate behaviors by both teachers and age appropriate models
- Explicit instruction in *Why, With Whom, Where, When, and How* the behavior being taught should be used
- Role playing and life like practice
- Extensive and repeated practice
- Explicit feedback and reinforcement
- Practice in multiple settings to encourage generalization and transfer

When teaching adaptive social and behavior skills is part of the special education program for students with disabilities, parent input is a critical part of the planning process. The measurement of adaptive social behavior should consist of surveys of the child's behavior and skills in a number of diverse settings, including his class, school, home, neighborhood, and community. Since it is not possible for one person to observe a child in all of the primary environments, measurement of adaptive behavior depends on the feedback from a number of people. Because parents have many opportunities to observe their child in an assortment of settings, they are normally an excellent source of information about adaptive behavior. The most prevalent method for collecting information about a child's adaptive behavior skills in the home environment is to have a school social worker, school psychologist, or guidance counselor interview the parents using a formal adaptive behavior assessment rating scale. These individuals may interview the parents at home or they may hold a meeting at the school to talk with the parents about their child's behavior. Adaptive behavior information is also procured from school personnel who work with the student in order to understand how the child functions in the school environment.

When incorporating social skills and adaptive behaviors in the classroom context, one useful strategy is to provide choices that allow students to select the assignment, and the order in which they complete tasks. In addition, priming or pre-practice is an effective classroom intervention for students with disabilities. Priming entails previewing information or activities that a student is likely to have problems with before he or she begins working on that activity.

Partial participation or multi-level instruction is another strategy, and it entails allowing students with disabilities to take part in the same projects as the rest of their class, with specific adaptations to the activity so that it suits a student's specific abilities and requirements. Additional instructional practices include self-management, which entails teaching the student to function independently without relying on a teacher or a one-on-one aid. This strategy allows the student to become more involved in the intervention process, and it improves autonomy.

Cooperative groups are an effective instructional technique for teaching social skills. Working in groups has been shown to result in increased frequency, duration, and quality of social interactions.

Typically, one tactic for enhancing success in learning social skills within the academic setting is through cooperative establishment of classroom rules and contingency point systems that focus upon both areas at the same time. Rules, few in number, written in a positive direction, and designed jointly with students, help to set standards for acceptable behavior within the classroom. Contingency point systems are established to reinforce the occurrence of these behaviors, as well as other academic and social behaviors that are considered appropriate. Reinforcement contingencies are an important means of encouraging appropriate behaviors.

It is important to arrange the physical environment so that preventive discipline can occur. By this means, the teacher assumes responsibility for creating and maintaining an environment in which the needs of his/her charges are met. The teacher may modify the physical aspects of the room to create a warm, motivating atmosphere, adapt instructional materials to the respective functioning levels of the students, and deliver specialized services through the use of systematic, reinforcing methods and techniques. When instructional environments, materials, and techniques are implemented that respond to the academic needs of students, often the personal needs of the student are met as well, with a parallel effect of increased learning and appropriate social behaviors.

Skill 8.3 Demonstrating knowledge of strategies for enhancing self-esteem, self-advocacy, self-determination, and independence of students with disabilities

Self- Esteem

Self-esteem may be defined as the collective attitudes or feelings that one holds about oneself. Children with disabilities often perceive early in life that they are deficient in skills that seem easier for their peers without disabilities. They may also encounter expressions of surprise or even disgust from both adults and children in response to their differing appearances and actions, resulting in damage to the self-esteem. The special education teacher will want to direct special and continuing effort to improve each child's own perception of himself.

The poor self-esteem of a child with disabilities may cause that student at times to exhibit aggression or rage over inappropriate things. The teacher can ignore this behavior unless it is dangerous to others or too distracting to the total group, thereby reducing the amount of negative conditioning in the child's life. Further, the teacher can praise this child quickly and frequently for the correct responses that are given, remembering that these responses may require special effort on the student's part to produce. Correction, when needed, can be done tactfully, and in private.

The child whose poor self-esteem manifests itself in withdrawn behavior should be pulled gently into as many social situations as possible by the teacher. This child might be encouraged to share experiences with the class, to serve as teacher helper for projects, or to be part of small groups for tasks. Praise for performing these group and public acts is most effective if done immediately. The teacher can plan, in advance, to structure the classroom experiences so that aversive situations will be avoided. Thus, settings that stimulate the aggressive child to act out can be redesigned and situations that stimulate group participation can be set up in advance for the child who acts in a withdrawn manner.

Frequent, positive, and immediate are the best terms to describe the teacher feedback required by children with disabilities. Praise for very small correct acts should be given immediately, and repeated when each correct act is repeated. Constructive criticism or correction should be done, whenever possible, in private. The teacher should review the total day's interactions with students to ensure that the number and qualitative content of verbal stimuli is heavily on the positive side. While this trait is desirable in all good teaching, it is fundamental and utterly necessary to build the fragile self-concept of youngsters with disabilities.

Self- Advocacy

Learning about one's self involves the identification of learning styles, strengths and weakness, interests, and preferences. For students with mild disabilities, developing an awareness of the accommodations they need will help them ask for necessary accommodations on a job and in postsecondary education. Students can also help identify alternative ways they can learn.

Self-advocacy involves the ability to effectively communicate one's own rights, needs, and desires, and to take responsibility for making decisions that impact one's life.

There are many elements in developing self-advocacy skills in students who are involved in the transition process. Helping the student to identify future goals or desired outcomes in transition planning areas is a good place to start. Self-knowledge is critical for the student in determining the direction that transition planning will take.

The role of the teacher in promoting self-advocacy should include encouraging the student to participate in the IEP process as well as other key parts of his or her educational development. Self-advocacy issues and lessons are effective when they are incorporated into the student's daily life. Teachers should listen to the student's problems and ask the student for input on possible changes that he or she may need. The teacher should talk with the student about possible solutions, discussing the pros and cons of doing something. A student who self-advocates should feel supported and encouraged. Good self-advocates know how to ask questions and get help from other people. They do not let other people do everything for them.

Students need to practice newly acquired self-advocacy skills. Teachers should have students role play various situations such as setting up a class schedule, moving out of the home, or asking for accommodations needed for a course.

Skill 8.4 Demonstrating knowledge of resources, techniques, and procedures for transitioning students with disabilities into and out of school and alternative programs

Transitioning to School

Federal, State and local requirements for transition planning services are broken down for the Individualized Family Service Plan (IFSP) and Individualized Education Program (IEP). The IFSP provides early intervention services planning and documentation for an infant or toddler from birth to three years of age with a disability and her/his family. It also prepares all parties for the IEP process, which provides special education services planning and documentation for school aged students with exceptionalities aged three to twenty-one years.

The purpose and function of the IFSP and IEP are considered similar in nature. Both plans provide communication between active participants, written resources, services management and progress monitors. The IFSP and IEP both require a written plan developed by a multidisciplinary team to include parents input and participation based on assessments of unique needs. All early intervention services address identified needs of an infant or toddler, including the involved family in the IFSP, just as all special education and related services must be reflected in an IEP. Communication and collaboration are frequently quoted as the most significant challenges from people involved in the transition process.

The participants in the transition process include children and their families, service coordinators, early intervention practitioners involved in a child's future/pending/current IFSP program, IFSP teams and preschool teachers, early childhood special educators, related services practitioners, administrators and future/pending/current IEP teams. In order to facilitate transition success among these diverse groups of participants, skilled cross-agency communication with achievement based collaboration is required.

According to the National Early Childhood Transition Center (NECTC), individuals with disabilities experience the same difficulties with transitions as individuals who develop typically, but often to an even higher degree. Clearly, transition involves more than a child moving from one program to another. Goals should be written that will support important aspects in proactive transitioning from one program of development to another for the individuals and their families as suggested in the following quotes (Bredekamp & Copple, 1997; Hanson, 2005; Shotts et al, 1994; Rosenkoetter, 1995):

- Procedural supports should be developed to enhance successful transitions.
- Program decisions should meet individual needs.
- Services should be uninterrupted; appropriate services, equipment, and trained staff should be available in new settings

- Transition is actually a complex and gradual process rather than a specific event or product; this process begins long before the child moves to another setting or service program and it extends well after the child has engaged in the new services and activities
- Transition planning should prepare children, families and professionals.
- Transition practices should reduce stress for children, families and service providers.
- Transition should avoid any duplication in assessment and goal planning.
- Transition should be marked by ongoing communication and collaborative partnerships.
- Transition should be viewed as a process.
- Transition should meet legal requirements and make decisions in a timely manner.
- Transition should model non confrontational and effective advocacy that families can emulate throughout their children's lives.
- Transition should orient the child to promote a joyful move to the new setting and encourage success.

The NECTC scrutinizes and authenticates strategies involved in both early and latent childhood transitioning. NECTC supports positive school outcomes for individuals with disabilities. NECTC recognizes that there is still a lot to be learned regarding transition and have highlighted current and ongoing considerations listed here in bullets.

- A conceptual model for transition shared by all stakeholders should be enacted at the state level and if already enacted, it should be recognized and followed by participants in the transition process.
- A regular routine/schedule will help promote successful transitioning and will provide the individual with a sense of predictability and routine.
- Broad community support results in the highest quality services for ongoing education and transitioning of individuals.
- Contact with the individual's family and teacher before a transition is essential; meetings should involve time for listening to parents and should maintain a stress-free environment for all parties involved in the process.
- Family involvement in the child's program and education makes a difference, such as the family taking the individual to visit their new program.
- Following federal and state agency transition models and regulations provides a foundation with instruction for transitioning at the local level.
- Processes and procedures involved in transitioning must be collaborative between and among community agencies; to include who will be responsible for implementing procedures.
- Staff from sending and receiving programs must communicate with one another and the family regarding the individual's classroom experiences and their impending or ongoing needs.

- Staff from sending and receiving programs must visit each other's programs and settings to gain insight into the whole transition process.

Transition strategies should be tailored to meet individual needs rather than implementing a cross-functional program as a simple remedy and these strategies should be offered to families with their reactions/suggestions denoted in follow-up planning.

Transition for Students from Culturally Diverse Backgrounds
The comprehensive Bruns and Fowler's (2001) review of conceptual and empirical transition policies, published as a technical report for The Early Childhood Research Institute on Culturally and Linguistically Appropriate Services (CLAS), offered five critical factors to meet transition needs of children with disabilities and their families from culturally and linguistically diverse groups, as follows:

- **Collaboration** - An understanding of cultural traditions concerning education and interaction with professionals will assist in formulating realistic options for collaboration in transition planning, implementation and evaluation.
- **Communication** - Communication with families is critical during times of transition; pre-service and in service training efforts must support the understanding of inter and intra-group differences in communication styles.
- **Community Context** - An awareness and understanding of the community context is needed for planning, implementing and evaluating transition.
- **Continuity** - Continuity between home and program must be incorporated throughout the transition process.
- **Family Concerns** - Service providers, administrators, and policymakers must be responsive to family concerns when planning, implementing, and evaluating transitions.

The renewed portion of IDEA for IFSP and IEP plans regarding transition presents quite a few updates to Federal policies, such as the following: Develop a plan to prepare for the transition from early intervention services to preschool special education or other services, when appropriate.

Parents must give informed written consent before services may begin. If there is not agreement on all services, only agreed upon services will be provided.

Services must be initiated "as soon as possible" after the IFSP meeting. The IFSP must be reviewed at least every six months and evaluated at least annually at an IFSP meeting. Additionally, the parents may request a review of the IFSP at any time.

Close communication and collaboration between and among all participants in the transition process reduces the risk of fragmentation, duplication or discontinuity of services as well as unmet family needs. Effective relationships are necessary in successful transitions and this includes intra-agency, inter-agency and family-professional relationships (Rosenkoetter et al, 1994). Even at the IDEA federal level, the acknowledgement of the need to recognize and support all of the relationships associated with transition is agreed upon in resounding affirmation. There is a cyclical bond between relationships and communication, where communication builds and strengthens strong, positive relationships in support of that effective communication. Even in the event of family goal and service provider conflicts, prevention can be achieved through the establishment of respectful working relationships that follow federal, state and local mandates.

Post-Secondary Transitioning

Transition planning for post secondary activities is also mandated in the Individuals with Disabilities Education Act (IDEA). The transition planning requirements ensure that planning is begun as early as 14, and no later than age sixteen and continued through high school. Transition planning and services focus on a coordinated set of student-centered activities designed to facilitate the student's progression from school to post-school activities. Transition planning should be flexible and focus on the developmental and educational requirements of the student at different grades and times.

Transition planning is a student-centered event that necessitates a collaborative endeavor. In reference to secondary students, the responsibilities are shared by the student, parents, secondary personnel, and postsecondary personnel, who are all members of the transition team.

In most cases when transition is mentioned, it is referring to a child sixteen or over, but in some cases children younger than sixteen may need transition planning and assistance. Depending on the child's disability and its severity, a child may need assistance with transitioning to school from home, or to school from a hospital or institution or any other setting. In those cases, the members of the transition team may also include others such as doctors or nurses, social workers, speech therapists, and physical therapists.

It is important that the student play a key role in transition planning. This will entail asking the student to identify preferences and interests and to attend meetings on transition planning. The degree of success experienced by the student in postsecondary educational settings depends on the student's degree of motivation, independence, self-direction, self-advocacy, and academic abilities developed in high school.

In order to contribute to the transition planning process, the student should:

- Understand his/her disability and the impact it has on learning and work;
- Implement achievable goals;
- Present a positive self-image by emphasizing strengths, while understanding the impact of the disability;
- Know how and when to discuss and ask for needed accommodations;
- Be able to seek instructors and learning environments that are supportive; and
- Establish an ongoing personal file that consists of school and medical records, individualized education program (IEP), resume, and samples of academic work.

Transition planning involves input from four groups: the student, parents, secondary education professionals, and postsecondary education professionals. The primary function of parents during transition planning is to encourage and assist students in planning and achieving their educational goals. Parents also should encourage students to cultivate independent decision-making and self-advocacy skills.

The result of effective transition from a secondary to a postsecondary education program is a student with a disability who is confident, independent, self motivated, and striving to achieve career goals. This effective transition can be achieved if the team consisting of the student, parents, and professional personnel work as a group to create and implement effective transition plans.

The transition team of a student entering the workforce may also include community members, organizations, company representatives, vocational education instructors, and job coaches.

Transition services will be different for each student. Transition services must take into account the student's interests and preferences. Evaluation of career interests, aptitudes, skills and training may be considered.

The transition activities that have to be addressed, unless the IEP team finds it uncalled for, are: (a) instruction (b) community experiences, (c) the development of objectives related to employment skill and other post-school areas, and (d) daily living skills.

Instruction – The instruction part of the transition plan deals with school instruction. The student should have a portfolio completed upon graduation. They should research and plan for further education and/or training after high school. Education can be in a college setting, technical school, or vocational center. Goals and objectives created for this transition domain depend upon the nature and severity of the student's disability, the students interests in further education, plans made for accommodations needed in future education and training, identification of post-secondary institutions that offer the requested training or education.

Community Experiences – this part of the transition plan investigates how the student utilizes community resources. Resources entail places for recreation, transportation services, agencies, and advocacy services. It is essential for students to deal with the following areas:

- Recreation and leisure – examples: movies, YMCA, religious activities.
- Personal and social skills - examples: calling friends, religious groups, going out to eat.
- Mobility and transportation - examples: passing a driver's license test or using public transportation.
- Agency access - examples: utilizing a phone book and making calls.
- System advocacy- example: have a list of advocacy groups to contact.
- Citizenship and legal issues - example: registering to vote.

Development of Employment -This segment of the transition plan investigates becoming employed. Students should complete a career interest inventory and have the opportunity to investigate different careers. Many work-skill activities can take place within the classroom, home, and community. Classroom activities may concentrate on employability skills, community skills, mobility, and vocational training. Home and neighborhood activities may concentrate on personal responsibility and daily chores. Community based activities may focus on part-time work after school and in the summer, cooperative education or work-study, individualized vocational training, and volunteer work.

Daily Living Skills – This segment of the transition plan is also important. Living away from home can be an enormous undertaking for people with disabilities. Numerous skills are needed to live and function as an adult. In order to live as independently as possible, a person should have an income, know how to cook, clean, shop, pay bills, get to a job, and have a social life. Some living situations may entail independent living, shared living with a roommate, supported living or group homes. Areas that may need to be looked into include: personal and social skills; living options; income and finances; medical needs; community resources and transportation.

The impact of transition planning on a student with a disability is very great. The student should be an active member of the transition team, as well as the focus of all activities. Students often think that being passive and relying on others to take care of them is the way to get things done. Students should be encouraged to express their opinions throughout the transition process. They need to learn how to express themselves so that others listen and take them seriously. These skills should be practiced within a supportive and caring environment.

Skill 8.5 Demonstrating knowledge of how to incorporate instructional and assistive technologies into IEPs in various settings (e.g., school, home)

IDEA provides the following definition of an Assistive Technology device: "Any item, piece of equipment or product system, whether acquired commercially off the shelf, modified, or customized, that is used to increase, maintain or improve functional capabilities of children with disabilities."

Almost anything can be considered assistive technology if it can be used to increase, maintain, or improve the functioning of a person with a disability. Some areas in which Assistive Technology (AT) may be used are:

- Communication
- Hearing
- Vision
- Environmental management
- Body movement
- Working with academic concepts related to reading, writing, or math
- Playing
- Memory
- Work or vocational skills
- AT devices can increase the following for a person with a disability:
- Level of independence
- Quality of life
- Productivity
- Performance
- Educational/vocational options
- Success in regular education settings

Assistive technology Services

In addition, the use of AT may decrease the amount of support services a student needs to be successful.

In addition to providing the devices, the LEA is also required to provide services to support the use of AT. IDEA '97 defines Assistive Technology Services as: "The term 'assistive technology service' means any service that directly assists a child with a disability in the selection, acquisition, or use of an assistive technology device." These services may include:

- **Evaluation** of the needs the child: The evaluation should include a functional evaluation of the child in his/her customary environment.
- **Providing** for the acquisition of assistive technology devices the child: this could be by purchasing or by leasing.

- **Selection and maintenance** of the AT device: included in this area could be the design, fitting, customizing, adapting applying, repairing, or replacing as needed to support the needs of the child.
- **Coordination** with other therapies, or interventions, such as those associated with existing education and rehabilitation plans and programs.
- **Training or technical assistance for the student** and/or the family of the student.
- **Training or technical assistance for professionals** including school personnel, employers, or any other individual who provide service to the student with a disability.

ACADEMIC AND LEARNING AIDS:

Reading:

Colored Overlays: Acetate overlays alter the contrast between text and the background paper. For students with visual perceptual difficulties, this low tech option may increase the student's ability to decipher what is written on a page.

Reading Window: Assists students who have difficulty with tracking. Reading windows are usually made of cardboard or stock paper. A "frame" the size of a standard line of text is cut out, forming a "window". The student moves the window down the page of text, highlighting one row at a time.

Hand-Held Spell Checker or Talking Dictionary: Provides support for students with reading or spelling difficulties. The student types a difficult word into the device and the word is spoken aloud by the device.

Audio-Tape or CD Textbooks: For students who have difficulty reading traditional texts, or for the student with a visual impairment, a textbook in an audio format may be used. Audio textbooks have become widely available and many CD versions provide indices, links, and a means of highlighting and "taking notes."

Talking Word Processing Program: These are generally software applications that provide speech output of the text displayed on a computer monitor. Options for reading the text may be word for word, line by line, or paragraph by paragraph. Some programs offer an option for the spell check to speak the list of options, allowing the student to hear the correct version of the word. Programs such as Write OutLoud by Don Johnston and Intellitalk II by IntelliTools are among the well known programs.

Writing

Modified Paper: For some students, bolder lines are helpful. Another option is tactile paper, where there is a raised line that the student can feel. Graph paper is often useful for math problems, or to improve legibility by placing one letter in each box.

Pencil Grips: Pencil grips are often used with students with fine motor difficulties to provide a more supported means of holding a pencil.

Adapted Tape Recorders: Students who have difficulty with writing may use a tape recorder to provide an oral product or to tape class notes. Adapted recorders with indexing features allow the student to pause the recorder and mark specific points for future reference.

Portable Word Processors: Although they do not have all the capabilities of a computer, portable word processors provide students with an alternative means to type rather than write. The information can be stored within the device and can be downloaded onto a computer for saving. Advantages of portable word processors, other than price, include durability and long battery life. Popular brands of portable word processors include AlphaSmart, Laser PC 6 and Quickpad.

Word Prediction Software: Used for students with difficulty in spelling and grammar. After the first letter or two of a word are typed, the computer predicts the word. One of the benefits for slow typing or students with physical impairments is that the numbers of keystrokes the student has to type in are reduced. A popular word prediction program is Co:Writer by Don Johnston. Some such programs offer the option to insert a prearranged list of key words for the student to use.

Voice Recognition Software: The student speaks the text into a microphone on the computer and the speech is converted to text. This type of technology is currently found in many applications outside of education. Voice dictation software includes Dragon naturally Speaking by Lernout & Hauspie and Via Voice from IBM.

Math

Calculators: Some students benefit from the use of a calculator. Adapted calculators with large buttons are appropriate for students with physical disabilities. Talking calculators are also available and useful for students with visual impairments.

On-Screen Electronic Worksheets: For students who have difficulty with the paper and pencil tasks of writing out math problems, products such as Math Pad by IntelliTools offer the option of allowing worksheets in an on-screen format.

Aids to Daily Living: In addition to academic areas, AT devices can be used to assist in the activities of daily living.

Adapted Eating/Drinking Utensils: For students with physical impairments, adapted eating and drinking utensils can assist the student in independent feeding. Some electronic eating utensils are also available. Companies such as Sammons Preston specialize in this type of equipment.

Home Maintenance: Adapted tools to help with tasks related to food preparation are available from companies such as Sammons Preston.

Self-Care Aids: Self-care aids include items that assist the person with a disability in tasks such as dressing, grooming, and toileting. Dressing aids include zipper grips for assisting with zipping, button hooks to aid in buttoning and unbuttoning. Grooming aids include hairbrushes, toothbrushes with adaptive handles. Toileting aids include adapted toilet seats and safety bars for transferring on and off the toilet.

Many students with disabilities require assistive technologies in order to be successful within the regular curriculum or environment. As with any form of technology, assistive devices are constantly being changed and updated; therefore, it is important to stay as up-to-date as possible. It is also essential to search out within a district to discover who to contact to provide help in finding the necessary technologies to allow student success.

When considering adding technology for students with special needs, it is important to conduct a multi-disciplinary evaluation to ensure that specific student strengths are utilized in providing appropriate technology. This might include consulting such people as an assistive technology specialist, an occupational therapist, a physical therapist, a speech pathologist, or other designated professionals with specific training.

Consider the needs of the student and those working with the device. For instance, an augmentative communication device is only as good as it is easy for the student to use and access. The ease with which the person in school and at home can program it is also a factor. If the device is too complicated to program with phrases or to make changes to when necessary, it will be less than ideal in the school setting.

Also, always start with the least restrictive device. If, for example a student requires information to be visually presented at the same time it is orally presented, an overhead/smart board might be the best choice. There are other students in the classroom who will benefit from this type of modification, as well, and the student with special needs will not have to be isolated or pointed out to his or her classmates.

If any form of assistive technology (even simply typing assignments instead of handwriting them) is required, it is essential to include it in the child's IEP. While many teachers and parents will follow the special educator's word and implement what is best for the child with no difficulties, it can provide future teachers with beneficial information. While the IEP is legally binding and therefore mandates the users to implement what is written in it, it also contains a wealth of information for people who are working with that child.

Determination of Student Need for Assistive Technology
Oftentimes, the special educator will identify the need for consultation or testing in an area in which a student is having difficulty. Testing or other professional evaluation may result in the trial or ongoing use of some form of assistive technology as listed on the student's IEP.

Development of Student Skill Using Specific Assistive Technology
Students who have been identified as needing assistive technology require training in the use of the equipment. Sometimes, a therapist or consultant will "push in" to the classroom, providing training for the student in the classroom setting. Other times, the student will practice using the assistive technology in a separate setting until a level of experience/expertise is reached. The assistive technology may then be used in the special education or inclusion classroom.

Communication of Expected Skill Level in Classroom
As students begin to use assistive technology in the classroom, the desired use (Including activity, location, and time) should be outlined for the special educator so that misunderstandings do not result in a student misusing or under-using the technology. The student, then, will have a level of accountability and be functioning to the best of his or abilities.

Training of School Personnel on Use of Assistive Technology
Although special educators are often trained in using a variety of assistive devices, advances in technology make it necessary for professionals to participate in ongoing training for new or unfamiliar equipment. This training may be conducted by a knowledgeable therapist or consultant in the school district, or school personnel may need to attend workshops off campus.

Teachers in future years can look back and see what worked in previous years, or if the student moves, the new personnel will understand what specific devices and needs the student has. They will thus be better able service those needs from the beginning. In the end, the IEP is an important document wherein all information pertaining to the student, including assistive technology needs, should be conveyed.

OBJECTIVE 9 UNDERSTAND STRATEGIES FOR MANAGING THE LEARNING ENVIRONMENT

Skill 9.1 Applying knowledge of strategies for creating a safe, supportive, and positive classroom climate that fosters respect for diversity and positive interactions among all students

Classroom Climate of Mutual Respect

Awareness of cultural diversity and beliefs will help the special educator understand how best to communicate school goals with his or her students' families. As understanding and communication grow, family support will help the student become more successful in academics. The teacher's responsibility to learn about and understand the background of all students was addressed earlier in this guide. However, it is not enough for the teacher to understand and respect each student's background and individuality. It is also important for the teacher to ensure that *other students—all of them*—learn to understand and respect each student's background and individuality.

While some students will have learned such attitudes at home, many will not have done so. It may be necessary for the teacher to implement specific activities and procedures to help build a supportive cohesive classroom climate. Activities and games that help students learn about one another and identify both differences and similarities are helpful at the start of the year. It may help to have students participate in activities that revolve around a form of group identity.

It may be necessary to explicitly teach students how to respond to one another in positive, supportive ways. Rewarding courtesy and mutual support can be helpful. Earlier sections on methods of teaching students to listen to one another can be modified to assist here, too. It is essential that students realize that everyone is different and that we do not all need to do things the same way.

The Role of Rules and Standards in Classroom Climate

According to Henley, Ramsey, and Algozzine (1993, 1995), positive student behavior is facilitated by the teacher through techniques such as the following: Provide students with cues about expected behavior. Both verbal and non-verbal signals may become a part of the general classroom routine. The teacher provides cues about acceptable and unacceptable behavior in a consistent manner.

Provide appropriate and necessary structure. Based upon individual differences and needs, structure should be built into the environment. Children with aggressive and anxious traits may need a high degree of structure, while others with less significant conditions will require lesser, but varied, amounts of structure. Structure is related to teacher direction, physical arrangement of environment, routine and scheduling, and classroom rules.

Involve each student in the learning process. Allow them to manipulate things, to explore surroundings, to experiment with alternative solutions, to compare findings with those of classmates, and to pose questions and seek answers. This approach helps to instill an internal focus of control while meaningfully involving the child in the learning process.

Enable the student to experience success. If the student is not provided tasks or activities in which success can be experienced, the teacher can expect misbehavior or withdrawal.

Having successful experiences are vital in developing feelings of self-worth and confidence in attempting new activities. (Jones & Jones, 1986).

Use interest boosting. If signs of disinterest or restlessness occur, the teacher quickly shows interest in the student. Conversing with the student may stimulate renewed interest or enthusiasm.

Diffuse tension through humor. A humorous comment may bring forth laughter that lessens the tension in a stressful situation.

Help the student hurdle lessons that produce difficulty. The teacher can get a student back on track by assisting in the answering of difficult problems. Thus, the hurdle is removed and the student is back on task.

Use signal interference. Cue the student with signals so that a potential problem can be extinguished. Individualized signals may be designed and directed toward specific students.

Incorporate antiseptic bouncing when it is obvious that a student needs to be temporarily removed from the classroom situation. This technique is useful in dispelling uncontrollable laughter or hiccups and in helping the student get over feelings of anger, or disappointment. This approach involves no punishment, and removal may be in the form of delivering a message, getting a drink of water, or other chores that appear routine.

Use teacher reinforcing. The teacher "catches the child engaged in appropriate behavior" and reinforces him at that time. For example, the teacher praises the student's task-oriented behavior in an effort to keep him from getting off task. Employ planned ignoring. Unless the behavior is of a severe, harmful, or self-injurious nature, the teacher purposefully ignores the child. This strategy helps to extinguish inappropriate behavior by removing a viable reinforcer, that of teacher attention. The key is to deliver substantial reinforcement for appropriate behavior.

Use teacher commanding. The teacher uses direct verbal commands in an effort to stop the misbehavior. This technique should not be continued, however, if the student does not stop the inappropriate behavior upon the first instance his is told to do so. Inappropriate behavior will probably worsen upon repeated verbal commands.

Try teacher focusing. The teacher expresses empathy or understanding about the student's feelings, situation, or plight. The teacher uses inquiry to obtain information from the student, and then offers reasons or possible solutions to the problem.

Skill 9.2 Demonstrating knowledge of strategies for addressing common barriers to accessibility and acceptance faced by students with disabilities and ways to design and adapt physical and learning environments to promote students' active participation, academic success, self-advocacy, and independence

Please refer to Skill 8.3 for additional details on self advocacy.

Physical Environment (Spatial Arrangements)

The physical setting of the classroom contributes a great deal to the propensity for students to learn. An adequate, well-built, and well-equipped classroom will invite students to learn. This has been called "invitational learning." This is even more important when students with disabilities are involved. Among the important factors to consider in the physical setting of the classroom are the following:

a) **Adequate physical space**: A classroom must have adequate physical space so students can conduct themselves comfortably. Some students are distracted by windows, pencil sharpeners, doors, etc. Some students prefer the front, middle, or back rows. The needs of students with disabilities may be critical here. Wheelchairs need space to get around. Blind students need furniture to remain in fixed locations, etc.
b) **Repair status**: The teacher has the responsibility to report any items of classroom disrepair to maintenance staff. Broken windows, falling plaster, exposed sharp surfaces, leaks in ceiling or walls, and other items of disrepair present hazards to students.
c) **Lighting adequacy**: Another factor that must be considered is adequate lighting. Report any inadequacies in classroom illumination. Some students may require full-spectrum lighting due to a visual impairment. Should these lights be in a room, reporting their failure as soon as possible will enable that student to have continuity in the learning environment.
d) **Adequate entry/exit access**: Local fire and safety codes dictate entry and exit standards. In addition, all corridors and classrooms should be wheelchair accessible for students and others who use them. Older schools may not have this accessibility.
e) **Ventilation/climate control**: Another consideration is adequate ventilation and climate control. Some classrooms in some states use air conditioning extensively. Sometimes it is so cold as to be considered a distraction. Specialty classes (such as science) require specialized hoods for ventilation. Physical Education classes have the added responsibility for shower areas and specialized environments that must be heated, such as pool or athletic training rooms.

f) **Coloration**: Classrooms with warmer subdued colors contribute to students' concentration on task items. Neutral hues for coloration of walls, ceiling, and carpet or tile are generally used in classrooms, so distraction due to classroom coloration is minimized.

In the modern classroom, there is a great deal of furniture, equipment, supplies, appliances, and learning aids to help the teacher teach and students learn. The classroom should be provided with furnishings that fit the purpose of the classroom. The kindergarten classroom may have a reading center, a playhouse, a puzzle table, student work desks/tables, a sandbox, and any other relevant learning/interest areas.

Whatever the arrangement of furniture and equipment may be, the teacher must provide for adequate traffic flow. Rows of desks must have adequate space between them for students to move and for the teacher to circulate. All areas must be open to line-of-sight supervision by the teacher.

In all cases, proper care must be taken to ensure student safety. Furniture and equipment should be situated safely at all times. No equipment, materials, boxes, etc. should be placed where there is danger of falling over. Doors must have entry and exit accessibility at all times.

Noise level should also be considered as part of the physical environment. Students vary in the degree of quiet that they need and the amount of background noise or talking that they can tolerate without getting distracted or frustrated. Thus, a teacher must maintain an environment that is conducive to the learning of each child.

Human Barriers to Accessibility

In many cases the most difficult barriers to accessibility for students with disabilities are not physical barriers; they are the attitudes of others. Students with disabilities often face intolerance and stereotypical attitudes from both other children and from teachers and adults. it is often necessary to educate general education students about disabilities and to help them learn about similarities and acceptance, as well. Sometimes even teachers have attitudes that provide obstacles to students with disabilities (See Skill 9.4).

Instructional Arrangements

Instructional arrangements can also affect the degree to which students feel accepted. Learning styles refer to the ways in which individuals learn best. Physical settings, instructional arrangements, available materials, techniques, and individual preferences are all factors in the teacher's choice of instructional strategies. Information about the student's preferences can be done through a direct interview or a Likert-style checklist where the student rates his or preferences. By taking a student's instructional preferences into account, the teacher shows an acceptance of those preferences as legitimate and of value.

Some students work well in large groups; others prefer small groups or one-to-one instruction with the teacher, aide, or volunteer. Instructional arrangements also involve peer-tutoring situations with the student as tutor or tutee. The teacher also needs to consider how well the student works independently with seatwork. If the student is able to work in a manner that "feels right" to him or her, the student will feel like an accepted, valued member of the class.

Skill 9.3 Demonstrating knowledge of classroom management strategies, including structuring and managing daily routines (e.g., transitions between lessons or classes) to optimize students' time on task and facilitate students' effective use of instructional time

Classroom management plans should be in place when the school year begins. Developing a management plan takes a proactive approach—that is, deciding on what behaviors will be expected of the class as a whole, anticipating possible problems, and teaching the behaviors early in the school year.

Behavior management techniques should focus on positive procedures that can be used at home as well as at school. Involving the students in the development of the classroom rules lets the students know the rationale for the rules, and allows them to assume responsibility for them. Once the rules are established, enforcement and reinforcement for following the rules should begin right away.

Consequences should be introduced at the same time as the rules. They should be clearly stated and understood by all of the students. The severity of the consequence should match the severity of the offense, and must be enforceable. The teacher must apply the consequence consistently and fairly; students should know what to expect when they choose to break a rule.

Like consequences, students should understand what rewards to expect for following the rules. The teacher should never promise a reward that cannot be delivered. The teacher should also follow through with the reward as soon as possible. Consistency and fairness are necessary for rewards to be effective. Students will become frustrated and give up if they see that rewards and consequences are not delivered timely and fairly.

About four to six classroom rules should be posted where students can easily see and read them. These rules should be stated positively, and describe specific behaviors so they are easy to understand. Certain rules may also be tailored to meet target goals and IEP requirements of individual students. (For example, a new student who has had problems with leaving the classroom may need an individual behavior contract to assist him or her with adjusting to the class rule about remaining in the assigned area.) As the students demonstrate the behaviors, the teacher should provide reinforcement and corrective feedback. Periodic "refresher" practice can be done as needed, for example, after a long holiday or if students begin to "slack off." A copy of the classroom plan should be readily available for substitute use, and the classroom aide should also be familiar with the plan and procedures.

The teacher should clarify and model the expected behavior for the students. In addition to the classroom management plan, a management plan should be developed for special situations, (e.g., fire drills) and transitions (e.g., going to and from the cafeteria). A periodic review of the rules, as well as modeling and practice, may be conducted as needed (such as after an extended school holiday).

Procedures that use social humiliation, withholding of basic needs, pain, or extreme discomfort should never be used in a behavior management plan. Emergency intervention procedures used when the student is a danger to him or herself or others are not considered behavior management procedures. Throughout the year, the teacher should periodically review the types of interventions being used, assess the effectiveness of the interventions used in the management plan, and make revisions as needed for the best interests of each child.

Motivation

Before the teacher begins instruction, he or she should choose activities that are meaningful, relevant, and at the appropriate level of student difficulty.

Teacher behaviors that motivate students include:

Maintaining success expectations through teaching, goal setting, establishing connections between effort and outcome, and self-appraisal and reinforcement; having a supply of intrinsic incentives such as rewards, appropriate competition between students, and the value of the academic activities.

Focusing on students' intrinsic motivation through adapting the tasks to students' interests, providing opportunities for active response, including a variety of tasks, providing rapid feedback, incorporating games into the lesson, and allowing students the opportunity to make choices, create, and interact with peers.

Stimulate students' learning by modeling positive expectations and attributions. Project enthusiasm and personalize abstract concepts. Students will be better motivated if they know what they will be learning. The teacher should also model problem-solving and task-related thinking so students can see how the process is done.

For adolescents, motivation strategies are usually aimed at getting the student actively involved in the learning process. Since the adolescent has the opportunity to get involved in a wider range of activities outside the classroom (e.g., job, car, being with friends), stimulating motivation may be the focus even more than academics.

Motivation may be achieved through extrinsic reinforcers or intrinsic reinforcers. This is accomplished by allowing the student a degree of choice in what is being taught or how it will be taught. The teacher should, if possible, obtain a commitment either through a verbal or written contract between the student and the teacher. Adolescents also respond to regular feedback, especially when that feedback shows that they are making progress.

Rewards for adolescents often include free time for listening to music, recreation, or games. They may like extra time for a break or exemption from a homework assignment. They may receive rewards at home for satisfactory performance at school. Other rewards include self-charting progress and tangible reinforcers. In summary, motivational activities may be used for goal setting, self-recording of academic progress, self-evaluation, and self-reinforcement. See Objective 25.07 for more on use of reinforcement.

Transitions and Time on Task

Schedule development depends on the type of class (elementary or secondary) and the setting (regular classroom, resource room, separate class). There are, however, general rules of thumb that apply to both types and settings:

- Allow time for transitions, planning, and setups.
- Aim for maximum instructional time by pacing the instruction quickly and allotting time for practice of the new skills.
- Proceed from short assignments to long ones, breaking up long lessons or complex tasks into short sessions or step-by-step instruction.
- Follow a less preferred academic or activity with a highly preferred academic activity.
- In settings where students are working on individualized plans, do not schedule all the students at once in activities that require a great deal of teacher assistance. For example, have some students work on math or spelling while the teacher works with the students in reading (as it usually requires more teacher involvement).
- Break up a longer segment into several smaller segments with a variety of activities.

Additionally, teachers who keep students informed of the sequencing of instructional activities maintain systematic transitions because the students are prepared to move on to the next activity. For example, the teacher says, "When we finish with this guided practice together, we will turn to page twenty-three and each student will do the exercises. I will then circulate throughout the classroom helping on an individual basis. Okay, let's begin." Following an example such as this will lead to systematic smooth transitions between activities, because the students will be turning to page twenty-three when the class finishes the practice without a break in concentration.

Another method that leads to smooth transitions is to move students in groups and clusters rather than seat them one-by-one. This is called "group fragmentation." For example, if some students do seat work while other students gather for a reading group, the teacher moves the students in pre-determined groups. Instead of calling the individual names of the reading group, which would be time consuming and laborious, the teacher simply says, "Will the blue reading group please assemble at the reading station. The red and yellow groups will quietly do the vocabulary assignment I am now passing out." As a result of this activity, the classroom is ready to move on in a matter of seconds rather than minutes.

Additionally, the teacher may employ academic transition signals, which are defined as any "teacher utterance that indicate[s] movement of the lesson from one topic or activity to another by indicating where the lesson is and where it is going." For example, the teacher may say, "That completes our description of clouds, now we will examine weather fronts." Like the sequencing of instructional materials, this keeps the student informed on what is coming next so he or she will move to the next activity with little or no break in concentration.

Students with disabilities may benefit from having a daily schedule at their desk that tells them what lessons or movements will occur at what times. This is particularly true of students whose schedule requires moving around a bit. Therefore, effective teachers manage transitions from one activity to another in a systematically oriented way by efficiently managing instructional matter, sequencing instructional activities, moving students in groups, and employing academic transition signals. Through an efficient use of class time, achievement is increased because students spend more class time engaged in on-task behavior.

Transition refers to changes in class activities that involve movement. Examples are:

- Breaking up from large group instruction into small groups for learning centers and small-group instructions
- Classroom to lunch, to the playground, or to elective classes
- Finishing reading at the end of one period and getting ready for math the next period
- Emergency situations such as fire drills

Successful transitions are achieved by using proactive strategies. Early in the year, the teacher pinpoints the transition periods in the day and anticipates possible behavior problems (such as students habitually returning late from lunch). After identifying possible problems with the environment or the schedule, the teacher plans proactive strategies to minimize or eliminate those problems. Proactive planning also gives the teacher the advantage of being prepared, addressing behaviors before they become problems, and incorporating strategies into the classroom management plan right away. Transition plans can be developed for each type of transition, and the expected behaviors for each situation taught directly to the students.

Skill 9.4 Analyzing the ways in which teacher attitudes and behaviors affect individuals with and without disabilities and recognizes effective strategies for establishing and maintaining rapport with all students.

Influence of Teacher Attitudes

The attitude of the teacher can have either a positive and negative impact on student performance. A teacher's attitude includes the expectations that the teacher may have toward the student's potential performance, as well as how the teacher behaves toward the student. This attitude, combined with expectations, can impact the student's self-image as well as his or her academic performance.

Negative teacher attitudes toward students with disabilities are detrimental to the handicapped students mainstreamed in general education classrooms. The phenomenon of a self-fulfilling prophecy is based on the attitude of the teacher. The term 'self-fulfilling prophecy' in the educational context refers to the research documented phenomenon in which a teacher's expectations about a student strongly influence both the teacher's perceptions of the student, and the student's self image and behavior. Teachers are more likely to see, to notice, behaviors that reinforce their expectations, so when evaluating a student's behavior they are simply more likely to report and record those behaviors that fit their expectations. Therefore, if the teacher expects the student to fail, the student is more likely to be *judged* to have failed, regardless of the student's objective behaviors, while that same student might be *judged* to have succeeded if the teacher expected him to succeed, because the teacher in each case is more likely to see and record behaviors that fit expectations.

In addition, the teacher's expectations can have a powerful effect on the student's self image and confidence about success or failure. A student, who feels the teacher's high expectations both for behavioral standards and for the student's ability to meet them, will typically make more of an effort and be less likely to give up than a student who feels the teacher already considers him a failure. This effort and confidence (or lack of each) contributes to a self-fulfilling prophecy effect in the classroom.

This phenomenon also occurs in more subtle ways. Even without realizing it, teachers communicate their expectations of individual students. In turn, the students may adjust their behaviors to match the teacher's expectations. Based on this, the teacher's expectations of what will happen affect what actually does happen.

Researchers in psychology and education have investigated this occurrence and discovered that many people are sensitive to verbal and nonverbal cues from others regarding how they expect to be treated. As a result, they may consciously and subconsciously change their behaviors and attitudes to conform to another person's hopes. Depending on the expectation, this can be either advantageous or detrimental.

The teacher's attitude toward a student can be shaped by a number of variables including race, ethnicity, disability, behavior, appearance, and social class. All of these variables can impact the teacher's attitude toward the student and how the student will achieve academically.

Teachers have the responsibility to prevent any of their negative attitudes toward students from impacting how they perceive the students and how they interact with them. If the teacher is able to communicate to all of his or her students that they all have great potential and is optimistic regarding this, then the students should excel in some aspect of their educational endeavors. This continues to be true for as long as the teacher is able to make the student believe in him or herself.

It can be hard for teachers to maintain a positive attitude at all times with all students. However, it is important to be encouraging to all students at all times, as every student has the potential to be successful in school. Consistent encouragement can help turn a C student into a B or even A student. At the same time, negative feedback can lead to failure and loss of self esteem.

Teachers should utilize their verbal communication skills to ensure that the things they communicate to students are said in the most positive manner possible. For example, instead of saying, "You talk too much," it would be more positive to state, "You have excellent verbal communication skills and are very sociable." Teachers have a major influence on what happens in their classrooms because they are the primary decision makers. They set the tone for how the information they distribute is absorbed. They also serve as models to other students in the room who may well imitate their attitudes or behavior—for good or bad.

In order for teachers to rise above their prejudices and preset attitudes, it is important that teachers are given training and support services to enable them to deal with students who come from challenging backgrounds or present challenging behaviors.

Skill 9.5 Demonstrating knowledge of strategies for preparing students to live harmoniously and productively in a culturally diverse world, including strategies for creating a learning environment that enables students to retain and appreciate their own and others' linguistic and cultural heritages

Effective teaching and learning for students begins with teachers who can demonstrate sensitivity for diversity in teaching and in relationships within school communities. Student portfolios should include work that has multicultural perspective and inclusion, enabling students to share cultural and ethnic life experiences in their learning. Effective teachers are responsive to including cultural and diverse resources in their curriculum and instructional practices.

Exposing students to culturally sensitive room decorations and posters that show positive and inclusive messages is one way to demonstrate inclusion of multiple cultures. Teachers should also continuously make cultural connections that are relevant and empowering for all students; they should also communicate academic and behavioral expectations. Cultural sensitivity must be communicated beyond the classroom with parents and community members to establish and maintain relationships.

It is also important to be sure this acceptance and appreciation of diversity is considered when selecting teaching materials and texts. Teachers should be aware of the "background assumptions" present in what they choose to present in class. They may not choose material that is openly negative toward a particular group, but is that group represented in the text? How is it represented? Teachers need to avoid materials that further stereotypes or present images that lack diversity.

Diversity can be further defined as the following:

- Differences among learners, classroom settings, and academic outcomes
- Biological, sociological, ethnic, socioeconomic, and psychological differences, as well as different learning modalities and styles among learners
- Differences in classroom settings that promote learning opportunities such as collaborative, participatory, and individualized learning groupings
- Expected learning outcomes that are theoretical, affective, and cognitive for students

Teachers should establish a classroom climate that is culturally respectful and engaging for students. In a culturally sensitive classroom, teachers maintain equity and fairness in student interactions and curriculum implementation. Assessments include cultural responses and perspectives that become further learning opportunities for students. Other artifacts that could reflect teacher/student sensitivity to diversity might consist of the following:

- Student portfolios reflecting multicultural/multiethnic perspectives
- Journals and reflections from field trips or guest speakers from diverse cultural backgrounds
- Printed materials and wall displays from multicultural perspectives
- Parent/guardian letters in a variety of languages, reflecting cultural diversity
- Projects that include cultural history and diverse inclusions
- Disaggregated student data reflecting cultural groups

Classroom climate of professionalism that fosters diversity and cultural inclusion The target of diversity allows teachers a variety of opportunities to expand their experiences with students, staff, community members, and parents from culturally diverse backgrounds. This allows their experiences to be proactively applied in promoting cultural diversity inclusion in the classroom. Teachers are able to engage and challenge students to develop their own diversity skills in building character and relationships with cultures beyond their own. In changing the thinking patterns of students to become more culturally inclusive in the 21st century, teachers are addressing the globalization of our world.

Cultural Factors and Perspectives that Affect Relationships
The mobile nature of society today provides a broader mixture of cultures around the country. Students moving from school to school may experience different curricula and different school cultural factors. As educators expect the students to adapt, they must also remember that the schools themselves must also consider the student's individual cultural influences.

Cultural relationships, morals, and values are not unique to students with disabilities. However, it is important to keep in mind that in certain cultures, individual differences may be thought of very differently than that of the current school. Many cultures now accept disabilities and realize the value and capability of students with them; however, there are still some cultures and beliefs that shield and hide those who appear to be different. When discussing a child's disabilities with the parents or guardians, it is important to keep in mind their views on disabilities.

Additionally, acculturation is not something that occurs overnight. It takes years for students to become acculturated. Students who move from a foreign country and do not speak English can take up to seven years to become proficient in English. This is not a disability; it is the natural progression of language acquisition. The timeline can be similar for other aspects of culture. When considering the identification of students who are not succeeding in school, teachers must take into consideration these types of cultural factors. There are a number of acculturation surveys that can be used to help guide the teacher in examining the role of culture in the academic performance of the student.

Community agencies can often help schools bridge these cultural gaps. Reaching out to families by including appropriate translators/translations, encouraging parents to share their heritage and traditions with the school and other students, and respecting that differences of what is acceptable will help all involved parties.

Beyond language, it is important to respect and provide accommodations for other cultural factors. Holidays may be significantly different for certain ethnicities. Another area may even include the food served in the cafeteria; if the culture requires that foods are, for example, Kosher or vegetarian, the school may need to make reasonable modifications.

The general issues that surround multiculturalism within schools are simply exacerbated when dealing with disabilities. Identification of a disability naturally increases the stress level and can damage the relationships; therefore, it is more important to extend any possible method to secure positive interactions. Keeping all of these issues in min—as well as the issues specific to the culture—will ensure a more productive educational process for all.

Skill 9.6 Demonstrating knowledge of how to use technology for planning and managing the teaching and learning environment

Part of being a teacher today means being able to perform the simplest and most complicated tasks of the job on a computer. Most schools take attendance electronically; the teacher may need to take a few minutes during class to enter attendance into a computer. Additionally, if a teacher is going to write a letter to all the parents, a standard form (template) may already exist on the database that will allow for individualizing the message to each parent. It may also address envelopes or create mailing labels to the parents.

Grade books can be found in electronic formats. Many school districts use programs like "Easy Grade Pro" and "Grade Quick." Some districts make their teacher's grade books accessible to parents on a daily basis by using web-based programs such as TeacherEase. This provides teachers with a reason not to fall behind in grading. Many schools have individual classroom sites on their website where events and homework are put up online.

Large textbook companies often include electronic lesson planners as part of their packaging. These may come with prepackaged lessons that assist teacher preparation and allow for teachers to individualize their needs. They also train teachers to find the work in PDF (digital format) and attach it directly to the lesson, which allows for easy access to what must be copied for the lesson that day.

Most of these programs stated above require the teacher to spend time learning the system. This most likely means that teachers will have to attend an in-service and/or find a colleague to go to for answers. Remember, these are not shortcuts; they are tools of the trade.

The most important thing a teacher must remember when using this type of technology is that a hardcopy (print out) is his or her salvation when the system goes down. Save information often and plan to print out the work at least weekly.

Teachers of students with disabilities now have access to technology that can assist them to meet the needs of these students. Scanners attached to computers can enlarge or rearrange worksheets or materials to meet the needs of individual students, print them on special paper, etc. The internet provides easy access to images from clipart to photographs that can be used to help illustrate concepts and make them more concrete. Since the teacher of students with disabilities may often need to redesign worksheets and lessons, or design them from scratch, word processors can make this task much simpler.

OBJECTIVE 10 UNDERSTAND THE DEVELOPMENT AND IMPLEMENTATION OF EFFECTIVE BEHAVIOR MANAGEMENT AND BEHAVIOR INTERVENTION STRATEGIES FOR STUDENTS WITH DISABILITIES

Skill 10.1 Identifying individualized expectations for the personal and social behavior of students with disabilities in given settings

When considering the personal and social behavior of students with disabilities, it is important to be specific and detailed in reporting these expectations in various settings. These expectations can be included in the student's IEP or the Behavior Intervention Plan (BIP).

Students who are struggling with behavior often misread social settings and the nonverbal cues people provide to each other. In this way, their troubles can often increase (this is due to inappropriate understanding on their part, rather than outward defiance). Children with autism also have difficulties in reading social situations and using appropriate behavior.

It is important to clearly develop a plan wherein students are taught the expectations of different settings. In this way, students can begin to make generalizations and develop more appropriate behavioral strategies. Understanding in detail that what may be acceptable at home in private may not be acceptable in McDonald's sometimes takes numerous repetitions, but is invaluable for certain students.

Students may need to practice or use role playing strategies to begin to make these types of generalizations. Field trips or other practical experiences may be the most beneficial format for ensuring student success.

Developing a plan, which has been individualized for the student, can be helpful, as well. Sometimes, visual aids can be used to ensure success. A note card with helpful reminders is another tool to help students remember expectations for their personal and social behaviors. A different set of reminders may need to be provided for each setting the student will be integrated into for a placement.

This type of training can begin at very young ages. Students in preschool and elementary school can begin to realize the difference in behavioral expectations depending upon the setting. Assemblies or other large group activities can provide the public setting for students. Lunch and recess are also good times to work on these types of behavioral skills.

As the child ages, mock interviews, field trips, and frank, honest discussions may be strategies of more use. In any case, students often require direct teaching of these skills; skills most of us take for granted. A teacher may hear a colleague ask why a student doesn't understand why it's inappropriate to do "that" in the classroom. In this situation, the answer may be as simple as no one taught the student it was wrong.

Skill 10.2 Demonstrating knowledge of how to use performance data and information from all stakeholders to modify the learning environment to manage behaviors

The special education teacher has the additional role of being an advocate for assigned students. It is particularly important when there are students moving from room to room, for teachers to listen to the input of all who have interactions with that student. This includes parents, each of the student's teachers, and service providers. As professionals, teachers look for what appears to be causing a problem. What is the antecedent to the behavior? If this can be seen uniformly with those who work with the student, a behavior plan can be easily written. However, student behavior is often influenced by those around them.

For example, Johnny may talk all the way through Algebra with Mrs. Desmond and behave the same with four of his other teachers, but when he is with Mr. Hammond, he may be well behaved. When effective teachers get together and discuss a student's needs, they almost always discover something that works and acknowledge what they know does not work. A discussion about why Johnny does well in Mr. Hammond's class would be the best way to address this issue. Just what does Mr. Hammond do that is different? If Mr. Hammond has assigned Johnny to sit in the front row and in every other class he sits in the back, a possible solution to try would be preferential seating in the front of the room.

Sometimes, parents will ask questions about how to address behaviors. Listen to them. They may be asking about something the student needs help with in school. Formulating a plan together with the parents, as well as with other staff and teachers, creates a team approach. It provides a level of consistency that will help prevent a student from successfully manipulating the individual teacher.

Talk to colleagues to find out what is successful. Find out what consistently does not work. If a change in seating works, or if providing opportunities for movement or "planned ignoring" are successful in more than just one classroom, these actions should be given a uniform trial. In this manner, team approaches to behavioral issues often provide a way for students to learn appropriate behaviors in a shorter period of time.

Skill 10.3 Demonstrating knowledge of ethics, laws, rules, and procedural safeguards related to planning and implementing behavior management and discipline for students with and without disabilities

According to IDEA law, a student can be removed from school for disciplinary reasons for a period of time not exceeding ten consecutive school days. Removals of less than ten consecutive days may be implemented as long as those removals do not represent an alteration of placement for the student.

The IEP team and additional qualified staff must assess whether the behavior in question is part of the student's disability before a disabled student's placement can be modified as a result of disciplinary action. If the student's behavior is assessed to be part of the student's disability, the student's placement cannot be modified as part of a disciplinary tactic. The IEP team may assess that a modification of placement is required in order to provide a free, appropriate public education (FAPE) in the least restrictive environment.

The district has to give services to a student with a disability who has been taken from his or her current placement for more than ten school days in the school year as a result of disciplinary action. School staff can place a student in an interim alternative educational setting without the consent of the parent for the same time frame that a student without a disability could be placed, but not more than 45 calendar days (e.g., if the student brings a weapon or firearm to school, knowingly possesses or uses illegal drugs, or sells or solicits the sale of a controlled substance while at school).

IDEA Regulations indicate that a functional behavioral assessment FBA) has to be done before a student can be removed from a placement. After the FBA is performed, the IEP team must convene to create the positive behavior intervention plan that addresses the behavior in question and make sure that the plan is put into place. Information from the FBA is utilized to create meaningful interventions and plan for instruction in replacement behaviors. The IEP team must review the positive behavior intervention plan and how it is implemented to decide if changes are needed to make the plan more effective.

Functional Behavior Assessment (FBA)
A Functional Behavior Assessment (FBA) is a method of gathering information. The information that is collected is utilized to assess why problem behaviors occur. The data will also help pinpoint things to do that will help alleviate the behaviors. The data from a functional behavioral assessment is used to create a positive Behavioral Intervention Plan (BIP).

The Individuals with Disabilities Education Act (IDEA) specifically calls for a functional behavior assessment when a child with a disability has his or her present placement modified for disciplinary reasons. IDEA does not elaborate on how an FBA should be conducted, as the procedures may vary dependent on the specific child. Even so, there are several specific elements that should be a part of any functional behavior assessment.

The first step is to identify the particular behavior that must be modified. If the child has numerous problem behaviors, then it is important to assess which behaviors are the primary ones that should be addressed. This should be narrowed down to one or two primary behaviors. The primary behaviors are then described so that the components of the relevant behavior are clear to everyone involved in the child's treatment. The most typical order of procedures is as follows:

Identify and come to an agreement about the behaviors that need to be modified. Find out where the behaviors are most likely to happen and where they are not likely to happen. Identify what may trigger the behaviors to occur.

The team will ask these types of questions: What is unique about the surroundings where behaviors are not an issue? What is different in the locations where the problem conduct occurs? Could they be linked to how the child and teacher get along? Does the presence of other students or the amount of work a child is requested to do trigger the difficulty? Could the time of day or a child's frame of mind affect the behaviors? Was there a bus problem or an argument in the hallway? Are the behaviors likely to happen in a precise set of conditions or a specific location? What events seem to encourage the difficult behaviors?

Assemble data on the child's performance from as many resources as feasible. Develop a hypothesis about why difficult behaviors transpire. Ask what function the behaviors serve, what the child *gets* from the behaviors. A hypothesis is an educated deduction, based on data. It helps foretell in which location and for what reason problem behaviors are most likely to take place, and in which location and for what reason they are least likely to take place. Single out other behaviors that can be taught that will fulfill the same purpose for the child. Test the hypothesis. The team develops and utilizes positive behavioral interventions that are written into the child's IEP or behavior intervention plan.

Assess the success of the interventions. Modify or fine tune as required. If children have behaviors that place them or others at risk, they may require a crisis intervention plan. Crisis interventions should be developed before they are required. The team should determine what behaviors are crises and what they (and the child) will do in a crisis. By having a plan that guides actions, teachers can assist children through difficult emotional circumstances.

Essential Elements of a Behavior Intervention Plan
A Behavior Intervention Plan is utilized to reinforce or teach positive behavior skills. It is also known as a behavior support plan or a positive intervention plan. The child's team normally develops the Behavior Intervention Plan. The essential elements of a behavior intervention plan are as follows:

- Skills training to increase the likelihood of appropriate behavior
- Modifications that will be made in classrooms or other environments to decrease or remove problem behaviors
- Strategies to take the place of problem behaviors and institute appropriate behaviors that serve the same function for the child
- Support mechanisms to help the child use the most appropriate behaviors

The IEP team determines whether the school discipline procedures need to be modified for a child or whether the penalties need to be different from those written into the policy. This decision should be based on an assessment and a review of the records, including the discipline records or any manifestation determination review(s) that have been concluded by the school.

A child's IEP or behavior intervention plan should concentrate on teaching skills. Sometimes school discipline policies are not successful in rectifying problem behaviors. That is, the child does not learn what the school staff intended through the use of punishments such as suspension. The child may learn instead that problem behaviors are useful in meeting a need, such as being noticed by peers. When this is true, it is difficult to defend punishment, by itself, as effective in changing problem behaviors. One of the most useful questions educators can ask when they have concerns about the discipline recommendations for a child is: "Where is the data to support the recommendations?" Special education decisions are based on data. If school staff wants to use a specific discipline procedure, they should check for data that support the use of the procedure.

Skill 10.4 Demonstrating knowledge of the principle of using the least intrusive behavior-management strategy consistent with the needs of students with disabilities and the procedures for reviewing, evaluating, and amending behavior management and intervention strategies

Please refer to Skill 9.3 for details on evaluating intervention strategies in BIPs.

It is important that the physical environment be arranged so that preventive discipline can occur. By this means, the teacher assumes responsibility for creating and maintaining an environment in which the needs of his or her charges are met. The teacher may modify the physical aspects of the room to create a warm, motivating atmosphere; adapt instructional materials to the respective functioning levels of the students; and deliver specialized services through the use of systematic, reinforcing methods and techniques. When instructional environments, materials, and techniques are implemented that respond to the academic needs of students, the personal needs of the student are often met as well, with a parallel effect of increased learning and appropriate social behaviors.

Classroom Interventions
Classroom interventions anticipate student disruptions and nullify potential discipline problems. Every student is different and each situation is unique; therefore, student behavior cannot be matched to specific interventions. Good classroom management requires the ability to select appropriate interventions strategies from an array of alternatives. The following nonverbal and verbal interventions were explained in Henley, Ramsey, and Algonzzine (1993):

Nonverbal Intervention - The use of nonverbal interventions allows classroom activities to proceed without interruption. These interventions also enable teachers to avoid "power struggles" with students. these can be arranged in advance with either the class as a whole or individual students, as appropriate.

Body Language - Teachers can convey authority and command respect through body language. Posture, eye contact, facial expressions, and gestures are examples of body components that signal leadership to students. the teacher must be sure that body language can be correctly interpreted particularly by students with disabilities or students from other cultures.

Planned Ignoring - Many minor classroom disturbances are best handled through planned ignoring. When teachers ignore attention-seeking behaviors, other students often do likewise.

Signal Interference - There are numerous nonverbal signals that teachers can use to quiet a class. Some of these are eye contact, snapping fingers, a frown, shaking the head, or making a quieting gesture with the hand. A few teachers present signs like flicking the lights, putting a finger over the lips, or winking at a selective student.

Proximity Control - Teachers who move around the room merely need to stand near a student or small group of students, or gently place a hand on a student's shoulder to stop a disturbing behavior. Teachers who stand or sit as if rooted are compelled to issue verbal directions in order to deal with student disruptions.

Removal of Seductive Objects - Some students become distracted by objects. Removal of those objects may eliminate the need some students have to handle, grab, or touch objects that take the focus of their attention away from instruction.

Verbal Interventions - Because nonverbal interventions are the least intrusive, they are generally preferred. Verbal Interventions are useful after it is clear that nonverbal interventions have been unsuccessful in preventing or stopping disruptive behavior.

Humor - Some teachers have been successful in dispelling discipline problems with a quip or an easy comment that produces smiles or gentle laughter from students. This does not include sarcasm, cynicism, or teasing, which increase tension and often create resentment.

Sane Messages - Sane messages are descriptive and model appropriate behavior. They help students understand how their behavior affects others. "Karol, when you talk during silent reading, you disturb everyone in your group," is an example of a sane message. Communicating such messages privately to students has proven to have a greater effect than when they are given in front of a class.

Restructuring - When confronted with student disinterest, the teacher may make the decision to change activities. This is an example of an occasion when restructuring could be used by the teacher to regenerate student interest.

Hypodermic Affection - Sometimes, students get frustrated, discouraged, and anxious in school. Hypodermic affection lets students know they are valued. Saying a kind word, giving a smile, or just showing interest in a child often gives the encouragement that is needed. This is most effective if you do it daily as your students enter your classroom.

Praise and Encouragement - Effective praise should be directed at student behavior rather than at the student personally. "Catching a child being good" is an example of an effective use of praise that reinforces positive classroom behavior. Comments like, "You are really trying hard," encourage student effort.

Alerting - Making abrupt changes from one activity to another can bring on behavior problems. Alerting helps students to make smooth transitions by giving them time to make emotional adjustments to change.

Accepting Student Feelings - Providing opportunities for students to express their feelings—even those that are distressful—helps them to learn to do so in appropriate ways. Role playing, class meetings or discussions, life space interviews, journal writings, and other creative modes help students to channel difficult feelings into constructive outlets.

The teacher must have a strategy for use with the child who persists in negative behavior outbursts that are not controlled by the above, less intrusive interventions. One system is to intervene immediately and break the situation down into three components. First, the teacher requires the child to identify the worst possible outcome from the situation, the thing that he or she fears. To do this task, the child must be required to state the situation in the most factual way he or she can. Second, he or she is required to state what would really happen if this worst possible outcome happened, and to evaluate the likelihood of it happening. Third, he or she is asked to state an action or attitude that can be taken, after examining the consequences in a new light. This process has been termed *rational emotive therapy.*

Skill 10.5 Demonstrating knowledge of strategies for increasing students' self-awareness, self-control, and self-management

Strategies to address self-awareness, self-control, and self-management require the teacher to address the student's self-concept and level of self esteem. Please refer to Skill 8.3 for more on student self-esteem.

Self-Control and Self-Management

Intrinsic rewards are the best method for creating behavioral changes. The difficulty in creating affective intrinsic rewards is that the student needs to understand what the reward is, as well as why he or she should consider it to be a reward. Simple tasks, such as self-monitoring by students filling in their own points on a behavior chart or recording a daily assigned action, provide such a method.

Self-management requires the ability to observe and note one's own behavior. It requires the ability to define what is wrong and what is the desired behavior. It requires looking at the consequences of specific behaviors. It requires the student to have the ability to control his or her behavior at specific times. If a student is able to understand these concepts, self-management programs can and should be developed to address behavioral issues.

Creating and monitoring such a system still requires observation and praise for the desired behaviors, but what should truly be praised is the control the student is exerting over past behaviors. Speaking to the student about these behaviors requires confidentiality—the ability to talk to the student without others listening. The student needs to hear both praise and criticism, but he or she does not need to be embarrassed because the teacher is praising a behavior others may normally exhibit.

Skill 10.6 Demonstrating knowledge of strategies for crisis prevention, intervention, and management

Crisis Prevention

According to the Center for Effective Collaboration and Practice, most schools themselves are safe, but violence from surrounding communities has begun to make its way into the schools. Fortunately, there are ways to intervene and prevent crises in our schools.

Administrators, teachers, families, students, support staff, and community leaders must be trained and/or informed on the early warning signs of potentially harmful behavior within the school population. However, it should also be emphasized that teachers should not use these warning signs to inappropriately label or stigmatize individual students simply because they may display some of the following warning signs.

Early Warning Signs

Social withdraw
Excessive feelings of isolation and being alone
Excessive feelings of rejection
Being a victim of violence
Feelings of being picked on and persecuted
Low school interest and poor academic performance
Expression of violence in writings and drawings
Uncontrolled anger
Patterns of impulsive and chronic hitting, intimidating, and bullying behaviors
History of discipline problems
Past history of violent and aggressive behavior
Intolerance for differences and prejudicial attitudes
Drug use and alcohol use
Affiliation with gangs
Inappropriate access to, possession of, and use of firearms
Serious threats of violence
Early warning signs and imminent warning signs differ; imminent warning signs require an immediate response. Imminent warning signs indicate that a student is very close to behaving in a way that is potentially dangerous to self and/or others.

Imminent Warning Signs

Serious physical fighting with peers or family members
Severe destruction of property
Severe rage for seemingly minor reasons
Detailed threats of lethal violence
Possession and/or use of firearms and other weapons
Other self-injurious behaviors or threats of suicide

When imminent signs are seen, school staff must follow the school board policies in place. These typically include reporting the behavior to a designated person or persons before handling anything alone.

Intervention and Prevention Plan
Each school system's plans may be different, but the plan should be derived from some of the following suggestions:

Share responsibility by establishing a partnership with the child, school, home, and community. Schools should coordinate with community agencies to coordinate their prevention plan (they should also partner to render services to students who may need assistance). The community involvement should include child and family service agencies, law enforcement and juvenile justice systems, mental health agencies, businesses, faith and ethnic leaders, and other community agencies.

Inform parents and listen to them when early warning signs are observed. Effective and safe schools make persistent efforts to involve parents by routinely informing them about school discipline policies, procedures, and rules; informing them about their children's behavior (both good and bad); involving them in making decisions concerning school-wide disciplinary policies and procedures; and encouraging them to participate in prevention

Maintain confidentiality and parents' rights to privacy. Parental involvement and consent is required before personally identifiable information is shared with other agencies, except in the case of emergencies or suspicion of abuse.

Develop the capacity of staff, students, and families to intervene. Schools should provide the entire school community—teachers, students, parents, and support staff—with training and support in responding to imminent warning signs, preventing violence, and intervening safely and effectively. Interventions must be monitored by professionals who are competent in the approach.

Support students in being responsible for their actions. Schools and members of the community should encourage students to consider themselves responsible for their actions, and actively engage them in planning, implementing, and evaluating violence prevention initiatives.

Simplify staff requests for urgent assistance. Many school systems and community agencies have complex legalistic referral systems with timelines and waiting lists. This should be a simple process that does not prevent someone from requesting assistance immediately.

Drill and practice. Schools are now required to have drills and provide practice to ensure that everyone is informed of the proper procedure to follow if emergencies occur. In addition to violence caused by a student, the emergency can also be an intruder in the builder, a bomb threat, or fire.

Skill 10.7 Demonstrating knowledge of various reinforcement techniques and identifying strategies for planning and implementing individualized reinforcement systems and environmental modifications

Reinforcement is the procedure in which a desirable or pleasant event follows a behavior and increases the probability or rate of that behavior. Positive reinforcement refers to the relationship between a behavior and a consequence; a positive reinforcer is the consequence. A positive reinforcer increases or maintains the future rate and/or probability of occurrence of a behavior.

In order to be effective, it must be:

- Administered contingently upon the production of the desired behavior
- Administered immediately following the production of the desired behavior
- Worthwhile in size and appropriate to the subject
- Administered in such a manner that satiation does not occur

There are two major types of reinforcers that may be used in the school setting: primary reinforcers and secondary reinforcers.

Primary Reinforcers
Primary reinforcers may be referred to as those stimuli that have biological importance to an individual. They may be described as natural, unlearned, unconditioned, and innately motivating. For example, youngsters do not have to be taught that eating tasty foods or drinking refreshing drinks will make them feel good, because they are naturally appealing to most people (Alberto & Troutman, 1990; Zirpoli & Melloy, 1993).

As a category, primary reinforcers include foods, liquids, sleep, shelter, and love. One of the most common and appropriate reinforcers for use in the classroom are food and liquids. Edible reinforcers have been found to be strong motivators for students with low functioning abilities, for younger students, and for students who are learning a new behavior.

The necessity for the student to be in a state of deprivation is a major drawback in the use of primary reinforcers. However, a state of hunger is not required in order for treats or special foods to be effective as reinforcers.

The opposite condition of deprivation is satiation. The deprivation state that existed before the instructional session may no longer exist; thus, the stimulus may cease to be an effective motivator.

Some suggestions for preventing satiation include:

- Vary reinforcers with instructional tasks
- Shorten the instructional sessions, and presentations of reinforcers will decrease
- Alternate reinforcers (e.g., food, then juice)
- Decrease the size of edibles presented
- Have an array of edibles available

Always remember, teachers must be cautious in the administration of edibles.

Medical records may need to be consulted prior to using food reinforcers in the classroom. A student may be on a special diet, have lactose intolerance or allergic reactions to certain foods, or may be susceptible to diabetic reactions. Liquid reinforcers increase the necessity for toileting breaks. Certain cereals or bite size fruits may be better reinforcers than candy (the sugar content and size are easier to control). Teachers also need to remember that what is reinforcing for one student is not necessarily reinforcing for another.

Secondary Reinforcers
Secondary reinforcers are reinforcers that are not necessarily naturally reinforcing to most people. Their value is learned: conditioned through an association—or pairing—with activities, praise, body language, and attention. A token economy system is included under secondary reinforcers.

The combined use of primary and secondary reinforcers is known as pairing. A primary reinforcer is paired with a secondary reinforcer; by this method, secondary reinforcers become of value to the student. For example, when the teacher pairs verbal praise with the delivery of an edible like cereal or cookies to a child, the verbal praise takes on some of the reinforcement value of the treat. In this case, the teacher is attempting to fade-out, or decrease, the use of a food as a reinforcer, and fade-in, or increase, the value of verbal praise. If the teacher is successful in doing this, verbal praise will become a secondary reinforcer capable of maintaining or increasing the desired behavior (Albern & Troutman, 1990; Zirpoli & Melloy, 1993).

This conditioning process is important for several reasons:

- The student may become temporarily satiated with the primary reinforcer.
- It is not always possible for the teacher to achieve deprivation of the reinforcer.
- The student may become dependent upon the primary reinforcer.

Using Various Types of Reinforcers in the School Setting
It is a generally accepted fact that teachers need to create positive learning environments that will meet their students' special needs and accommodate individual learning styles. The need to develop appropriate antecedent stimuli (e.g., classroom arrangement, task assignments, and instructions preceding performance) is considered to be of much importance; however, emphasis is placed heavily on the consequential events that follow a behavior. This can be seen in the basic rules of behaviorism: (1) behavior that is reinforced tends to occur more frequently; (2) behavior that is no longer reinforced will be extinguished; (3) behavior that is punished will occur less often. Thus, teachers must systematically be able to use reinforcers that are available to all children during the normal course of a school day.

Social Reinforcement
Social reinforcement refers to the behaviors of others that directly influence the increase in a child's behavior. The range of potential social reinforcers includes verbal expressions that convey approval of the students' accomplishments (e.g., praise such as "I like the way you stayed at your desk," or "You did a great job!"), nonverbal expressions (e.g., winking, smiling), teacher proximity to student (e.g., hug, pat on the back), and the granting of privileges that carry status for the student among his or her peers. Social reinforcement can be used as a planned teaching technique, or it can be given spontaneously.

The advantages of using social reinforcement are many. It is easy to use, absorbing little of the teacher's time and effort, and it is available in any setting. The fact that teachers are persons who possess high status in the students' eyes makes it especially appropriate for use. Social reinforcement rarely incurs criticism, is unlikely to satiate, and can be generalized to most situations. The main disadvantage is that it may not be strong enough reinforcer; thus, teachers may need to pair it with a tangible reinforcer.

Activity Reinforcement
Activity reinforcement refers to the involvement in preferred activities. The systematic use of activity reinforcers is described by the Premack Principle. It states that any activity that a student voluntarily does on a frequent basis (e.g., a high interest activity) can be used as a reinforcer for any activity in which the student seldom participates (e.g., running errands, decorating a bulletin board, leading a group activity, earning free time). Additional examples of activity reinforcers include activities that students voluntarily participate in when given the chance, selected chores, favored involvement in the classroom (e.g., captain of a team, use of craft center, access to the computer, extra free time), and peer activities (e.g., listening to music, singing, dancing, playing chess).

Major advantages in using activity reinforcers include their ready availability and unlimited accessibility, thus preventing satiation. If a student tires of one activity, there are many others that can be used. Special needs children are less likely to be considered "different" when engaged in earned activity time, and activity reinforcers can be combined with social reinforcers. Furthermore, once activity reinforcers are identified with the learning environment, they can be acquired with little effort. Disadvantages in the use of activity reinforcers are few, but might include the need for handling delayed gratification and the possibility of interrupting other classroom activities. In addition, some activity reinforcers may not always be available.

Token Reinforcement
A system whereby children are given immediate reinforcement by means of an object that can be exchanged for a reinforcer of value at a future time is called token reinforcement. In using this system, the token is delivered contingent on a desired response. Tokens should be durable, practical, and easily dispensed. They can be in the form of objects (e.g., poker chips, play money, stars, or tickets), or they can be symbols like happy faces, check marks, or points.

Used alone, tokens have little or no value or power. Their reinforcing value is attained by virtue of their being exchanged for a variety of reinforcing rewards, known as backup reinforcers. The backup reinforcers must be items desired by all the students using the token reinforcement system. An array of items—tangible objects such as trinkets, school supplies, edibles, as well as activities—needs to be available for selection,.

Use of a token economy system has advantages. They provide a concrete means for immediate reinforcement and an observable record of accomplishments. Tokens can be given without interfering with classroom activities, and their use is generally acceptable by teachers, peers, and parents.

Use of this system necessitates a well-organized management system that does require time and energy to operate successfully. Other considerations include dependency upon receiving concrete, immediate reinforcement, the need to acquire an assortment of desirable backup reinforcers, and the inability to readily generalize this system into another environment. However, many teachers have found the token reinforcement system to be of great benefit in modifying student behavior and report that the advantages far outweigh required efforts on their part.

Tangible Reinforcement

As the name suggests, the use of tangible items as consequential reinforcement for desired behavior is called tangible reinforcement. This system can be used by itself or as a part of another system such as token reinforcement. Tangible items dispensed in the educational setting are typically those that can be used or consumed in the classroom for academic activities, including pencils, paper, erasers, or items that can be consumed during free activity time, like baseball cards, game items, trinkets, or posters.

Tangible reinforcers are considered desirable by children because they are concrete items. Therefore, their high reinforcing value enhances their effectiveness. This primary advantage, however, must be weighed in relation to possible disadvantages. Tangible reinforcers can be costly and hard to acquire, must be age appropriate, and, if given only to special needs students, may make them appear different from their peers. Children must receive this type of reinforcement less frequently, or else satiation will occur. The less frequent aspect, however, means that immediate reinforcement based on contingent behavior is unlikely to occur unless the tangible reinforcers are part of a token economy.

Many teachers pair tangible reinforcers with activity or social reinforcers, and therefore eventually fade the tangible rewards in lieu of using intangible means of reinforcement.

Schedules of Reinforcement

Schedules of reinforcement refer to when the delivery of reinforcement occurs. A **continuous schedule** of reinforcement is used with new behaviors. Continuous reinforcement is given every time the behavior occurs. It is useful for building new behaviors. Once the new behavior has become established, a more infrequent type of reinforcer is desirable to maintain the behavior and to avoid satiation.

Intermittent or partial reinforcement schedules are those when reinforcement follows some, but not all, correct or desirable behaviors. Intermittent schedules: (1) require greater numbers of correct responses for reinforcement; (2) require the maintenance of appropriate behavior over longer periods of time; and (3) are more resistant to extinction.

Ratio refers to the number of times a target behavior occurs as the determinant for the timing of the delivery of the reinforcer. **Interval** refers to the amount of time before a target behavior occurs as the determinant for the timing of the delivery of the reinforcer. A fixed number of behaviors or amount of time may be required; a variable number of behaviors or amount of time may also be established. The four schedules reflecting these components are as follows:

Fixed Ratio. A fixed ratio schedule requires that a person be reinforced every time he or she completes a fixed number of correct responses. For example, Tom must complete 10 math problems before he receives a point for staying on task.

Variable ratio. A variable ratio schedule requires that a person be reinforced when he or she completes a variable number of responses. The number of responses required for reinforcement varies every time. For example, as the teacher circulates among students working on math problems, reinforcement may occur upon completion of the second, fifth, or eighth math fact.

Fixed Interval. In a fixed interval schedule, the person must (1) wait for a fixed time to pass, during which responses are not reinforced, and (2) make a response after that time that will be reinforced. For example, a student receives a token or verbal praise following the elapse of a specified number of minutes if he or she is in the correct seat at that instance during reading period.

Variable Interval. In a variable interval schedule, the person must (1) wait for a varying length of time to pass during which responses have no effect, and (2) make a response after that time that will be reinforced. For example, a student is reinforced if he or she is in the correct seat following two, five, 10, or 20 minutes of working on an assigned task in reading.

In general, ratio schedules result in higher rates of responding or behavior, than interval schedules and they tend to have a brief pause after reinforcement. Variable schedules produce higher rates of response than fixed schedules and are better at making the new behavior resistant to extinction. The variable ratio schedule results in the highest rate of behavior as well as the greatest resistance to extinction. This is particularly relevant when helping a child learn new behaviors as it is important that the behavior continue to occur even when there is no one present to reinforce it on a regular basis.

Skill 10.8 Demonstrating knowledge of how to integrate academic instruction with behavior management, including knowledge of nonaversive techniques for controlling targeted behavior and maintaining the attention of students with disabilities

Positive behavioral interventions and supports (PBS) is IDEA's preferred strategy for handling challenging behaviors of students with disabilities. IDEA requires PBS to be considered in all cases of students whose behavior impedes their learning or the learning of others.

IDEA requires that "in the case of a child whose behavior impedes his or her learning or that of others," a student's IEP team, while developing an IEP (initial development, review, or revision), is required to "consider, when appropriate, strategies, including positive behavioral interventions, strategies, and supports to address that behavior."

PBS involves the use of positive behavioral interventions and systems to attain socially significant behavior change. PBS has four interrelated components: systems change activities, environmental alterations activities, skill instruction activities, and behavioral consequence activities. These come together to form a behaviorally-based systems approach to enhance the ability of schools, families, and communities to create effective environments that improve the link between research-validated practices and the environments in which teaching and learning occur.

Skill 10.4 and 10.7 describe positive means of behavior management in more detail. Skill 10.3 discusses the use of Functional Behavioral Assessments and Behavior Intervention Plans when the initial positive efforts are not successful.

OBJECTIVE 11 UNDERSTAND PRINCIPLES AND METHODS OF PLANNING AND DELIVERING INSTRUCTION FOR STUDENTS WITH DISABILITIES

Skill 11.1 Demonstrating knowledge of how to adapt or create learning plans for students with disabilities (e.g., sensory, mobility, cognitive, behavioral, pragmatic) in a variety of settings (e.g., classroom, resource room, community) using specialized materials, curricula, and resources

Just as no two snowflakes are the same, no two children demonstrate exactly the same skills. In this way, school systems need to consider the strengths of all students. Finding the strengths of students is something that all educators need to address.

When we look at the physical abilities of students with special needs, we must take into considerations ways to adapt the instruction and settings to maximize their ability to access the same information as other students with no physical differences.

Keeping in mind that there can be numerous physical conditions that could prevent a student from accessing the regular curriculum, it is important to be flexible in thinking and problem solving. Students may simply need items enlarged or put on tape if they have visual or auditory difficulties. In some cases, in-room audio systems can be utilized to address auditory discrimination issues; these also have a research base for helping students with Attention Deficit Disorder.

Still other times, it may be necessary to rearrange the physical layout of the room to allow enough space for walkers or wheelchairs to be maneuvered. Some children may require special pencils, pencil grips, or even regular access to an augmentative communication device to be able to participate. There are special chairs and additive seating devices that can be used to help position the students correctly.

Finding equipment is only half the battle. Sometimes, discussions with non-disabled peers are critical components overlooked by schools. Helping others to understand how to provide what is necessary without enabling is a daunting task, but one well worth undertaking. It is when everyone understands and has the opportunity to ask appropriate questions that they can truly accept others into their world without unnecessary stigma.

The many adaptations are available from a variety of sources. Schools contract with or hire their own speech therapists, occupational therapists, physical therapists, and hearing and vision specialists. Accessing the knowledge these professionals can provide can be the missing critical element to finding the appropriate needs for students to become integral members of the learning community.

Skill 11.2 Applying knowledge of how to select, adapt, and use research-based instructional methods and materials to address the strengths and needs of students with disabilities

Instructional Methods
Many of the techniques useful to students with disabilities might be described and "just good teaching practice—but more if it." The chosen curriculum should introduce information in a cumulative sequence but not introduce too much new information at a time. Students with disabilities may need a reduced rate of presentation or presentation in smaller units. Review difficult material and practice to aid retention. Students with disabilities may need much more review (see overlearning, below). New vocabulary and symbols should be introduced one at a time, and the relationships of components to the whole should be stressed. Students with disabilities may need concrete or multimedia presentation and illustration of concepts. Students' background information should be recalled to connect new information to the old. Students with disabilities may need that background to be created for them. Finally, teach strategies or algorithms first and then move on to tasks that are more difficult. Learning new material and retaining it. Students with disabilities may need templates and problem solving lists to help with

Addressing Students' Needs
There are a number of procedures teachers can use to address the varying needs of the students. Some of the more common procedures:

Vary assignments: A variety of assignments on the same content allows students to match learning styles and preferences with the assignment. If all assignments are writing assignments, for example, students who are hands-on or visual learners are at a disadvantage unrelated to the content base itself.

Cooperative learning: Cooperative learning activities allow students to share ideas, expertise, and insight in a non-threatening setting. The focus tends to remain on positive learning rather than competition. When incorporating students with special needs into cooperative learning groups, it is important to ensure that each student plays a role that is both useful to the group and within their capabilities.

Structure environment: Some students need and benefit from a clear structure that defines the expectation and goals of the teacher. The student knows what is expected and when, and can work and plan accordingly.

Clearly stated assignments: Assignments should be clearly stated, along with the expectation and criteria for completion. Many students with disabilities benefit from written assignments or assignments and instructions presented pictorially. Reinforcement and practice activities should not be a guessing game for the students. The exception to this is, of course, those situations in which a discovery method is used.

Independent practice: Independent practice involving application and repetition is necessary for thorough learning. Students learn to be independent learners through practicing independent learning. These activities should always be within the student's abilities to perform successfully without assistance. Students with disabilities may need materials modified to make the tasks appropriate to their needs and skills (see above).

Repetition: Very little learning is successful with a single exposure. Learners generally require multiple exposures to the same information for learning to take place. However, this repetition does not have to be dull and monotonous. In conjunction with #1 above, varied assignments can provide repetition of content or skill practiced without repetition of specific activities. This helps keep learning fresh and exciting for the student.

Overlearning: As a principle of effective learning, overlearning recommends that students continue to study and review after they have achieved initial mastery. The use of repetition in the context of varied assignments offers the means to help students pursue and achieve overlearning. This strategy is particularly important for students with many forms of disability (e.g., short or long term memory deficits, difficulty with multistep procedures, algorithms, abstractions).

Effective curriculum design assists the teacher from teacher demonstration to independent practice. Components of curriculum design include:

- Quizzes or reviews of the previous lesson
- Step-by-step presentations with multiple examples
- Guided practice and feedback
- Independent practice that requires the student to produce faster responses

Selecting Appropriate Materials
Regardless of which instructional approaches are selected as the most appropriate for the learner, the materials in that approach must match the learner's functioning level and style. Texts and workbooks are typically designated for grade level difficulty. Kits and supplementary materials contain instructions that specify certain progressive levels of difficulty.

Teachers should be familiar with the overall scope and sequence of major subjects (e.g., reading, spelling, and math) in the academic areas, from readiness abilities through higher-order learning skills. Since the exceptional students that a teacher instructs will vary in abilities, the sequence in which skills are developmentally approached, and the overall hierarchical range of the curricula from kindergarten through 12th grade, must be known in order to plan for entry-level instruction.

Some authorities (Radabaugh & Yukish, 1982) assert that grade levels specified for instructional materials, especially those developed for exceptional students, may be inaccurate. In attempting to evaluate the instructional level of teaching materials, several questions should be asked by the teacher.

First of all, does the publisher state the readability level of the material, and does the readability level remain consistent throughout? If not, the teacher may need to determine readability level and select texts appropriate for each student.

Is there more than one book or story lesson for each level? Students with disabilities may need much more practice at each level than students without disabilities. The teacher may need to find additional texts to provide this additional practice.

Is there an attempt to control the use of content-specific vocabulary? Is the interest level appropriate for the content, illustrations, and age of the students who will use the material? This is very important since many students with disabilities have the *interests* of their age peers, but much lower reading or cognitive levels. In addition, it is customary to provide *grade level curriculum topics* in content areas (e.g., Solar System in third grade, or the Constitution in fourth), so it is important to find content materials that are presented in a form students with disabilities can access.

The purpose for reading has a great deal to do with whether the material is on a comfortable or difficult level. There are instances when the reader should not encounter many new words or sentences written in a difficult manner. Wiederholt, Hammill, & Brown (1983) list these times as (1) practicing reading (e.g., pleasure, future discussion); (2) working independently; (3) focusing on one or more aspects of comprehension; and (4) reading orally before an audience.

More difficult material may be appropriate when analyzing how a student attempts to read unknown words or new material. Material in which the student is applying skills that have previously been taught must likewise present sufficient difficulty, otherwise the student's performance may merely reflect recall of the content.

Unfortunately, as students progress into higher grade levels, many special educators become involved in tutoring. This is due to the reading difficulty of the subject content assigned, and the lack of time for building foundation skills while assisting with required academic subject content.

One of the major tasks of a special educator is to find an appropriate match between materials and students, particularly in reading, as this skill is necessary in most subject areas. The customary practice is to obtain a measured reading level, either from a diagnostic type of assessment tool or from an individual reading inventory (IRI).

In addition to the instructional level, two other levels are determined when using an IRI: the independent reading level and the student's level of frustration. The IRI consists of a series of grade level passages and a corresponding list of vocabulary words. Starting with the last level at which all vocabulary words presented are recognized, the student is asked to read the story passage silently and then out loud. Following his or her oral reading, the student is asked to answer predetermined comprehension questions. The student continues in this manner until he or she arrives at a level of frustration. This level of difficulty is considered reached whenever the teacher records 10 errors in a sample of approximately 100 running words, and comprehension questions are answered at the 50 percent level. Instruction should occur on the level where five errors are recorded during the reading sample, and comprehension questions are answered correctly at 75 percent. The student is encouraged to select library books and to pursue other types of comfortable reading at his or her independent reading level, where the student misses only one word while reading the passage, and 90 percent of the answers are considered correct. These criteria (Wiederholt, Hammill, & Brown, 1983) appear in the table below.

Reading Levels

LEVEL	WORD RECOGNITION IN CONTEXT (percent)	COMPREHENSION (percent)	OBSERVABLE BEHAVIOR
Independent	99	90	Ease in reading
Instructional	95	75	No signs of frustration
Frustration	90	50	Signs of tension

Some publishing companies include IRIs along with their basal reading series. However, the teacher can easily construct the inventory him or herself. In so doing, it is suggested that passages be taken from the middle of each text in the series, ranging from the preprimer to the fifth or sixth grade level. Passages should be chosen that read as complete stories. Suggested approximate length of passages is 50 words at the preprimer level; 100 words at the primer, first, and second levels; and 100 to 150 words at the upper levels. Though one selection at each level to be read orally by the student may be considered by some authorities to be sufficient, an alternative guideline would be to choose two stories, one for oral reading and one for silent reading, at each level.

Word recognition tests serve three major purposes. First, a learner's sight vocabulary can be identified; second, applied word-attack skills can be pinpointed; third, initial reading instruction levels can be attempted.

Teachers can use commercially prepared word recognition lists arranged by grade level difficulty, or teacher-made lists may be developed. Glossaries included in basal readers, from which 20 to 25 words are selected at random, can also be used. For example, after dividing the total number of words by 20 or 25, every "n^{th}" word is written on the word list.

The predetermined comprehension questions are asked after a student reads a selection from his or her estimated instructional level. It is suggested that five to ten questions be developed, with fewer questions used at the lower reading levels (e.g., preprimer, primer, first), and more questions at the upper grade range (e.g., fifth, sixth). Questions should include vocabulary and higher level thinking skills (e.g., evaluation, appreciation), as well as those more typically asked to reflect lower level thinking abilities (e.g., literal recognition or recall).

Content area reading material has historically presented a challenge to teachers of students with disabilities. Since content areas taught are typically determined by state grade standards, school textbooks are written at a reading level that makes them inaccessible to many students with disabilities. Skill 11.6 presents strategies to modify or rewrite such texts, however, more and more of today's educational publishers are providing content area texts written at simpler reading levels, often with decoding and comprehension components integrated into the material. Rigby, National Geographic Windows on Literacy, and Time For Kids Magazine are three such examples.

An informal **math** inventory is constructed based on grade level skills delineated on scope and sequence charts. Sample problems are written that represent many different types of skills (e.g., computation, operations, fractions, measurement, time) at many grade levels. Some diagnostic math tests (e.g., Key Math Diagnostic Arithmetic Test-Revised, Brigance Diagnostic Inventory of Basic Skills, and Wide Range Achievement Test-Revised) are suitable models from which ideas for developing sample problems can be obtained for use in teacher made inventories. Math scope and sequence charts present objectives from which items can be selected for sampling skills. Student performance on the math inventory supplies the teacher with a guide for identifying entry level instructional skills.

When selecting math texts and presenting problems, it is important to remember that students with some disabilities may be able to master computation, but struggle with the language of math. When presented with "word problems," they struggle to understand what is needed, and even when they properly solve the problem, they may not be able to explain what they did (typically a requirement on high stakes tests). These students may need extra practice on word problems that use grade level computation, but are written in simpler language, gradually leading the student to understanding more sophisticated math language. Sometimes word problems designed for a lower grade will help; other times, it will be necessary for the teacher to rewrite grade level problems to make them more accessible.

Evaluating Instructional Material

A great amount of time and research has been devoted to developing criteria for selecting instructional materials that meet the needs of special students (Henley, Ramsey, & Algozzine, 1996; Morsink, 1984). The criteria listed by some authorities in this area (e.g., Brown, 1983; Hammill & Bartel, 1986; Mercer & Mercer, 1993; Smith, 1983) can be helpful to teachers as they select materials that are relevant to the needs of their students, and will be useful once selected. The effectiveness of materials, of course, can be increased by adapting the way they are used.

Relevance

Materials selected for use with exceptional students should be pertinent to their needs, regardless of their categorical assignment. Hammill and Bartel (1986) recommend an examination of the following factors when evaluating relevance:

- Are the skills and concepts required of the student present so that success can be realized?
- Does the student's performance level correspond with the skill sequence?
- Is there a history of success or failure with use of certain methods? Does the student react positively or negatively to particular modes of instruction (e.g., multimedia versus print only)?

- Are there characteristics that imply needs (e.g., orthopedic restrictions, family problems, ethnic or cultural diversity)?

Brown (1975) listed 35 factors that should be considered in selecting curriculum materials for disabled learners. Criteria relating more directly to relevance include the following:

- What range of student difference does the material encompass?
- Are there readiness behaviors specified that are prerequisites for the student(s)?
- Has any effort been made to assess or control the complexity of the language, either receptively or expressively?
- Is the material obviously intended for younger children, or has it been adapted for use with older students (e.g., high interest, low vocabulary)? Does the teacher have to develop or provide background experiences, information, or interests for some students?
- What processes have been used, and what results are available to determine readability or learner interest?
- What are the target populations for whom the materials were developed? Are they identified?
- Is it possible to isolate sensory channels as a major instructional variable?

In summary, the teacher will need to develop ways of determining whether criteria related to the relevancy of the materials for use with his or her special needs students is met. The teacher will need to examine the materials in relation to the academic, behavioral, developmental, and physical needs of students; their learning styles; and the behavioral objectives specified on their individualized education programs (IEPs).

Utility

Usefulness or practicality is another criterion essential for evaluating instructional materials to be used with special needs students. When considering the utility, Brown (cited in Smith, 1983) suggests that questions similar to the following be asked:

- What is the comprehensiveness of breadth of the program? Is it useful in meeting the needs of students, or does it supplement existing programs?
- Is the material sequenced so that mastery can be achieved before progressing to the next step, or are materials spiraled so that areas of difficulty can be left temporarily, and then returned to later?
- Is the presentation of instruction paced for various groups or individuals? Are modifications made within the material so that those who need more or different experiences at various points can receive them?
- Are the materials useful in their organizational schemata (e.g., units, page arrangements, illustrations)?

- Is the material teacher-directed or student-directed? Are materials practical for self-directed use, and if so, how is feedback received (e.g., programmed materials with self-correcting answers) and progress monitored (e.g., self-charting)?
- Other questions that might be asked when considering the utility of instructional materials follow:
- Can the material be used to accomplish a number of objectives? Is the material convenient to use for its intended purposes?
- Will reasonable demands be made on the teacher's time when using these materials? Does the material allow for flexibility of scheduling?
- Will additional equipment or supplies be needed to utilize the materials effectively? Does it contain many components? If so, can it be stored or transported easily?
- Can the material be incorporated into other programs? Can it be adapted to many levels of instruction?

Skill 11.3 Demonstrating knowledge of strategies for helping students with disabilities maintain and generalize skills across learning environments

Transfer of learning occurs when experience with one task influences performance on another task. Positive transfer occurs when the required responses and stimuli are similar, such as moving from baseball or handball to racquetball, or field hockey to soccer. Negative transfer occurs when the stimuli remain similar, but the required responses change, such as shifting from soccer to football, tennis to racquetball, or boxing to sports karate.

Instructional procedures should stress the similar features between the activities as well as the dimensions that are transferable. Specific information should emphasize when stimuli in the old and new situations are the same or similar, and when responses used in the old situation apply to the new.

To facilitate learning, instructional objectives should be arranged in order of their patterns of similarity. Objectives involving similar responses should be closely sequenced; thus, the possibility for positive transfer is stressed. Likewise, learning objectives that involve different responses should be programmed within instructional procedures in the most appropriate way possible. For example, students should have little difficulty transferring handwriting instruction to writing in other areas; however, there might be some negative transfer when moving from manuscript to cursive writing. By using transitional methods and focusing on the similarities between manuscript and cursive writing, negative transfer can be reduced.

Generalization

Generalization is the occurrence of a learned behavior in the presence of a stimulus other than the one that produced the initial response (novel stimulus). It is the expansion of a student's performance beyond conditions initially anticipated. Students must be able to generalize what is learned to other settings (e.g., reading to word problems in math, resource room to regular classroom). Ultimately, of course, it is essential that students be able to transfer what they learn in school to the job and daily life setting they will encounter when they leave school.

Generalization training is a procedure in which a behavior is reinforced in each of a series of situations until it generalizes to other members of the same stimulus class. Stimulus generalization occurs when responses, which have been reinforced in the presence of a specific stimulus (the discriminative stimulus, or SD) occur in the presence of related stimuli (e.g., bathrooms labeled women, ladies, dames). In fact, the more similar the stimuli, the more likely it is that stimulus generalization will occur.

This concept applies to intertask similarity, in that the more one task resembles another; the greater the probability the student will be able to master it. For example, if Johnny has learned the initial consonant sounds of "b" and "d," and he has been taught to read the word "dad," it is likely that when he is shown the word "bad," he will be able to pronounce this formerly unknown word upon presentation.

Generalization may be enhanced by the following:

- Using many examples in teaching to deepen application of learned skills
- Using consistency in initial teaching situations, later introducing variety in format, procedure, and use of examples
- Having the same information presented by different teachers, in different settings, and under varying conditions
- Including a continuous reinforcement schedule at first, later changing to delayed and intermittent schedules as instruction progresses
- Teaching students to record instances of generalization and to reward themselves at that time
- Associating naturally occurring stimuli when possible. Arranging for real life practice or practice in diverse settings is beneficial.

Skill 11.4 Applying knowledge of strategies for teaching students with disabilities how to use self- assessment, problem solving, metacognitive skills, and other cognitive strategies to identify and meet their own needs

Please refer to Skill 8.3 for a discussion of self advocacy.

Metacognitive Functioning
Metacognition is the advanced cognitive ability to think about thinking and learning, the degree to which a student is aware of his or her own learning strategies and processes. Many, many students with disabilities lack adequate metacognitive skills and need direct instruction in how to acquire and use them. Initially, teachers can use informal process measures to gain information about a student's metacognitive knowledge associated with a particular task, such as analyzing visual aids. The teacher can give the student a task involving analysis of visual aids then interview the student with direct and open-ended questions. In these interviews, the teacher attempts to answer the following three questions:

What does the student know about the metacognitive processes involved in using visual aids? This addresses the student's knowledge of the function of visual aids and whether the student uses background knowledge to predict or clarify the information in the visual aid.

If the student knows that certain strategies are needed to analyze an aid, does the student know how to perform those strategies?

What variables influence the student's ability or lack of ability to make efficient use of process strategies?

A teacher-made process assessment can be done with a visual aid and a structured, teacher-prepared interview. Interviews begin with global or general questions that measure what the student knows without being prompted to recall specific techniques. Examples of global or general questions are:

- What types of information can graphics tell you?
- What sorts of things make graphics useful?
- What should you do if you cannot figure out a graphic?
- Following the global/general questions, the teacher can move on to specific questions about specific strategies and components of the strategies, Examples of specific questions would be:
- What does "Identify what is important?" mean in this illustration?
- How do you know what part is important, or How do you know that is the important part?
- How do you know what part of the text this illustration is showing? What does the illustration show you that is not in the text?

Beginning with general questions lessens the possibility that the student will answer what he believes the teacher wants to hear. During the specific question stage, the teacher can explore specific aspects of the student's use of the process in more detail. It may be necessary to simplify the questions and, of course, make them relevant to the specific strategy being discussed.

This procedure can be used to help students think about their own thinking and learning in many contexts. The series of questions might be designed to help with interpreting social cues, or math word problems, etc.

A major focus of special education is to prepare students to become working, independent members of society. IDEA 2004 (Individuals with Disabilities Education Act) also includes preparing students for *further education*. Certain skills beyond academics are needed to attain this level of functioning.

Affective and social skills transcend to all areas of life. When an individual is unable to acquire information on expectations and reactions of others, or if the individual misinterprets those cues, he or she is missing an important element needed for success as an adult in the workplace and community. Special education should incorporate a level of instruction in the affective/social area, as many students will not develop these skills without instruction, modeling, practice, and feedback.

Affective and social skills taught throughout the school setting might include social greetings; eye contact with a speaker; interpretation of facial expression, body language, and personal space; the ability to put feelings and questions into words; and use of words to acquire additional information, as needed.

Skill 11.5 Demonstrating knowledge of strategies for modifying classroom tests and for helping students with disabilities learn how to prepare for and take tests (e.g., development of learning strategies, study skills, and test-taking strategies)

Please refer to Skill 5.2 for detailed information on modifications that can be made on various assessments and tests.

Authentic Assessments
Authentic assessments, as mentioned in Skill 5.5, may be performance based assessments and may include real life activities. Differentiating authentic assessments for students with disabilities should be based on the student's strengths and on the student's learning process. Consider the following when differentiating authentic assessments for students with disabilities:

Consider the amount of content to be covered. A student will disabilities, for example, could be required to complete three out of five questions.

Consider the levels of Bloom's taxonomy. Design the assignment so students with different cognitive domains can complete the assignment, although the higher order thinking skills are differentiated based on student ability.

Consider the type of product. Provide choices for alternative ways to present the information learned. Some students may provide a written product, such as a report, while others may choice to make a poster or diorama covering the same topic.

Traditional Classroom Assessments
Traditional classroom assessments are necessary to determine students' success in meeting unit standards. Tests and quizzes should be developed prior to beginning the unit. End of unit tests can be given as a pretest to the unit to facilitate grouping and differentiation for instruction.

The general education teacher typically develops the tests and quizzes. The special education teacher makes accommodations for students with disabilities by changing the format. The special education teacher might also make modifications for some students by altering the content.

Alternative Assessments
In *alternative assessments*, students create an answer or a response to a question or task. In traditional, inflexible assessments, students choose a prepared response from among a selection of responses, such as matching, multiple-choice, and true or false. When implemented effectively, an alternative assessment approach will exhibit the following characteristics, among others:

- Requires higher-order thinking and problem-solving
- Provides opportunities for student self-reflection and self-assessment
- Uses real world applications to connect students to the subject
- Provides opportunities for students to learn and examine subjects on their own and collaborate with their peers.
- Encourages students to continue learning beyond the requirements of the assignment
- Clearly defines objective and performance goals
- Allows students to demonstrate their knowledge using their individual strengths rather than through a "one size fits all" method.

Teachers are learning the value of giving assessments that meet the individual abilities and needs of students. After the teacher has provided instruction, discussion, questioning, and practice, rather than assigning one task to all students, he or she asks students to generate tasks that will show their knowledge of the information presented. Students are given choices and, thereby, have the opportunity to demonstrate more effectively the skills, concepts, or topics that they as individuals have learned. For example, following a unit on the life of a famous historical figure, students might choose from among "tests" such as a traditional written report, a poster illustrating important events and contributions of the individual, a timeline of event, a cause and effect web or diagram analyzing the individual's contributions, a skit or oral presentation, a comic book style summary, etc. It has been established that student choice increases student originality, intrinsic motivation, and higher mental processes.

Test Taking Strategies
Many students with disabilities lack coherent strategies for taking tests so even when they know the material; they are unable to show their knowledge on a traditional test. Although the teacher can design more appropriate assessments within the class, and make standard modifications of high stakes tests, students with disabilities may not be able to avoid taking at least some traditional tests—the kind on which they struggle so much. The teacher can help them improve their performance, and be more comfortable taking such tests by explicitly teaching test taking strategies.

The specific strategies to be used on a given test will depend upon the nature of the test. However, there are some strategies that will often be useful:

- Read all choices on a multiple choice question before choosing. This simple strategy will nearly always improve performance. Most tests ask for the **best** answer, and this means that there may be more than one answer that fits. The student must compare them to see which is best.

- Eliminate choices you know are wrong. It is hard to make a list of choices that are all equally likely. There will usually be some more unlikely than others. In addition, the student is likely to have at least some information about the question. Students can cross out choices they are sure are wrong. When they cross out impossible choices, their odds of getting the question right improve.

- Skip and go back to questions you do not understand the first time through. USE information in other questions to help you answer confusing questions. If, for example, question #4 asks, "What kept Bobby from finding the treasure chest when he looked in the attic," then you automatically know he did NOT find it when he looked in the attic, and this information may help you answer another question about how he did find it, and so forth.

- Many tests do not penalize wrong answers any more than omitted answers. If the student knows this about a test, then the student should be sure to answer ALL questions even if he is not sure of the answer.

- Underline key information in the question before answering it and look for answers (in multiple choice format) that refer to that information.
- When answering open response questions, learn how to turn the question around to make a topic sentence.

- Turn the question into a statement. You probably read it that way or heard the teacher say it; this may help you remember it.

- Try reading the questions BEFORE reading the material. This is a simple way to help you focus on the most relevant parts of what you are learning.

Teachers can teach mini-lessons on each of these strategies and use sample tests or old tests, or test preparation examples from published sources (e.g., Time For Kids, Scholastic, many commercially available sources) for practice. The teacher can walk the students through one example or model and "think aloud" strategy as she completes a sample. Then students can try it themselves on these practice materials. Materials that do not have high stakes value and are not used for grading also do not produce as much stress and students are more likely to be successful, learn the strategies, and be less stressed on the "real" tests.

Skill 11.6 Applying knowledge of how to modify instruction, adapt materials, and provide feedback based on formative assessment and student feedback (e.g., by scaffolding instruction, integrating student-initiated learning experiences into ongoing instruction)

Please refer to Skill 6.2 and Skill 6.4 for more on using Assessment to drive instruction.

Identifying Basic Instructional Approaches
Instructional alternatives to help students with learning problems may be referred to as compensatory techniques, instructional adaptations, or accommodation techniques. A problem-solving approach to determining what modifications should be made centers around: (a) the requirements of the course, (b) the requirement(s) that the student is not meeting, (c) factors interfering with the student's meeting the requirements, and (d) the identification of possible modifications. Of course, a student's IEP or 504 documents may spell out such modifications.

Many of the adaptations and modifications helpful to students with disabilities can be seen in terms of Cummins'(1994) analysis of the cognitive demands of a task or lesson. Such adaptations can be designed to either lighten the cognitive burden of a task or make it easier for the student to carry that burden. Cummins' work with students with limited English proficiency (LEP) led him to analyze tasks in terms of two variables: amount of context, and cognitive demand. Lessons or tasks that have a lot of context for a student will be easier for that student than tasks with little or no context; the more context, the easier the task. Cognitive demand is a measure of how much information must be processed quickly. A cognitively demanding task requires processing lots of information all at once or in rapid succession and is more demanding or difficult. Cognitively undemanding tasks or lessons present only single pieces of information or concepts to process, and they separate tasks or lessons into discrete, small steps. When making changes to accommodate students with special needs, it is helpful to focus on changes that will move the task or lesson from a cognitively demanding, low context arena to one of high context and reduced cognitive demand.

Adaptations or changes designed to help the student(s) meet the requirements of a class or standard can take place in a number of areas of curriculum and setting. The following are some of the primary areas in which a special education teacher may need to make changes.

Adapting the Overall Instructional Environment
The teacher can modify the classroom instructional environment in several ways.

I. **Adapt for Individual Student Variables**: Some students with disabilities benefit from sitting close to the teacher or away from windows. Others (with ADHD, for example) might benefit from wiggle seats or fiddle objects, others from an FM system or cubicles that reduce distractions. Seating that reduces distractions serves also to reduce the cognitive load of lessons, by removing the need for the students to block distractions themselves.

II. **Adapt Classroom Organization**: Many students with learning disabilities benefit from a highly structured environment in which physical areas (e.g., supplies, reading, math, and writing) are clearly labeled and a schedule for the day prominently displayed. Individual schedule charts can be useful if some students follow different schedules, such as leaving for a resource room or specialized therapy periodically. Such schedules reduce the cognitive load required to simply get through the day, and provide increased context for the student navigating the daily routine. The teacher can also vary grouping arrangements (e.g., large group, small group, peer tutoring, or learning centers) with student needs in mind.

III. **Adapt Classroom Management**: The teacher can vary grading systems, reinforcement systems, and even the rules to accommodate the varying needs of the students. Early teaching and practice of daily classroom routines can be particularly helpful to students with certain learning disabilities or emotional problems. It may be helpful to pay extra attention to the transitions between tasks, lessons or parts of the day. Some students benefit from having clear stimuli (a bell, hand signal, or flag, e.g.) to signal changes and transitions. Attention and time spent on such routines early in the year can pay big dividends in classroom management later in the year. The specific techniques required will depend upon the needs of the students.

Questions can be used to involve all students in class discussions. The higher-level questions should be asked of the high-ability students and less demanding ones of lower-ability students. Questions can be used to have students stretch their thinking and challenge them to extend what they have learned. Opening the lesson with a question can stimulate interest in the upcoming activity and get the students thinking about what will happen in the lesson. Throughout the lesson, teacher questions are usually one of these types:

Lower level for recall or recognition of basic facts. (Who wrote White Fang?)
Descriptive or comparison questions are used for the acquisition of specific information and organization of information. (Compare the lifestyle of the Native Americans in Mexico before and after the arrival of the Spanish in the1500s).

Explanation questions and synthesis/summary questions are used to interpret information and draw conclusions. (How did the novels of Charles Dickens influence social reform in England?)

Judgmental/open-ended questions require one to apply divergent thinking and evaluate the quality or truth of a relationship or conclusion. (If farmers were not allowed to use some sort of pesticide on their crops, what effect would that have on food prices?

When students with disabilities are included in the classroom it is important for the teacher to keep their needs in mind when asking questions. If the teacher knows a particular student will not be able to remember very much about the lesson, she might call on that student first so that his/her response is not 'taken' by someone else. Likewise, when calling on a student with disabilities the teacher should carefully consider the cognitive level of the question as described above and be sure to ask a question that is within the ability of the student to answer.

Techniques for Modifying Content Area Texts
Materials, usually textbooks, are frequently modified because of reading level. The goal of modification is to present the material in a manner that the student can more readily understand, while preserving the basic ideas and content. Modifications of course material may take the form of:

Simplifying Texts
Use a highlighter to mark key terms, main ideas, and concepts. In some cases, a marker may be used to delete nonessential content.

Cut and paste. The main ideas and specific content are cut and pasted on separate sheets of paper. Additional headings or other graphic aids can be inserted to help the student understand and organize material.

Supplement with graphic aids or tables.

Supplement with study guides, questions, and directed previews.
Use self-correcting materials.

Allow additional time, or break content material into smaller, more manageable units.

Rewriting Content Material
In some cases, it might be necessary to simply rewrite the content material to make it accessible to students with reading disabilities. Though the specific modifications will depend upon individual student needs, one of the most common requirements will be finding or revising text for learners who cannot read at grade level or who have difficulty comprehending what they read in content areas such as science and social studies. The most common specific learning disabilities involve reading difficulties. In order for such students to have equal access to the grade level curriculum in content areas, it is often necessary to revise printed material so students can access it at their reading comprehension level. Whether selecting published materials, or revising them for the students, these guidelines should be followed in order to increase context, reduce cognitive demand, and provide content material that students with learning disabilities can access.

Avoid complex sentences with many relative clauses.

Avoid the passive tense.

Try to make the topic sentence the first sentence in a paragraph.

Make sure paragraphs have a concluding sentence that restates the topic sentence in another way.

Use simple, declarative sentences that have only one main idea or concept at a time.

Use simple, single syllable, concrete words rather than more complex words (e.g., "an arduous journey" should be "a hard trip").

Eliminate nonessential information in favor of the main concepts necessary to teach.

Try to use only one tense in all the sentences.

Add diagrams and illustrations whenever possible and deliver information through labels rather than complete sentences.

Whenever possible, include multisensory elements and multimodalities in the presentation.

Avoid unfamiliar names and terms that will "tie up" the students' cognitive efforts (e.g., while the student is trying to figure out how to read the name " Aloicious" he/she will miss the point of the sentence; change the name to "Al")

Taped Textbooks
Textbooks can be taped by the teacher or aide for students to follow along. In some cases, the students may qualify for recordings of textbooks from agencies such as Recordings for the Blind. Modern technology includes most textbooks on CDs that can be highlighted and searched for index items and key words.

Parallel Curriculum
Projects such as Parallel Alternative Curriculum (PAC) or Parallel Alternative Strategies for Students (PASS) present the content at a lower grade reading level and come with tests, study guides, vocabulary activities, and tests.

Supplementary Texts
Book publishers, such as Steck-Vaughn, Rigby, Scholastic, and National Geographic Windows on Literacy publish series of content-area texts that have been modified for reading level, amount of content presented on pages, highlighted key items, and visual aids.

Other Ways to Select and Modify Materials to Match Learning Needs
The first step in the process would be to make informal assessments of the areas the student is having trouble with, as well as learning styles and preferences. If the materials come with a scope and sequence, or a summary of objectives and skills, the teacher can select those portions that match the student's needs. Since commercial materials are not always written with special needs students in mind, there are general things that teachers can do to make these materials easier to use:

- Review the materials and add advance organizers, cues, prompts, and feedback steps as necessary to make sure that the lesson contains the elements of explicit teaching procedures.
- Tape record directions, stories, or specific lessons so that the student can listen and play them back as needed.
- Clarify written directions by underlining key phrases or direction words. If the directions are too lengthy or wordy, simplify or rewrite them.
- For students who are anxious about seeing what appears to be too much work, tear out individual pages or present portions of the assignment.
- Students who are distracted by the visual stimulus of a full page can cover the sections that they are not working on at the moment.
- Change the response directions to underlining, multiple-choice, or marking or sorting if the student has a problem with handwriting. If necessary, give extra space for writing answers.
- Develop reading guides, outlines of lectures, graphic organizers, and glossaries for content area materials that do not contain them.
- Develop a method of marking a place in consumable materials, such as the use of post-it notes or arrows.
- Use tape recorders, computer-assisted instruction, overhead projectors with transparencies, Language Masters, and self-correcting materials.

Enhancing Visual Aids

In order to facilitate instructions for students with disabilities via visual images and messages, teachers should ensure that learning is visible and explicit. Key information and learning objectives should be highlighted. Tasks and activities should be broken down into steps. Learning games can be used to provide practice of concepts. Numerous methods should be utilized for students to show what they have learned. Students can produce news releases, comic strips, collages, advertisement, websites, maps, diorama, or other visual tasks to demonstrate learning of instructional objectives.

Teachers should plan for modifications of the lessons to appeal to the visual learner. They should access a variety of resources and collaborate with other teachers and professionals. Teachers should make sure they know their students so they can adapt the lesson to target various students' learning styles. The integration of technology, such as computers, Internet, multimedia displays, audio video equipment, art and visual equipment, computer assisted instruction is important when creating visual images.

The pacing of the lesson should be adjusted based on the feedback received from the students.

One method of making learning visual to the student is to provide a written list of steps and ensure that students monitor their own work as they finish each step. Auditory instructions should be supported with visual and tactile cues. Teachers should visually model how to complete tasks.

Students should be given ample opportunity to use and incorporate visual technologies into assignments and activities. The use of multi-media technology, graphics, video, sound, computer technology, Internet, CD-Rom, and computer software should be reflected in classroom lessons.

Skill 11.7 Demonstrating knowledge of strategies for differentiating instruction based on students' academic and social abilities, attitudes, interests, and values

Differentiated instruction is an educational philosophy that embraces the varied learning styles of individual students. In differentiated instruction, instruction is designed to meet the unique needs of each learner, utilizing the student's strengths and addressing state standards requirements.

Reasons to Differentiate Instruction

Student Interest
Effective differentiated instruction can be based on the student's interest. Students with disabilities may have interests similar to their nondisabled peers but students with certain types of disabilities may have unique or alternative interests.

One reason to know a student's interest is to be able to motivate the student. Surveys, checklists, or questionnaires can be utilized to determine students' interests. Conversation and observation can also provided insight into what is interesting and motivating for an individual student.

Student Learning Profile
Effective differentiated instruction incorporates the student's learning profile. A student's learning profile is unique to that individual and includes strengths and weaknesses which may enhance or inhibit learning. Knowing a student's learning style helps the teacher understand how a student learns best.

Multiple Intelligences:
Howard Gardner describes eight different types of intelligences that can be helpful in assessing r students' learning styles. Supporting students by utilizing the various types of intelligences can help pinpoint student strengths. The eight intelligences identified by Howard Gardner:

- Vertical/Linguistics Learners: Like to read, listen, discuss, and communicate with others through speaking and writing.
- Logical/Mathematical Learners: Love numbers of all sorts not only in math, think conceptually and see patterns, like to solve problems, reason, and analyze.
- Visual/Spatial Learners: Need mental pictures and images, graphic organizers, pictures, webs, diagrams, and mind maps.
- Bodily/Kinesthetic Learners: Need action, hands-on activities, manipulation of materials
- Musical Learners: Respond to pitch, rhythm, tone, musical patterns and singing, may or may not have musical skills, but respond strongly to music.

- Interpersonal Learners: Like to motivate others, organize, work with others.
- Intrapersonal Learners: Thoughtful and reflective, closely examine ideas, work alone, like independence.
- Naturalist Learners: Use surroundings to succeed, observe how systems work, effective manipulators of situations, connections with the natural world, observe, and investigate.

Processing Systems
The brain uses seven processing systems to acquire, store, and retrieve information. These processing systems are the same for everyone. While everyone has strengths and weaknesses in their processing systems, those strengths and weaknesses have a greater impact on learning for students with disabilities. The seven processing systems include:

Attention
Memory
Visual/Spatial
Sequential
Language
Motor Functioning
Higher-Order Thinking

Skill Level
Differentiating instruction based on student skill level is a common and effective practice for teachers. Using on-going assessment, teachers can identify the skill level of the individual student to determine the instructional level. The instructional level must match the skill level of the student in order for the student to derive the greatest benefit from instruction. If the instructional level is too low, the student is not challenge. If the instructional level is too high, the student may not be able to comprehend new skills and knowledge.

Factors Affecting Skill Level
Students with disabilities often exhibit reading deficits that impact learning at all grade levels and in all content areas. The teacher may be concerned with presenting higher level, challenging content to a student who has reading difficulties. Differentiated instruction provides for instructional presentation using a variety of skills and accommodations that allow the student with a disability to participate in higher level instruction.

Students with poor decoding skills may process more information by listening. The information could be presented on a computer with voice output, books on tape/CD, or read aloud by the teacher or peer. Accommodations such as these allow the student to access the curriculum and meet the state standards.

For these students with comprehension deficits, consideration must be given to the type of processing deficit. Information can be presented using visuals, such as graphic organizers, video clips or hands-on-activities. If a student has a deficit in higher-order thinking, he/she may be a candidate for lowering the number of concepts taught and/or breaking broad concepts into simpler concepts (which leads to a modification of the state standards).

Students with disabilities will also have varying skill levels in math, writing and background knowledge in content areas. Decisions about providing accommodations and modifications should follow the procedures of determining deficits and deciding the appropriate means to access state standards.

OPTIONS FOR DIFFERENTIATING INSTRUCTION

In recent years, increasing emphasis has been put on incorporating at least some principles of differentiated instruction into classrooms with students of mixed ability. Tomlinson (2001) states that teachers must first determine where the students are with reference to an objective, then tailor specific lesson plans and learning activities to help each student learn as much as possible about that objective. The effective teacher seeks to connect all students to the subject matter through multiple techniques with the goal that each student will relate to one or more techniques and excel in the learning process. Differentiated instruction encompasses modifying curriculum in several areas.

There are several options to consider with determining how to differentiate instruction.

Content
Products and Assessments
Materials
Activities

Content: What is the teacher going to teach? Or, perhaps better put, what does the teacher want the students to learn? Utilize state developed curriculum maps to determine the content to be covered and how much time will be spent on the unit. Based on the content, the understandings, essential questions, knowledge, and skills for the unit are developed. The second step is to develop the assessment instructions (e.g., quizzes, products, projects, tests) that will be used to evaluate student learning. Then the teachers determine what instructional strategies and materials are needed to teach the content. Finally, teachers determine what type of learning activities will be utilized. Differentiating content means that students have access to aspects of the content that pique their interest, with a complexity that provides an appropriate challenge to their intellectual development, but does not go beyond their frustration level. When students with special needs are included in a classroom, this often means modifying a lesson plan so that it has several levels. One common way to structure such levels is the following:

A Basic level might address the content of the objective at a cognitively less demanding level (e.g., knowledge, the lowest level on Bloom's taxonomy). Example: The student or student group matches names to planets on a diagram, or they correctly define key vocabulary.

A Moderate level could address the content at a higher level than basic, but still a fairly low level (e.g., comprehension). Example: After learning that the Earth orbits the sun due to the Sun's greater gravity, challenge the student or student group to give other examples of objects orbiting others and explain why in their own words.

A Mastery level might address the objective at the level most students should reach given state standards (e.g., Analysis). Example: The student or student group compares two planets based on a set of variables.

An Advanced level would address the objective at a higher level aimed at gifted students who can go beyond the required curriculum (e.g., the highest level on Bloom, Evaluation). Example: The student or student group is given a real or fictional theory of planetary movement and asked to evaluate its accuracy in light of the facts they have learned in the unit.

Once the unit of instruction is planned, the teachers determine how each student with a disability will be able to actively participate in the unit. Utilizing the student's IEP, the teacher can plan for the student with a disability in regard to strengths and weaknesses, disability area, processing deficits, and required accommodations and/or modifications.

Process: The classroom management techniques where instructional organization and delivery are maximized for the diverse student group. These techniques should include dynamic, flexible grouping activities, where instruction and learning occur as whole-class, teacher-led activities and in a variety of small group settings, such as teacher guided small group, peer learning and teaching (while teacher observes and coaches), or independent centers or pairs. Such techniques should also include strategies for anchor activities and smooth transitions from activity to activity.

One of the key concepts associated with differentiating instruction is flexible grouping. Flexible groups provide teachers with the ability to match student skill level, interest and learning profile to instruction and learning activities. Teachers should carefully consider various ways to group students, keeping in mind student skills and behaviors as they relate to the teaching and learning activities.

Flexible groups include:

Random Groups
Cooperative
Skill Level or Instructional Level
Reading Level
Interest
Learning Profile
Student Choice

Product: The expectations and requirements placed on students to demonstrate their knowledge or understanding. The type of product expected from each student should reflect that student's own capabilities. A student's IEP will provide guidelines on the best way to assess the student's progress as well as any testing accommodations that must be made. Earlier skill sections have addressed modifications to testing materials. Consider the following when determining accommodations and modifications for testing:

- Review the student's strengths and weaknesses
- Consider the student's learning profile
- Determine whether the assessment is to measure content or skills
- Options for differentiating tests and assessments based on the student's learning processing deficits include:
- Attention: Administer individually or in a small group, allow student to use a cubicle
- Memory: Provide a word bank, allow extended time, allow open book/note tests
- Visual-Spatial: Color code portions of the tests, cut tests into pieces, fewer problems per page, allow the student to finish and turn in one page at a time.
- Sequential: Provide formulas, allow use of a calculator, use graphic organizers
- Language: Read test to student, use software to read to student, allow more time, simplify wording on the test, allow oral answers to written essay questions
- Motor Function: Allow use of word processor, transcribe student response, allow oral testing
- Higher Order Thinking: Use graphic organizers, use picture prompts, highlight type of question

Materials and Activities
Consideration of materials used for instruction is another means to differentiate instruction for students with disabilities. In addition to textbooks, materials can include software and other assistive technology to support students. Such materials include:

Off level texts
Teacher adapted materials
Web based materials
Highlighted materials or texts
Reading pens
Calculator/multiplication chart
Manipulatives
Models
Books on tape
Text reader software

Activities include all teaching and learning experiences that support students in meeting the curriculum standards. Activities require students to respond in some way to information using their processing systems. Differentiation of activities is based on the strengths and needs of the student.

SUBAREA III. WORKING IN A PROFESSIONAL ENVIRONMENT

OBJECTIVE 12 UNDERSTAND HOW TO COMMUNICATE AND COLLABORATE WITH STUDENTS WITH DISABILITIES AND THEIR FAMILIES TO HELP STUDENTS ACHIEVE DESIRED LEARNING OUTCOMES.

Skill 12.1 Demonstrating familiarity with typical concerns of parents/guardians of students with disabilities and recognizes effective strategies for addressing such concerns

Most parents share some basic goals for their children. They want their children to grow up to be healthy, happy members of society who lead independent lives with productive employment. Parents of students with disabilities are no different, although the path that their children take may have additional turns and obstacles along the way.

Health

Many children with disabilities have associated health problems or are at risk for health problems. Many also take medication(s) routinely for health or behavioral conditions.

Parents of students with disabilities are concerned with their children's long-range health, the cost of health care (as children and as adults), and the effects of medication on their child's behavior, health, and school work.

It is not uncommon for special education students to take some medication while at school. Providing the school with the needed medication may be a financial strain for the family. Just the fact that others will be aware of the child's health and medications can also be a parental concern.

Parents are often concerned because their children and teachers may have difficulties identifying changes in health and in communicating possible changes in medication reactions. IEPs often include objectives for the child to communicate changes in his or her health and effects of medication.

Happiness

The quality of life for more severely disabled children is different than that of the general population. Even students with less severe physical conditions (e.g., a learning disability) may have lower self-esteem and feelings of being "stupid" or "different" because they leave the inclusion classroom for some special education services. Students with disabilities often have difficulty making friends, which can also impact happiness.

Parents of students with disabilities (as all parents) feel the emotional impact of the disability on their children. Parents are anxious to help their children feel good about themselves and fit in the general population of their peers.

Social goals may be included on the IEP. Some students (particularly those on the autism spectrum) may have a time (per the IEP minutes) to meet with a speech and language pathologist to work on social language. Other students may meet regularly (again, per IEP minutes) with the social worker to discuss situations from the classroom or general school setting.

Independence
Initially, parents of students with disabilities may be somewhat overprotective of their children. Soon after, however, most parents begin to focus on ways to help their children function independently.

Young children with disabilities may be working on self-care types of independence such as dressing, feeding, and toilet use. Elementary students may be working on asking for assistance, completing work, being prepared for class with materials (e.g., with books or papers). High school students may be working on driving, future job skills, or preparation for post-secondary education.

Job Training
IDEA 2004 addresses the need for students with disabilities to be prepared for jobs or post-secondary education in order to be independent, productive members of society.

Job training goals and objectives for the student with a disability may be vocational (such as food service, mechanical, carpentry, etc). Job training goals for other students may include appropriate high school coursework to prepare for a college program.

Productivity
Ultimately, the goal of the parents and school is for the student to become a productive member of society who can support him or herself financially and live independently. This type of productivity happen when the student becomes an adult with a measure of good health, positive self-esteem, the ability to interact positively with others, independent personal and work skills, and job training.

Particular Stages of Concern
Parents of students with special needs usually deal with increased concerns when the child reaches a new age or stage of development. Some of these development stages include: when the child is first identified as having a disability, entrance into an early childhood special education program, kindergarten (when it is evident that the disability remains despite services received thus far), third grade (when the student is expected to use more skills independently), junior high school, and entrance into high school.

Additional IEP goals and objectives may be warranted at these times, as the student is expected to use a new set of skills or may be entering a new educational setting.

It should be noted that parents are often more concerned when a younger, non-disabled sibling surpasses the child with the disability in some skill (such as feeding or reading). Previously, the parents may not have fully been aware of what most children can do at a particular age.

Skill 12.2 Demonstrating knowledge of strategies for helping students with disabilities and their parents/guardians become active participants on the educational team (e.g., during assessment, during the development and implementation of an individualized program)

Parents can be excellent sources of information and history about a student. As such, an educator must realize the importance of the parents of a child in order to provide adequate services to the student. To ensure the participation of the parent in the educational team, there must be constant contact during all stages of the special education process.

The first contact a teacher has with parents should be before the school year starts. While the teacher may be required to send a letter out stating the required supplies for the class, this does not count as an initial contact.

Parents are used to hearing that their child has done something bad/wrong when they receive a phone call from a teacher. Whenever possible, parents should be contacted to give positive feedback. When you call John's mother and say, "John got an A on the test today," you have just encouraged her to maintain open communication lines with you. Try to give three positive calls for every negative call you must give.

Effective communication between the teacher and parents/families

Effective communication with student parents and families is of critical importance to educational success. Research has shown that the more families are involved in a child's educational experience, the more that child will succeed academically. Families know students better than almost anyone and are a valuable resource for teachers of exceptional students. Often, an insight or observation from a family member or his or her reinforcement of school standards or activities means the difference between success and frustration in a teacher's work with children. Suggestions for relationship building and collaboration with parents and families include the following:

- Use laypersons' terms when communicating with families and make the communication available in the language of the home.
- Search out and engage family members' knowledge and skills in providing educational and therapeutic services to the student.
- Explore and discuss the concerns of families and help them find tactics for addressing those concerns.
- Plan collaborative meetings with children and their families and help them become active contributors to their educational team.
- Ensure that communications with and about families are confidential and conducted with respect for their privacy.

- Offer parents accurate and professionally presented information about the pedagogical and therapeutic work being done with their child. It is sometimes necessary to provide professional guidance about the child's disability or the techniques that will help. For example, the parent of a third grade child who reads at the first grade level checks out library books at the third grade level and insists that the child labor through trying to read them in the hope this will improve the child's reading skills. The teacher needs to explain that while it would be helpful for the parent to read that third grade level book **to** the child, books chosen for the **child** to read should be easy enough for the child to read about 95% of the text independently, even if this is below grade level. The teacher might help the parent find material that is age appropriate but written at the child's level.
- Keep parents abreast of their rights, of the kinds of practices that might violate them, and of available recourse if needed.
- Acknowledge and respect cultural differences.

One common difficulty occurs when teachers assume that involvement in education simply means that the parents show up to help at school events or participate in parental activities on campus. With this belief, many teachers devise clever strategies to increase parental involvement at school. However, just because a parent shows up to school and assists with an activity does not mean that the child will learn more. Many parents work all day long and cannot assist in the school. Teachers, therefore, have to think of different ways to encourage parental and family involvement in the educational process.

Quite often, teachers have great success with involving families by just informing families of what is going on in the classroom. Newsletters are particularly effective at this. Parents love to know what is going on in the classroom. In newsletters teachers can provide suggestions on how parents can help with the educational goals of the school. For example, teachers can recommend that parents read with their children for twenty minutes per day. Teachers can also provide suggestions on what to do when their children come across difficult words or when they ask a question about comprehension. This gives parents practical strategies. In addition, when working with students with special needs, it is a good idea to give frequent updates on the student's progress. Many IEPs require this on specific intervals. It is also helpful if a means (daily notebook, response sheet, etc.) is provided where parents can alert the teacher to issues at home that might impact the student (e.g., Johnny took his medication late or a change in home routine has upset him).

Parent conferences

Parent-teacher conferences are scheduled at regular intervals throughout the school year. These provide excellent opportunities to discuss students' progress, what they are learning, and how these accomplishments may relate to future plans for their academic growth. It is not unusual for the parent or teacher to ask for a conference outside of the scheduled parent-teacher conference days. These meetings should be looked at as opportunities to provide momentum to that student's success.

The parent-teacher conference is generally for one of three purposes. First, the teacher may wish to share information with the parents concerning the performance and behavior of the child. Second, the teacher may be interested in obtaining information from the parents about the child. Such information may help answer questions or concerns that the teacher has. A third purpose may be to request parent support or involvement in specific activities or requirements. In many situations, more than one of the purposes may be involved.

Planning the conference

When a conference is scheduled, whether at the request of the teacher or parent, the teacher should allow sufficient time to prepare thoroughly. Collect all relevant information, samples of student work, records of behavior, and other items needed to help the parent understand the circumstances. It is also a good idea to compile a list of questions or concerns you wish to address. Arrange the time and location of the conference to provide privacy and to avoid interruptions.

Conducting the conference

Begin the conference by putting the parents at ease. Take the time to establish a comfortable mood, but do not waste time with unnecessary small talk. Begin your discussion with positive comments about the student. Identify strengths and desirable attributes, but do not exaggerate.

As you address issues or areas of concern, be sure to focus on observable behaviors and concrete results or information. Do not make judgmental statements about parent or child. Share specific work samples, anecdotal records of behavior, etc., which demonstrate clearly the concerns you have. Be a good listener and hear the parent's comments and explanations. Such background information can be invaluable in understanding the needs and motivations of the child.

Finally, end the conference with an agreed plan of action between parents and teacher (and, when appropriate, the child). Bring the conference to a close politely but firmly and thank the parents for their involvement.

After the conference
A day or two after the conference, it is a good idea to send a follow-up note to the parents. In this note, briefly and concisely reiterate the plan or step agreed to in the conference. Be polite and professional; avoid the temptation to be too informal or chatty. If the issue is a long term one such as the behavior or on-going work performance of the student, make periodic follow-up contacts to keep the parents informed of the progress.

Modern technology has opened two more venues for communicating with parents. School/classroom websites are written with the intent of sharing regularly with parents and guardians. Many teachers now post their plans for the marking period and provide extra-credit assignments or homework from these websites. Email is now one of the major modes of communication. Most parents have email accounts and are more than willing to give their email addresses to teachers to be kept appraised of their child's academic progress.

Special events also provide opportunities for parental contact. Poetry readings, science fairs, and ice-cream socials, are a few examples of such events.

Skill 12.3 Demonstrating awareness of culturally responsive strategies for ensuring effective communication and collaboration among families of students with disabilities, school personnel, and representatives of community agencies

An educator must be aware of various cultures and be familiar with their different values and traditions. This will ensure no one is mistakenly offended or is misunderstood in any way. Effective communication strategies are required when dealing with families of students with disabilities. The communication strategies should be flexible and respond to the individual needs of the families.

Teachers traditionally communicate their educational philosophies to families through parent workshops or newsletters. However, these methods have their drawbacks. In many cases, workshops have low attendance when parents have problems with work schedules, transportation, or with getting outside help to take care of a student with disability. Newsletters may be thrown away or not read thoroughly; even when they are taken home, those that are only written in English may present difficulties for parents for whom English is not their first language.

Family school partnerships are developed when families are encouraged to spend more time in the classroom and are offered more information about their children's education. When families are in the classroom, they have the chance to observe teacher-student interactions, ask the teacher questions, and give feedback on curriculum or development. They also have an opportunity to meet other families.

As the structure of families in today's societies continue to change, teachers may need to try different family outreach strategies that target the new family structure, as what was done in the past may not be effective.
Teachers need to have a range of strategies for contacting parents. This includes using the telephone, email, letters, newsletters, classroom bulletin boards, and parent teacher conferences.

Teachers also need to be familiar with the student's home culture and have an appreciation for diversity by planning lessons and activities that are inclusive of the multi-cultural classroom. Through effective communication, teachers can involve parents as leaders and decision makers in the school. As more students with disabilities are included in the general education curriculum, both special and regular educators will need training that focuses on effectively interacting with parents of children with disabilities to involve them as equal partners in the educational planning and decision-making process for their children.

Effective Communication Skills

Communication occurs when one person sends a message and gets a response from another person. In fact, whenever two people can see or hear each other, they are communicating. The receiver changes roles and becomes the sender once the response is given. The communication process may break down if the receiver's interpretation differs from that of the sender.

Effective teaching depends on communication. By using good sending skills, the teacher has more assurance that he or she is getting the correct message across to the students. By being a model of a good listener, a teacher can help his or her students learn to listen and respond appropriately to others.

Attending Skills

The sender is the person who communicates the message; the receiver is the person who ultimately responds to the message.

Attending skills are used to receive a message. Some task-related attending skills that have been identified include: (1) looking at the teacher when information or instructions are being presented, (2) listening to assignment directions, (3) listening for answers to questions, (4) looking at the chalkboard, and (5) listening to others speak, when appropriate.

For some students, special techniques must be employed to gain and hold attention. For example, the teacher might first call the student by name when asking a question to assure the child is attending, or the teacher may ask the question before calling the name of a student to create greater interest.

Selecting students at random to answer questions helps to keep them alert and listening. Being enthusiastic and keeping lessons short and interactive assists in maintaining the attention of those students who have shorter attention spans. Some students may be better able to focus their attention when environmental distraction are eliminated or at least reduced; nonverbal signals can be used to draw students' attention to the task. Finally, arranging the classroom so that all students can see the teacher helps direct attention to the appropriate location.

Clarity of Expression

Unclear communication between the teacher and students with special needs sometimes contributes to problems in academic and behavioral situations. In the learning environment, unclear communication can add to the student's confusion about certain processes or skills he or she is attempting to master.

There are many ways in which the teacher can improve the clarity of communication. Giving clear, precise directions is one. Verbal directions can be simplified by using shorter sentences, familiar words, and relevant explanations. Asking a student to repeat directions or to demonstrate understanding of them by carrying out the instructions is an effective way of monitoring the clarity of expression. In addition, clarification can be achieved by the use of concrete objects, multidimensional teaching aids, and by modeling or demonstrating what should be done in a practice situation.

Finally, a teacher can clarify communication by using a variety of vocal inflections. The use of intonation juncture can help make the message clearer, as can pauses at significant points in the communication. For example, verbal praise should be spoken with inflection that communicates sincerity. Pausing before starting key words, or stressing those that convey meanings, helps students learn the concepts being taught.

Paraphrasing

Paraphrasing—restating what the student says using one's own words—can improve communication between the teacher and students. First, in restating what the student has communicated, the teacher is not judging the content—he or she is simply relating what he or she understands the message to be. If the message has been interpreted differently from the way intended, the student is asked to clarify. Clarification should continue until both parties are satisfied that the message has been understood.

The act of paraphrasing sends the message that the teacher is trying to better understand the student. Restating the student's message as fairly and accurately as possible assists the teacher in seeing things from the student's perspective. Paraphrasing if often a simple restatement of what has been said. Lead-ins such as "Your position is…" or "It seems to you that…" are helpful in paraphrasing a student's messages. A student's statement, "I am not going to do my math today" might be paraphrased by the teacher as, "Did I understand you to say that you are not going to do your math today?" By mirroring what the student has just said, the teacher has telegraphed a caring attitude for that student and a desire to respond accurately to the student's message.

To effectively paraphrase a student's message, the teacher should: (1) restate the student's message in his or her own words; (2) preface his or her paraphrasing with such remarks as, "You feel…" or "I hear you say that…"; and (3) avoid indicating any approval or disapproval of the student's statements. Johnson (1978) states the following as a rule to remember when paraphrasing: "Before you can reply to a statement, restate what the sender says, feels, and means correctly and to the sender's satisfaction" (p.139).

Descriptive feedback is a factual, objective (i.e., unemotional) recounting of a behavioral situation or message sent by a student. Descriptive feedback has the same effect as paraphrasing, in that: (1) when responding to a student's statement, the teacher restates (i.e., paraphrases) what the student has said or factually describes what he or she has seen; and (2) it allows the teacher to check his or her perceptions of the student and the student's message. A student may do or say something, but because of the teacher's feelings or state of mind, the student's message or behavior might be totally misunderstood. The teacher's descriptive feedback, which Johnson (1972) refers to as "understanding," indicates that the teacher's intent is to respond only to ask the student whether the statement has been understood, how the student feels about the problem, and how the student perceives the problem. The intent of the teacher is to more clearly "understand" what the student is saying, feeling, or perceiving in relation to a stated message or a behavioral event.

Evaluative feedback is verbalized perception by the teacher that judges, evaluates, approves, or disapproves of the statements made by the student. Evaluative feedback occurs when the student makes a statement and the teacher responds openly with "I think you're wrong," "That was a dumb thing to do," or "I agree with you entirely." The tendency to give evaluative responses is heightened in situations where feelings and emotions are deeply involved. The stronger the feelings, the more likely it is that two persons will each evaluate the other's statements solely from their own point of view.

Since evaluative feedback intones a judgmental approval or disapproval of the student's remark or behavior, it can be a major barrier to mutual understanding and effective communication. However, it is a necessary mechanism for providing feedback of a quantitative (and sometimes qualitative) instructional nature (e.g., test scores, homework results, classroom performance). In order to be effective, evaluative feedback must be offered in a factual, constructive manner. Descriptive feedback tends to reduce defensiveness and feelings of being threatened because it most likely communicates that the teacher is interested in the student as a person, has an accurate understanding of the student and what the student is saying, and encourages the student to elaborate and further discuss his or her problems.

In the learning environment, as in all situations, effective communication depends on good sending and receiving skills. Teaching and managing students involves good communication. By using clear, non-threatening feedback, the teacher can provide students with information that helps them to understand themselves better, at the same time providing a clearer understanding of each student on the teacher's part.

Skill 12.4 Demonstrating knowledge of family systems; the roles of families in the educational process; and the potential impact of differences in values, languages, and customs that can exist between the home and school

Role of the Family

Understanding the role of the family will assist a new educator with involving the parents in the educational team. The presence of a child with a disability within the family unit creates changes and possible stresses that will need to be addressed. Many parents feel the demands of the disabled child are greatly in excess of a non-disabled child's requirements. "A child (with a disability) frequently needs more time, energy, attention, patience, and money than the child (without a disability), and frequently returns less success, achievement, parent pride-inducing behavior, privacy, feelings of security and well-being" (Paul, 1981, p.6).

The family, as a microcosmic unit in a society, plays a vital role in many ways. The family assumes a protective and nurturing function, is the primary unit for social control, and plays a major role in the transmission of cultural values and mores. This role is enacted concurrently with changes in our social system as a whole. Paradoxically, parents who were formerly viewed as the cause of a child's disability are now depended on to enact positive changes in their children's lives. Siblings play an important role in fostering the social and emotional developments of a brother or sister with a disability. A wide range of feelings and reactions evolve as siblings interact. Some experience guilt over being the normal child and try to overcompensate by being the successful, perfect child for their parents. Others react in a hostile, resentful manner toward the amount of time and care the disabled sibling receives, frequently creating disruption as a way of obtaining parental attention.

The extended family, especially grandparents, can provide support and assistance to the nuclear family unit if they live within a manageable proximity. This support can take the form of childcare services for an evening or a few days, which can provide a means of reprieve for heavily involved parents.

Parents as Advocates

Ironically, establishing the parent-educator partnership, an action that is now sought by educators around the nation, came about largely through the advocacy efforts of parents. The state compulsory education laws began in 1918. They were adopted across the nation with small variances in agricultural regions. However, due to the fact that children with disabilities did not fit in with the general school curriculum, most continued to be turned away at the schoolhouse door, leaving the custodial services at state or private institutions as the primary alternative placement site for parents.

Educational policies reflected the litigation and legislation of the times, which overwhelmingly sided with the educational system and not with the family. After all, the educational policies reflected the prevailing philosophies of the times, including Social Darwinism (i.e., survival of the fittest). Thus, persons with disabilities were set apart from the rest of society—literally out of sight, out of mind. Those with severe disabilities were placed in institutions, and those with moderate disabilities were kept at home to do family or farm chores.

Following the two World Wars, the realization that disabling conditions could be incurred by a member of any family came to the forefront. Several celebrity families allowed stories to be published in national magazines about a family member with an identified disability, thus taking the entire plight of this family syndrome out of the closet. The 1950s brought about the founding of many parent and professional organization, and the movement continued into the next decade. Learning groups included the National Association of Parents and Friends of Mentally Retarded Children, which was founded in 1950 and later called the National Association for Retarded Children (it is now named the National Association of Retarded Citizens); the International Parents Organization, founded in 1957; and the parents' branch of the Alexander Graham Bell Association for Parents of the Deaf, founded in 1965. The Epilepsy Foundation of America was founded in 1967. The International Council for Exceptional Children had been established by faculty and students at Columbia University as early as 1922, and the Council for Exceptional Children recognized small parent organizations in the late 1940s.

During the 1950s, Public Law 85-926 brought about support for the preparation of teachers to work with children with disabilities so that these children might receive educational services.

The 1960s was the first period of time during which parents received tangible support from the executive branch of the national government. In 1960, the White House Conference on Children and Youth made the declaration that a child should only be separated from his or her family as a last resort. This gave vital support to parents' efforts toward securing a public education for their children with disabilities.

Parents as Partners

Parent groups are a major component in assuring appropriate services, co-equal with special education and community service agencies, for children with disabilities. Their role is individual and political advocacy, as well as socio-psychological support. Great advances in services for children with disabilities have been made through the efforts of parent advocacy groups. These groups have been formed to represent almost every type of disabling condition.

Family Systems

The special educator should be knowledgeable of family systems, as well as the impact of the systems on a family's response and contribution to the education of a child with special needs. The family systems theory, as outlined on the Bowen Center for the Study of the Family (http://www.thebowencenter.org/pages/theory.html), has been developed by Murray Bowen over recent decades. The Bowen Theory of Family Systems is outlined as follows.

Triangles refer to the impact on existing relationships between two people in a family when a third individual joins the family. In the case of a child with a disability, it could refer to the impact of the child's needs and associated physical, emotional, and financial stress on the marriage of the parents.

Differentiation of Self refers to the influence of family members to think alike and the individual's ability to think critically and independently while realizing the extent of his or her need for others.

For example, in a family with child who is deaf, the parents may be pressured by grandparents not to have the child undergo a cochlear implant, due to the invasive nature of the surgery. While the child's parents realize the importance of family support and relationships, parents with a strong differentiation of self will consider all the information and then make a decision that may go against the thoughts of the grandparents.

Nuclear Family Emotional System describes four basic relationship patterns that can develop or worsen because of tension. The patterns are marital conflict, dysfunction in one spouse, impairment of one or more children, and emotional distance. Because of the tension that results from the birth and parenting of a child with a disability, any or all of the relationship patterns may develop.

Family Projection Process refers to the parental projection of a perception (such as low self-esteem) or problem (learning disability) that results in the treatment of the child as such. With time, the projection may become a self-fulfilling prophecy. The projection process follows three steps:

1. The parent focuses on a child out of fear that something is wrong with him or her.
2. The parent interprets the child's behavior as confirming the fear.
3. The parent treats the child as if something is really wrong.

Multigenerational Transmission Process refers to the impact of parenting and the resulting differentiation of self on future generations. In the case of the parents of a child with a disability, parents who have developed a stronger differentiation of self are more likely to acknowledge their child's disability (regardless of extended family perception of the social stigma it may bring) and to consider all options of treatment and educational programming for their child.

Emotional Cutoff occurs when the individual distances him or herself from the family as an adult due to unresolved conflict. In the case of a child with a disability, a parent may distance him or herself from his or her own parents because of their ongoing opinion that the child with a severe disability should be institutionalized. By the emotional cutoff between the child's parent and grandparents, ongoing emotional and physical support may be jeopardized or lost completely.

Sibling Position is described in Bowen's work and is referenced as "incorporating the work of Walter Toman." According to sibling position, birth order reflects tendencies of children in later interactions. Firstborn children tend to be leaders; younger siblings tend to be followers.

Societal Emotional Process refers to the carryover of the above systems into all areas of personal interaction in the society (including the workplace and school). Hypothetical examples of how family systems affect students with disabilities and their families are given above. The special educator should be aware of these systems as he or she interacts with families on a regular basis and communicates with them regarding IEP planning and considerations.

Diversity in Cultural and Belief Systems

When interacting with families, it is important to keep in mind that culture and belief systems will have an impact on parental concerns and opinions about a child with a disability. For example, many mainstream American families would list future independence as a goal for a child with a disability. They hope that even a child with a severe disability will be able to live and work as independently as possible. However, from some cultural perspectives this goal would be unthinkable. The emphasis on extended family and the manner in which each cares for the other throughout all stages of life might lead some parents to look with horror on the prospect of a child with a disability ever living alone or functioning independently. Their assumption might be that the best and most appropriate goal is for the child to find a way to fit in and contribute to the family while being sheltered *at home* with siblings and relatives.

It is the educator's responsibility to learn as much as possible about the family and parental viewpoints on matters relevant to the child's education, and to listen carefully to the parents' viewpoint.

Research is beginning to document ways in which cultural minority parents interact with their children to support learning. The research focuses primarily on how these interactions differ from more main-stream approaches.

One recent study explored the non-traditional ways in which Hispanic parents are involved in their children's education; ways that are not necessarily recognized by educators as parent involvement. Further research is needed to delve more deeply into the ways these parents are involved and to consider why some families are not involved in traditional ways. Such studies might also suggest ways to train teachers to recognize these "non-traditional" forms of involvement.

OBJECTIVE 13 UNDERSTAND HOW TO COMMUNICATE AND COLLABORATE WITH COLLEAGUES, ADMINISTRATORS, SERVICE PROVIDERS, AND COMMUNITY AGENCIES TO HELP STUDENTS WITH DISABILITIES ACHIEVE DESIRED LEARNING OUTCOMES

Skill 13.1 Recognizing various roles and responsibilities that school personnel, service providers, and community agencies can take in planning an individualized program

The special educator is trained to work in a team approach. This starts at the initial identification of students who appear to deviate from what is considered to be normal performance or behavior for particular age- and grade-level students. The special education teacher serves as a consultant (or as a team member, depending on the school district) to the student support team. If the student is referred, the special education teacher may be asked to collect assessment data for the forthcoming comprehensive evaluation. This professional then generally serves on the multidisciplinary eligibility, individualized educational planning, and placement committees. If the student is placed in a special education setting, the special educator continues to coordinate and collaborate with regular classroom teachers and support personnel at the school-based level.

Support professionals are available at both the district- and school-based levels, and they contribute valuable services and expertise in their respective areas. A team approach between district ancillary services and local school-based staff is essential.

School Psychologist. The school psychologist participates in the referral, identification, and program planning processes. He or she contributes to the multidisciplinary team by adding important observations, data, and inferences about the student's performance. As the evaluation is conducted, he or she observes the student in the classroom environment, takes a case history, and administers a battery of formal and informal individual tests. The psychologist is involved as a member of a professional team throughout the stages of referral, assessment, placement, and program planning.

Physical Therapist. This person works with disorders of bones, joints, muscles, and nerves following medical assessment. Under the prescription of a physician, the therapist applies treatment to the students in the form of heat, light, massage, and exercise to prevent further disability or deformity. Physical therapy includes the use of adaptive equipment, as well as prosthetic and orthotic devices to facilitate independent movement. This type of therapy helps individuals with disabilities to develop or recover their physical strength and endurance.

Occupational Therapist. This specialist is trained in helping students develop self-help skills (e.g., self-care, motor, perceptual, and vocational skills). The students are actively involved in the treatment process to quicken recovery and rehabilitation.

Speech and Language Pathologist. This specialist assists in the identification and diagnosis of children with speech or language disorders. In addition, he or she makes referrals for medical or habilitation needs, counsels family members and teachers, and works with the prevention of communicative disorders. The speech and language therapist concentrates on rehabilitative service delivery and continuing diagnosis.

Administrators. Building principals and special education directors (or coordinators) provide logistical as well as emotional support. Principals implement building policy procedures and control designation of facilities, equipment, and materials. Their support is crucial to the success of the program within the parameters of the base school. Special education directors provide information about federal, state, and local policies, which is vital to the operation of a special education unit. In some districts, the special education director may actually control certain services and materials. Role clarification, preferably in writing, should be accomplished to ensure effectiveness of program services.

Guidance Counselors, Psychometrists, and Diagnosticians. These persons often lead individual and group counseling sessions, and are trained in assessment, diagnostic, and observation skills, as well as personality development and functioning abilities. They can apply knowledge and skills to multidisciplinary teams and assist in the assessment, diagnosis, placement, and program planning process.

Social Worker. The social worker is trained in interviewing and counseling skills. This person possesses knowledge of available community and school services, and makes these known to parents. He or she often visits homes of students, conducts intake and assessment interviews, counsels individuals and small groups, and assists in district enforcement policies.

School Nurse. This person offers valuable information about diagnostic and treatment services. He or she is knowledgeable about diets, medications, therapeutic services, health-related services, and care needed for specific medical conditions. Reports of communicable diseases, to which a health professional has access, are filed with the health department. A medical professional can sometimes obtain cooperation with the families of children with disabilities in ways that are difficult for the special education teacher to achieve.

General Education Teachers and Subject Matter Specialists. These professionals are trained in general and specific instructional areas, teaching techniques, and overall child growth and development. They serve as a vital component to the referral process, as well as in the subsequent treatment program if the student is determined eligible. They work with the students with special needs for the majority of the school day and function as a link to the children's special education and medical programs.

Paraprofessional. This staff member assists the special educator and often works in the classroom with the special needs students. He or she helps prepare specialized materials, tutor individual students, lead small groups, and provide feedback to students about their work.

Planning and Implementing an Individualized Program and Applying Effective Strategies for Working Collaboratively

The roles of the special education teacher and the general education teacher are to work together to ensure that students with disabilities are able to attain their educational objectives in the least restrictive environment. Some students are best served in the general education setting with additional accommodations, while other students may be best served in the special education setting. The educators must work together to decide what educational program is best suited for the student, as well as where the student can best meet his or her goals and objectives.

These decisions should be made during the student's IEP meeting. It is important that the special education teacher, the general education teacher, and other interested professionals (such as the speech/language pathologist) are in attendance at the meeting so they can discuss and collaborate on their roles in helping the student.

Lesson Plan Collaboration

According to Walther-Thomas et al (2000), "Collaboration for Inclusive Education," ongoing professional development that provides teachers with opportunities to create effective instructional practice is vital and necessary. "A comprehensive approach to professional development is perhaps the most critical dimension of sustained support for successful program implementation." The inclusive approach incorporates learning programs that include all stakeholders in defining and developing high quality programs for students. The figure at the top of the next page shows how an integrated approach of stakeholders can provide the optimal learning opportunity for all students.

Integrated Approach to Learning

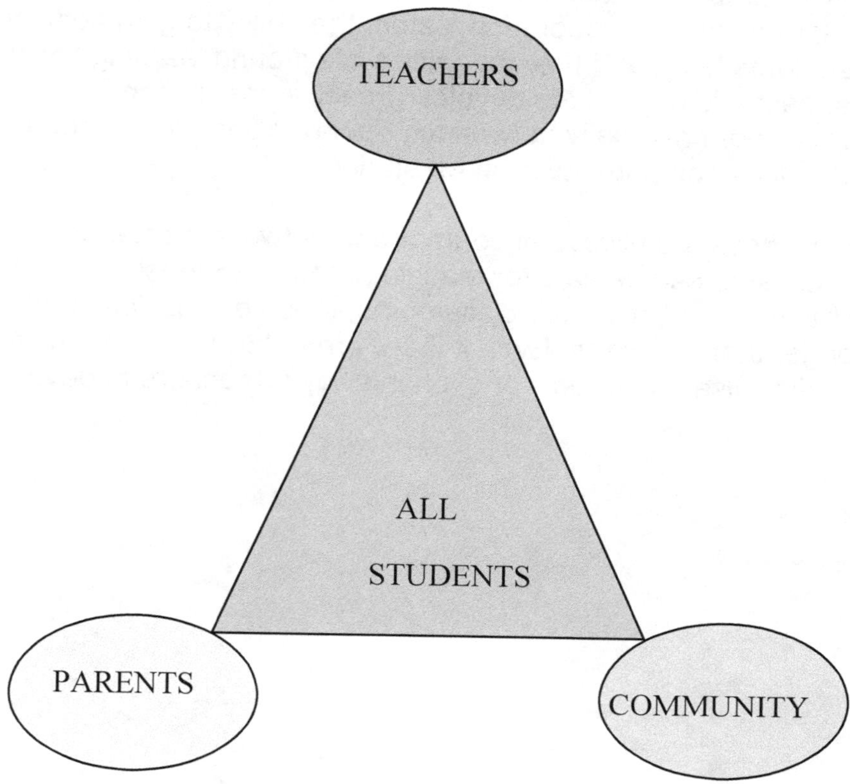

In the integrated approach to learning, teachers, parents, and community support become the integral apexes to student learning. The focus and central core of the school community is triangular as a representation of how effective collaboration can work in creating success for student learners. The goal of student learning and achievement now becomes the heart of the school community. The direction of teacher professional development in constructing effective instruction is clearly articulated in a greater understanding of facilitating learning strategies that develop skills and education equity for students.

Teachers need diversity in their instructional toolkits, which can provide students with clear instruction, mentoring, inquiry, challenge, performance-based assessment, and journal reflections on their learning processes. For teachers, having a collaborative approach to instruction fosters for students a deeper appreciation of learning, subject matter, and knowledge acquisition.

Implementing a consistent approach to learning from all stakeholders will create equitable educational opportunities for all learners.

Research has shown that educators who collaborate become more diversified and effective in implementation of curriculum and assessment of effective instructional practices. Collaboration fosters the ability to gain additional insight into how students learn and how modalities of differing learning styles can increase a teacher's capacity to develop proactive instruction methods. Teachers who team teach or have daily networking opportunities can create a portfolio of curriculum articulation and inclusion for students.

People in business are always encouraged to network in order to further their careers. The same can be said for teaching. If English teachers get together and discuss what is going on in their classrooms, those discussions make the "whole" much stronger than the parts. Even if there are not formal opportunities for such networking, it's wise for schools or even individual teachers to develop and seek them.

Skill 13.2 Recognizing the roles and responsibilities of the special education teacher in regard to seeking assistance from and collaborating with other professionals to support student learning

When making eligibility, program, and placement decisions about a student, the special education teacher serves as a member of a multidisciplinary team. Teachers are involved in every aspect regarding the education of individual students; therefore, they need to be knowledgeable not only about teaching and instructional techniques, but also about support services. These services will need to be coordinated, and teachers must be able to work in a collaborative manner.

The concept of mainstreaming students with special needs—that is, integrating them with their classmates in as many living and learning environments as possible—caught hold about the time that provisions for the Individuals with Disabilities Education Act (IDEA) were formulated in the early- to mid-70s. Even though mainstreaming is not specifically addressed in this legislation, the education of all children and youth with disabilities in the least restrictive environment is mandated. In addition, this important legislation defines special education, identifies related services that may be required if special education is to be effective, and requires the participation of parents and other persons involved in the education of children and youth with disabilities.

Close contact and communication must be established and maintained between the school district staff, each base school, and the various specialists (or consultants) providing ancillary services. These persons often serve special needs students in auxiliary (e.g., providing help) and supplementary (e.g., in addition to) ways. Thus, the principles and methods of special education must be shared with regular educators, and tenets and practices of general education must be conveyed to special educators. Job roles and the unique responsibilities and duties of support specialists like speech/language therapists, physical and occupational therapists, social workers, school psychologists and nurses, and others need to be known by all teachers.

Furthermore, the services that can be provided by community resources, and the support that can be given by parents and professional organizations, must be known to all in order for maximum education for exceptional students to occur. Professional services are offered on a local, state, and national level for most areas of disability. Teachers are able to stay abreast of most current practices and changes by reading professional journals, attending professional conferences, and maintaining membership in professional organizations.

Principles and Factors Related to the Coordination of Efforts

When professionals work together to provide services for students with disabilities, it is important that they work as a cohesive teaching unit that uses information sharing systems and proper scheduling procedures.

A system should be put into place for sharing program materials, tracking student mastery of goals and objectives, and supporting the various requirements of administrative and teaching staff. Because of the variety of learning objectives and the need to make the special education curriculum appropriate for each student, information sharing is critical. It is not uncommon for a teacher in one part of the school to be completely unaware of what another teacher is doing. Two teachers may have similar students with similar intensive needs, and by sharing information, lesson plans, and behavior modification strategies, the workload is shared and students benefit from a more cohesive program.

Professionals also need to work together to ensure that students with disabilities are receiving the services outlined in the IEP. The speech/language pathologist, the occupational therapist, the general education teacher, and the special education teacher may all be providing services to one student. In order to ensure that the proper time is allotted for each service, the professionals involved will have to work together to develop a schedule for the student to ensure that nothing is left out and all areas outlined in the IEP are addressed. This will also help when ensuring that students with disabilities who can be taught in groups are grouped with other students who may have the same requirements. This can only be effectively done when professional share schedules, student information, and student requirements. If they work together, they can accomplish a lot more then when working independently.

Working Within School Administrative Structures

The student's IEP must state the special education, supplementary aids, and services either to be provided to the student or on behalf of the student. The IEP should also contain a statement of the program modifications and support for school personnel that will allow the student to become involved in and progress through the general curriculum. In the past, students with disabilities were sometimes placed in the general education classroom for the sake of inclusion without any help or support. IDEA 1997 required that supplementary aids and services, accommodations, modifications, and supports play a more important role in a student's education.

The IEP should specify supports for school personnel. The decisions as to what kind of support is appropriate for a particular student are to be made on an individualized basis by the IEP team. The approach should be to create, from the beginning, a curriculum with built-in supports for diverse learners, rather than to fit supplementary aids and services, accommodations, modifications, or supports after the fact.

The IEP should include ways for the parent and the teacher to objectively measure the student's progress or lack of progress (regression) in the special education program. If the student is not receiving the services specified in his or her IEP, the student may not be able to meet the outlined goals. Careful monitoring and reporting of goals and objectives every grading period should help ensure that students receive the services to which they are entitled.

For example, if the student is entitled to additional services from a speech therapist, occupational therapist, or other specialist, the teachers should ensure that the specified services outlined in the IEP are being provided to the students. This can be done by working with the principal or other administrators to discuss how much time has been allotted for the additional services and to ensure that each student receives the time allotted and spelled out in the IEP.

Skill 13.3 Demonstrating knowledge of various models and strategies of collaboration (e.g., co-teaching, consultant teaching) and their implementation

INSTRUCTIONAL PLANNING FOR A VARIETY OF INCLUSIVE MODELS

According to IDEA 2004, students with disabilities are to participate in the general education program to the extent that it is beneficial for them. As students are included in a variety of general education activities and classes, the need for collaboration among teachers grows.

Co-Teaching
One model for general education teachers and special education teachers to use for collaboration is co-teaching. In this model, both teachers actively teach in the general education classroom. Perhaps both teachers will conduct a small science experiment group at the same time, switching groups at some point in the lesson. Perhaps in social studies, one teacher will lecture while the other teacher writes notes on the board or points out information on a map.

In the co-teaching model, the general education teacher and special educator often switch roles back and forth within a class period, or they may do so at the end of a chapter or unit. The special education teacher is responsible for ensuring that appropriate modifications and accommodations are made for special education students.

Push-In Teaching
In the push-in teaching model, the special educator teaches parallel material in the general education classroom. When the regular education teacher teaches word problems in math, for example, the special educator may work with some students on setting up the initial problems, followed by having them complete the computation. Another example would be in science; when the general education teacher asks review questions for a test, the special educator works with a student who has a review study sheet to find the answer from a group of choices. In the push-in teaching model, it may appear that two versions of the same lesson are being taught or that two types of student responses/activities are being monitored on the same material. The push-in teaching model is considered one type of differentiated instruction in which two teachers are teaching simultaneously.

Consultant Teaching
In the consultant teaching model, the general education teacher conducts the class after planning with the special educator how to differentiate activities so that the needs of the student with a disability are met.

In a social studies classroom using the consultant teaching model, both teachers may discuss what the expectations will be for a student with a learning disability and fine motor difficulty when the class does reports on states. They may decide that doing a state report is appropriate for the student; however, he or she may use the computer to write the report so that he or she can utilize the spell check feature and so that the work is legible.

INSTRUCTIONAL PLANNING FOR PULL OUT MODELS

Resource Room or Partial Pull out

The resource room is a specialized instructional setting where students go for short periods of special work, to learn specific skills and behaviors in which the student is deficient. The student spends the remainder of the day in the regular classroom. Generally, the resource room is inside the school environment where the child goes to be taught by a teacher who is certified in the area of disability. The accommodations and services provided in the resource room are designed to provide her access to an equal education in spite of her disability, and to help her catch up and perform with her peers in the regular classroom. In this case, she returns to the regular classroom for other subjects because this is the Least Restrictive Environment (LRE). The resource room is usually a bridge to mainstreaming.

Resource room time should be scheduled so that the student does not miss academic instruction in his/her classroom or miss desirable nonacademic activities. In schools where ESE teachers also co-teach or work with students in the regular classroom, the regular teacher will have to coordinate lesson plans with those of the special education teacher. Consultation time will also have to be budgeted into the schedule. For maximum effectiveness, the general education teacher and the special education teacher (in the Resource room) collaborate on differentiating the student's activities so they can be integrated into the mainstream classroom.

Substantially Separate Classrooms

In some cases a child's disability makes it impossible for the student to succeed in a mainstream classroom. Some students might need very specialized forms of instruction not available in the general education class, or have emotional, attention, or medical difficulties that prevent them from accessing the curriculum in a large group. For these students, a separate classroom where they receive all their academic instruction is required. Special education teachers and, often, additional aides staff these classes and deliver specialized services.

Even in such a separate classroom, however, collaboration between general education and special education teachers is very important. Children in these classrooms typically spend at least part of the day, for lunch, recess, enrichment and social activities, etc., with a general education class. In order for transitions to move smoothly teachers must coordinate times and activities. Often, the general education teacher will include the special education students in special projects where their work can be displayed with that of their grade peers. For example, when an entire grade level is doing display boards on dinosaurs or states, the special education teacher might modify the lesson so the students in the separate classroom produce a display, as well.

Skill 13.4 Recognizing the roles and responsibilities of paraprofessionals (e.g., related to instruction, intervention, and direct services) and demonstrates knowledge of strategies and procedures for observing, evaluating, and providing feedback to paraprofessionals

Paraprofessionals and General Education Teachers

Paraprofessionals and general education teachers are important collaborators with teachers of exceptional students. Although they may not have the theoretical experience to assure effective interaction with such students, they do bring valuable perspective to offer to and opportunities for breadth and variety in, an exceptional child's educational experience.

Paraprofessionals' true roles may be different in each school's system. Typically, a paraprofessional will provide assistance to students under direct supervision of the general education or special education teacher. Their duties may be, but are not limited to, providing small group or one-on-one instruction, incorporating assistive technology, or providing assistance to students with physical handicaps or minor medical conditions.

General education teachers also offer curriculum and subject matter expertise and a high level of professional support, while paraprofessionals may provide insights born of their particular familiarity with individual students. The Council for Exceptional Children (CEC) suggests that special education teachers can best collaborate with general education teachers and paraprofessionals by:

- Offering information about the characteristics and needs of children with exceptional learning needs.
- Discussing and brainstorming ways to integrate children with exceptionalities into various settings within the school community.
- Modeling best practices, instructional techniques, and accommodations, as well as coaching others in their use.
- Keeping communication about children with exceptional learning needs and their families confidential.
- Consulting with these colleagues in the assessment of individuals with exceptional learning needs.
- Engaging them in group problem solving and in developing, executing, and assessing collaborative activities.
- Offering support to paraprofessionals by observing their work with students, as well as offering feedback and suggestions.

Skill 13.5 Recognizing effective strategies for collaborating with school personnel, service providers, and community agencies to integrate students with disabilities into various settings and demonstrates knowledge of strategies for evaluating the effectiveness of collaborative activities

Related Service Providers and Administrators

Related service providers and administrators offer specialized skills and abilities that are critical to an exceptional education teacher's ability to advocate for his or her student, to meet a school's legal obligations to the student, and to meet legal obligations to the student's family. Related service providers (e.g., speech, occupational, and language therapists; psychologists; and physicians) offer expertise and resources unparalleled in meeting a child's developmental needs. Administrators are often experts in the resources available at the school and local education agency levels, as well as the culture and politics of a school system. They can be powerful partners in meeting the needs of exceptional education teachers and students.

A teacher's most effective approach to collaborating with these professional includes:

- Confirming mutual understanding of the accepted goals and objectives of the student with exceptional learning needs as documented in his or her IEP.
- Soliciting input about ways to support related service goals in classroom settings.
- Understanding the needs and motivations of each, and acting in support whenever possible.
- Facilitating respectful and beneficial relationships between families and professionals.
- Regularly and accurately communicating observations and data about the child's progress or challenges.

This section will specifically address the working relationship teachers should have with their colleagues in the classroom environment. There are six basic steps to having a rewarding collaborative relationship, whether the others are paraprofessionals, aides, or volunteers.

While it is understood that there are many types of colleagues who may be assisting in a classroom, this section will summarize their titles as "classroom assistant."

Get to know each other. The best way to start a relationship with anyone is to find time alone to get to know each other. Give a new classroom assistant the utmost respect and look at this as an opportunity to share talents and learn those of a coworker. Remember that this is the opportunity to find places of agreement and disagreement, which can help maintain and build a working relationship. Good working relationships require the knowledge of where each other's strengths and weaknesses are. This knowledge may create one of one of the best working relationships possible.

Remember that communication is a two-way street. As a professional educator, it is important to remember that one must actively communicate with others. This is especially important with classroom assistants. Listen to them and let them know that listening is taking place. Pay attention and make sure that the classroom assistant sees an incorporation of his or her thoughts. Encourage them to engage in conversations by asking for more information. Asking a classroom assistant for details and insights may help to further meet the needs of students. It is also an educator's responsibility to remove and prevent communication barriers in the working relationship. Avoid giving negative criticism or put downs. Do not "read" motivations into the actions of the classroom assistant. Learn about them through open communication.

Establish clear roles and responsibilities. The Access Center for Improving Outcomes of All Students K-8 has defined these roles in the following graph.

	Teacher Role	**Classroom Assistant Role**	**Areas of Communication**
Instruction	Plan all instruction, including expected goals/objectives in small groups Provide instruction in whole-class settings	Work with small groups of students on specific tasks, including review or re-teaching of content Work with one student at a time to provide intensive instruction or remediation on a concept or skill	Teachers provide specific content and guidance about curriculum, students, and instructional materials Classroom assistants note student progress and give feedback to teachers
Curriculum & Lesson Plan Development	Develop all lesson plans and instructional materials Ensure alignment with standards, student needs, and IEPs	Provide assistance in development of classroom activities, retrieval of materials, and coordination of activities	Mutual review of lesson plan components prior to class Teachers provide guidance about specific instructional methods
Classroom Management	Develop and guide class-wide management plans for behavior and classroom structures Develop and monitor individual behavior management plans	Assist with the implementation of class-wide and individual behavior management plans Monitor hallways, study hall, and other activities outside normal class	Teachers provide guidance about specific behavior management strategies and student characteristics Classroom assistants note student progress and activities and give feedback to teachers

"Working Together: Teacher-Paraeducator Collaboration" The Access Center for Improving Outcomes of All Students K-8, http://www.k8accesscenter.org/documents/RESOURCELIST3-1.doc

Plan together. Planning together lets the classroom assistant know they are considered valuable. It also provides a timeline of expectations that will aid in the overall classroom delivery to students. This also gives the impression to students that all authority figures are on the same page and know what is going to happen next.

Show a united front. It is essential to let students know that both adults in the room deserve the same amount of respect. Have a plan in place on how to address negative behaviors individually as well as together. DO NOT make a statement in front of the students that the classroom assistant is wrong. Take time to address issues regarding class time privately, not in front of the class.

Reevaluate your relationship. Feedback is wonderful. Stop every now and then and discuss how the team is working. Be willing to listen to suggestions. Taking this time may be the opportunity to improve the working relationship.

Additional Reading:

- "Creating a Classroom Team" http://www.aft.org/pubs-reports/psrp/classroom_team.pdf.
- "Working Together: Teacher-Paraeducator Collaboration" The Access Center for Improving Outcomes of All Students K-8, http://www.k8accesscenter.org/ documents/RESOURCELIST3-1.doc.

Skill 13.6 Demonstrating knowledge of strategies for providing information to general education teachers and other service providers in instructional methods, technology, and accommodations for students with disabilities

A student with a disability may require specialized instructional methods, use of specific technology, and/or other accommodations. These will be outlined in the student's IEP and should be familiar to all educators and staff members working with the student.

Inservices and workshops are often used to explain the above needs of a student to a group of professionals. These sessions may be conducted by the special education teacher. In some instances, the special educator may call upon another professional to conduct the in-service, or he or she may work with the other professional to make a joint presentation. This is sometimes the case with students with hearing impairments, when the audiologist conducts an in-service on how the hearing loss impacts classroom performance and how to use auditory training equipment. Another example might be an assistive technology consultant explaining the use of an augmentative communication device.

Explanation of disability and student IEP is important so that everyone working with the student is aware of and focusing on the same goals and objectives. Oftentimes, the general education teacher or other school staff will be listed as implementers of some of the IEP goals and objectives. These individuals should not only be aware of the goals, but should also be knowledgeable about how to keep record of student progress. The special educator is responsible for making sure that an appropriate type of documentation is being kept. He or she will often need to provide a chart or questionnaire to assist with this. Confidentiality is crucial and should be stressed when explaining the student's IEP, as well as addressing where (in a locked file cabinet) it should be kept.

Observation of the special education teacher in the class is often helpful for those who will be working with the special education student. If the IEP is discussed prior to such an observation, it will help the general education teacher be aware of what to watch for and to better formulate questions for clarification later.

Observation of the general education teacher or other service provider in their class and feedback is helpful once the student is in the general education setting or working with other service providers. The special educator can give feedback on the accommodations and methods being used as well as the student's progress. Observation of the student in these settings provides data needed for future IEP planning, and the feedback of the special educator assists the general education teacher in meeting the needs of the student.

Ongoing evaluation of student progress via the general education teacher can be done in a number of ways besides observation. The special education teacher may provide a questionnaire or checklist for the general education teacher. In addition, conversations and emails on student progress should be documented for reference in completing student progress reports and in IEP planning. It is the role of the special educator to communicate the importance of input from the general education teacher for these purposes.

Skill 13.7 Recognizing how to communicate effectively with school personnel about the characteristics and needs of students with disabilities

Please refer to Skill 13.1, Skill 13.2, Skill 13.4, Skill 13.5, and Skill 13.6, where these issues were discussed in detail.

OBJECTIVE 14 UNDERSTAND THE HISTORICAL, SOCIAL, AND LEGAL FOUNDATIONS OF THE FIELD OF SPECIAL EDUCATION.

Skill 14.1 Demonstrating knowledge of theories and philosophies that form the foundation for special education practice

Historical Aspects

Special education is precisely what the term denotes: education of a special nature for students who have special needs. The academic and behavioral techniques that are used today in special education are a culmination of "best practices." They evolved from a number of disciplines (e.g., medicine, psychology, sociology, language, ophthalmology, otology) to include education. Each of these disciplines contributed uniquely to its field so that the needs of special students might be better met in the educational arena.

Unfortunately, during the earlier part of the 1900s through the mid-1950s, too many educators placed in positions of responsibility refused to recognize their professional obligation for assuring <u>all</u> children a free, appropriate, public education. Today, doors can no longer be shut, eyes cannot be closed, and heads cannot be turned; due process rights have established for special needs students and their caregivers. Specific mandates are now stated in national laws, state regulations, and local policies. These mandates are the result of many years of successful litigation and political advocacy, and govern the delivery of special education.

What special educators <u>do</u> is one thing; <u>how</u> services are delivered is yet another. The concept of inclusion, which was advocated by Evelyn Deno and has been in existence since the early 1970s, stresses the need for educators to rethink the continuum of services. Many school districts developed educational placement sites, which contain options listed on this continuum. These traditional options extend from the least restrictive to the most restrictive special education settings. The least restrictive environment is the regular education classroom. The present trend is to team special education and regular classroom teachers in regular classrooms. This avoids pulling out students for resource room services, and provides services by specialists for students who may be showing difficulties similar to those of special education students.

Major Developments in the History of Special Education

Although the origin of special education services for children with disabilities is relatively recent, the history of public attitude toward people with disabling conditions was recorded as early as 1552. The Spartans practiced infanticide, which is the killing or abandonment of malformed or sickly babies. The ancient Greeks and Romans thought people with disabilities were cursed and forced them to beg for food and shelter. Those who could not fend for themselves were allowed to perish. Some with mental disabilities were employed as fools for the entertainment of the Roman royalty.

In the time of Christ, people with disabilities were thought to be suffering the punishment of God. Those with emotional disturbances were considered to be possessed by the devil, and although early Christianity advocated humane treatment of those who were not normal physically or mentally, many remained outcasts of society, sometimes pitied and sometimes scorned.

During the Middle Ages, persons with disabilities were viewed within the aura of the unknown, and were treated with a mixture of fear and reverence. Some were wandering beggars, while others were used as jesters in the courts. However, the Reformation brought about a change of attitude. Individuals with disabilities were accused of being possessed by the devil, and exorcism flourished. Many innocent people were put in chains and cast into dungeons.

The early seventeenth century was marked by a softening of public attitude toward persons with disabilities. Hospitals began to provide treatment for those with emotional disturbances and mental retardation. A manual alphabet for those with deafness was developed, and John Locke became the first person to differentiate between persons with mental retardation and those with emotional disturbance.

In America, however, the colonists treated people with severe mental disorders as criminals, while those who were harmless were left to beg or were treated as paupers. At one time, it was common practice to sell them to the person who would provide for them at the least cost to the public. When this practice was stopped, persons with mental retardation were put into poorhouses, where conditions were often extremely squalid.

The Nineteenth Century: The Beginning of Training

In 1799, Jean Marc Itard, a French physician, found a 12-year old boy who had been abandoned in the woods of Averyron, France. His attempts to civilize and educate the boy, Victor, established many of the educational principles presently in use in the field of special education, including developmental and multi-sensory approaches, sequencing of tasks, individualized instruction, and a curriculum geared toward functional life skills.

Itard's work had an enormous impact on public attitude toward individuals with disabilities. They began to be considered educable. During the late 1700s, rudimentary procedures were devised by which those with sensory impairments (e.g., deaf, blind) could be taught, closely followed in the early 1800s by attempts to teach students with mild intellectual disabilities and emotional disorders (at that time known as the "idiotic" and "insane"). Throughout Europe, schools for students with visual and hearing impairments were erected, paralleled by the founding of similar institutions in the United States. In 1817, Thomas Hopkins Galludet founded the first American school for students who were deaf, known today as Galludet College in Washington, D.C., one of the world's best institutions of higher learning for those with deafness. Galludet's work was followed closely by that of Samuel Gridley Howe, who was instrumental in the founding of the Perkins Institute in 1829 for students who were blind.

The mid-1800s saw the further development of Itard's philosophy of education of students with mental disabilities. Around that time, his student, Edward Seguin, immigrated to the United States, where he established his philosophy of education for persons with mental retardation in a publication entitled *Idiocy and Its Treatment by the Physiological Method* in 1866. Seguin was instrumental in the establishment of the first residential school for individuals with mental retardation in the United States.

State legislatures began to assume the responsibility for housing people with physical and mental disabilities—the institutional care was largely custodial. Institutions were often referred to as warehouses, due to the deplorable conditions of many. Humanitarians like Dorthea Dix helped to relieve anguish and suffering in institutions for persons with mental illnesses.

1900 - 1919: Specific Programs

The early twentieth century saw the publication of the first standardized test of intelligence by Alfred Binet of France. The test was designed to identify educationally sub-standard children, but by 1916, the test was revised by an American named Louis Terman. Through Terman, the concept of the intelligence quotient (IQ) was introduced. Since then, the IQ test has come to be used as a predictor of both delayed and advanced intellectual development.

At approximately the same time, Italian physician Maria Montessori was concerned with the development of effective techniques for early childhood education. Although she is known primarily for her contributions to this field, her work included methods of education for children with mental retardation, as well, and the approach she developed is used in preschool programs today.

Ironically, it was the advancement of science and the scientific method that led special education to its worst setback in modern times. In 1912, psychologist Henry Goddard published a study based on the Killikak family, in which he traced five generations of the descendants of a man who had one legitimate child and one illegitimate child. Among the descendants of the legitimate child were numerous mental and social disabilities. This led Goddard to conclude that mental retardation and social deviation were inherited traits, and therefore that persons with mental and social disabilities were a threat to society, an observation that he called the Eugenics Theory. Reinforcing the concept of retardation as hereditary was a popular philosophy called positivism, under which these unscientific conclusions were believed to be fixed, mechanical laws that were carrying mankind to inevitable improvement. Falling by the wayside was seen as the natural scientific outcome for the defective person in society.

Consequently, during this time, mass institutionalization and sterilization of persons with mental retardation (as well as criminals) were practiced. Nevertheless, public school programs for persons with retardation gradually increased during this same period. Furthermore, the first college programs for the preparation of special education teachers were established between 1900 and 1920.

1919 - 1949: Professionalism and Expansion of Services

Awareness of the need for medical and mental health treatments in the community increased during the 1920s. Halfway houses became a means for monitoring the transition from institution to community living; outpatient clinics were established to provide increased medical care. Social workers and other support personnel were dispensed into the community to coordinate services for the needy. The thrust toward humane treatment within the community came to an abrupt halt during the 1930s and 1940s, primarily due to economic depression and widespread dissatisfaction toward the recently enacted social programs.

Two factors related to the World Wars helped to improve public opinion toward persons with disabilities. The first was the intensive screening of the population of young men with physical and mental disabilities that were in the United States. The second was patriotism, which caused people to regard the enormous number of young men who returned from the wars with physical and emotional disabilities in a different light than they would have been regarded before that time. People became more sensitive to the problems of the veterans with disabilities, and this acceptance generalized to other groups in the special needs population.

With increased public concern for people with disabilities came new research. John B. Watson introduced behaviorism, which shifted the treatment emphasis from psychoanalysis to learned behavior. He demonstrated in 1920 that maladaptive (or abnormal) behavior was learned by Albert, an 11-month old boy, through conditioning. B.F. Skinner followed with a book entitled the *Behavior of Organisms,* which outlined principles of operant behavior (i.e., voluntary) behavior.

In 1922, the Council for Exceptional Children (first called the International Council for Exceptional Children) was founded. During the 1920s, many comprehensive statewide programs were initiated. The number of special education programs in public schools increased at a rapid rate until the 1930s, when the push for humane and effective treatment of people with disabilities began to diminish once again. This period of the Depression was marked by large-scale institutionalization and an overall lack of treatment. Part of the cause was inadequately planned programs and poorly trained teachers. WWII did much to swing the pendulum back in the other direction, however, and inaugurated the most active period in the history of the development of special education.

1950 - 1969: The Parents, the Legislators, and the Courts Became Involved

The first two decades of the second half of the century were characterized by increased federal involvement in general education, gradually extending to special education. In 1950 came the establishment of the National Association of Retarded Children, later renamed the National Association of Retarded Citizens (NARC). It was the result of the efforts among concerned parents who felt the need for an appropriate public education. Increased media coverage exposed the miserable conditions in some of the institutions devoted to caring for people with disabilities, especially those with intellectual and emotional disabilities, and treatment consequently became more humane.

It was at about this time that parents of children with disabilities discovered the federal courts as a powerful agent on behalf of their children. The 1954 decision in the Brown v. the Topeka Board of Education case guaranteed equal opportunity rights to a free public education for all citizens, and the parents of children and youth with disabilities insisted that their children be included in that decision. The court cases and public laws enacted as a result of court decisions are too numerous to include in their entirety. Collectively, they are part of a movement in U.S. Supreme Court history known as the Doctrine of Selective Incorporation, under which the states are compelled to honor various substantive rights under procedural authority of the 14th Amendment.

Skill 14.2 Demonstrating knowledge of the historical foundations of special education, including classic studies, landmark cases, major contributors, and important legislation (e.g., Individuals with Disabilities Education Improvement Act [IDEA], Section 504 of the Rehabilitation Act, Americans with Disabilities Act [ADA], No Child Left Behind [NCLB] Act)

The competencies in this section include the mandates (i.e., laws, regulations, policies) that apply to or have a bearing on the respective states and local districts, as well as the major provisions of federal laws implemented twenty or more years ago, including Public Laws 94-142 (1975), 93-112 (1973) and 101-476 (1990). These laws culminated into the comprehensive statute—IDEA (Individuals with Disabilities Education Act)—which requires the states to offer comprehensive special education service programs to students with disabilities, and to plan for their transition into the work world. Most local districts have elaborately articulated delivery systems, which are an extension of national or state Department of Education of Department of Public Instruction. Any inquires should be directed to the unit that administers programs for exceptional children.

Background

The U.S. Constitution does not specify protection for education. However, all states provide education, and thus individuals are guaranteed protection and due process under the 14th Amendment. The basic source of law for special education is the Individuals Disabilities Education Act (IDEA) and its accompanying regulations. IDEA represents the latest phase in the philosophy of educating children with disabilities. Initially, most children with disabilities did not go to school. When they did, they were segregated into special classes in order to avoid disrupting the regular class. Their education usually consisted of simple academics and later, training for manual jobs.

Significant Legislation and Supreme Court Cases with an Impact on Exceptional Student Education

By the mid-1900s, advocates for handicapped children argued that segregation was inherently unequal. By the time of PL 94-142, about half of the estimated eight million children with disabilities in the United States were either not being appropriately served in school or were excluded from schooling altogether. There were a disproportionate number of minority children placed in special programs. Identification and placement practices and procedures were inconsistent, and parental involvement was generally not encouraged. After segregation on the basis of race was declared unconstitutional in Brown v Board of Education, parents and other advocates filed similar lawsuits on behalf of children with handicaps. The culmination of their efforts resulted in PL 94-142. This section is a brief summary of that law and other major legislation, which affect the manner in which special education services are delivered to handicapped children.

Brown v. Board of Education (1954): While this case specifically addressed the inequality of "separate but equal" facilities on the basis of race, the concept that segregation was inherently unequal—even if facilities were provided—was later applied to disabilities.

The Cooperative Research Act (1954): Passed the first designation of general funds for the use of students with disabilities.

Public Law 85-926 (1958): Provided grants to institutions of higher learning and to state education agencies for training professional personnel who would, in turn, train teachers of students with mental retardation.

Elementary and Secondary Education Act (1965): Provided funds for the education of children who were disadvantaged and disabled (Public Law 89-10).

Educational Consolidation and Improvement Act-State Operated Programs PL 89-313 (1965): Provided funds for children with disabilities who are or have been in state-operated or state-supported schools.

Public Law 89-750 (1966): Authorized the establishment of the Bureau Education for the Handicapped (BEH) and a National Advisory Committee on the Handicapped.

Hanson v. Hobson (1967): Ruled that ability grouping (tracking) based on student performance on standardized tests is unconstitutional.

Handicapped Children's Early Education Assistance Act PL 90-538 (1968): Funded model demonstration programs for preschool students with disabilities.

Public Law 90-247 (1968): Included provisions for deaf-blind centers, resource centers and the expansion of media services for students with disabilities.

Public Law 90-576 (1968): Specified that ten percent of vocational education funds be earmarked for youth with disabilities.

Public Law 91-230 (Amendments to Public Law 89-10) (1969): Previous enactment relating to children with disabilities was consolidated into one act: **Education of the Handicapped**.

Pennsylvania Association for Retarded Citizens (PARC) v. Commonwealth of Pennsylvania (1972): Special education was guaranteed to children with mental retardation. The victory in this case sparked other court cases for children with other disabilities.

Mills v. Board of Education of the District of Columbia (1972): The right to special education was extended to all children with disabilities, not just mentally retarded children. Judgments in PARC and Mills paved the way for PL 94-142.

Section 504, Rehabilitation Act of 1973: Section 504 expanded an older law by extending its protection to other areas that receive federal assistance, such as education. Protected individuals must (a) have a physical or mental impairment that substantially limits one or more major life activities (e.g., self-care, walking, seeing, breathing, working, and learning); (b) have a record of such an impairment; or (c) be regarded as having such an impairment. A disability in itself is not sufficient grounds for a complaint of discrimination. The person must be otherwise qualified, or able to meet, the requirements of the program in question.

Goss v. Lopez (1975): Ruled that the state could not deny a student education without following due process. While this decision is not based on a special education issue, the process of school suspension and expulsion is obviously critical in assuring an appropriate public education to children with disabilities.

Education for All Handicapped Children Act PL 94-142 (1975): The philosophy behind these pieces of legislation is that education is to be provided to all children 6-18 who meet age eligibility requirements. All children are assumed capable of benefiting from education. For children with severe or profound disabilities, “education” may be interpreted to include training in basic self-help skills and vocational training as well as academics.

Gifted and Talented Children’s Act PL 95-56 (1978): Defined the gifted and talented population, and focused upon this exceptionally category, which was not included in Public Law 94-142.

Larry P. v. Riles (1979): Ordered the re-evaluation of black students enrolled in classes for educable mental retardation (EMR) and enjoined the California State Department of Education from the use of intelligence tests in subsequent EMR placement decisions.

Parents in Action on Special Education (PASE) v. Hannon (1980): Ruled that IQ tests are necessarily biased against ethnic and racial subcultures.

Board of Education v. Rowley, 1982: Amy Rowley was a deaf elementary school student whose parents rejected their school district’s proposal to provide a tutor and speech therapy services to supplement their daughter’s instruction in the regular classroom. Her parents insisted on an interpreter, even though Amy was making satisfactory social, academic, and educational progress without one.

... of the school district, the Supreme Court ruled that school ...vide those services that permit a student with disabilities to ... instruction. Essentially, the court ruled that the states are obligated ...vide a "basic floor of opportunity" that reasonably allows the child to benefit from social education.

Irving Independent School District v. Tatro 1984: IDEA lists health services as one of the "related services" that schools are mandated to provide to exceptional students. Amber Tatro, who had spina bifida, required the insertion of a catheter on a regular schedule in order to empty her bladder. The issue was specifically over the classification of clean, intermittent catheterization (CIC) as a medical service (not covered under IDEA) or a "related health service," which would be covered. In this instance, the catheterization was not declared a medical service, but a "related service" necessary for the student to have in order to benefit from special education. The school district was obliged to provide the service. The Tatro case has implications for students with other medical impairments who may need services to allow them to attend classes at the school.

Smith v. Robinson (1984): Concerned reimbursement of attorney's fees for parents who win litigation under IDEA. At the time of this case, IDEA did not provide for such reimbursement. Following this ruling, Congress passed a law awarding attorney's fees to parents who win their litigation.

Honig v. Doe (1988*)*: Essentially, students may not be denied education or exclusion from school when their misbehavior is related to their disability. The "stay put" provision of IDEA allows students to remain in their current educational settings pending the outcome of administrative or judicial hearings. In the case of behavior that is a danger to the student or others, the court allows school districts to apply their normal procedures for dealing with dangerous behavior, such as time-out, loss of privileges, detention, or study carrels.

Where the student has presented an immediate threat to others, that student may be temporarily suspended for up to ten school days to give the school and the parents' time to review the IEP and discuss possible alternatives to the current placement.

Public Law 99-457 (1986): Beginning with the 1991-1992 school year, special education programs were required for children ages three to five, with most states offering outreach programs to identify children with special needs from birth to age three. In place of, or in addition to an annual IEP, the entire family's needs are addressed by an Individual Family Service Plan (IFSP), which is reviewed with the family every six months.

Americans with Disabilities Act (ADA) 1990: Bars discrimination in employment, transportation, public accommodations, and telecommunications in all aspects of life, not just those receiving federal funding. Title II and Title III are applicable to special education because they cover the private sector (such as private schools) and require access to public accommodations. New and remodeled public buildings, transportation vehicles, and telephone systems now must be accessible to persons with disabilities. ADA also protects individuals with contagious diseases, such as AIDS, from discrimination.

IDEA: PL 101-476 (1990): The principles of IDEA also incorporate the concept of "normalization." Within this concept, persons with disabilities are allowed access to everyday patterns and conditions of life that are as close as possible or equal to those of their non-disabled peers. There are seven fundamental provisions of IDEA.

Free Appropriate Public Education (FAPE). Special Education services are to be provided at no cost to students or their families. The federal and state governments share any additional costs. FAPE also requires that education be appropriate to the individual needs of the students.

Notification and Procedural Rights for Parents. These include: right to examine records and obtain independent evaluations, right to receive a clearly written notice that states the results of the school's evaluation of their child, as well as whether the child meets eligibility requirements for placement or continuation of special services. Parents who disagree with the school's decision may request a **due process** hearing and a **judicial hearing** if they do not receive satisfaction through due process

Identification and Services to All Children. States must conduct public outreach programs to seek out and identify children who may need services.

Necessary Related Services. Developmental, corrective, and other support services that make it possible for a student to benefit from special education services must be provided. These may include speech, recreation, or physical therapy.

Individualized Assessments. Evaluations and tests must be nondiscriminatory and individualized.

Individualized Education Plans. Each student receiving special education services must have an **individualized education plan** developed at a meeting that is attended by a qualified representative of the local education agency (LEA). Others who should attend are the proposed special education teachers, mainstream teachers, parents, and, when appropriate, the student.

Least Restrictive Environment (LRE). There is no simple definition of LRE. LRE differs with the child's needs. LRE means that the student is placed in an environment that is not dangerous, overly controlling, or intrusive. The student should be given opportunities to experience what other peers of similar mental or chronological age are doing. LRE should be the environment that is the most integrated and normalized for the student's strengths and weaknesses. LRE for one child may be a regular classroom with support services, while LRE for another may be a self-contained classroom in a special school.

Florence County School Dist Four v. Shannon Carter (1993): Established that when a school district does not provide FAPE for a student with disability, the parents may seek reimbursement for private schooling. This decision has encouraged districts to be more inclusive of students with autism who receive ABA/Lovaas therapy.

Reauthorization of IDEA: PL 105-17 (1997): Required involvement of a regular education teacher as part of the IEP team. It provides additional strength to school administrators for the discipline of students with special needs.

In 1997, IDEA was revised and reauthorized as Public Law 105-17 as progressive legislation for the benefit of school age children with special needs, their parents, and those who work with these children. The 1997 reauthorization of IDEA made major changes in the areas of the evaluation procedures, parent rights, transition, and discipline.

The evaluation process was amended to require members of the evaluation team to look at previously collected data, tests, and information and to use it when deemed appropriate. Previous to IDEA 1997, an entire re-evaluation had to be conducted every three years to determine if the child continued to be a "child with a disability." This was changed to allow existing information/evaluations to be considered to prevent unnecessary assessment of students and reduce the cost of evaluations.

Parent participation was not a requirement under the previous IDEA for an evaluation team to make decisions regarding a student's eligibility for special education and related services. Under IDEA 1997, parents were specifically included as members of the group making the eligibility decision.

The IEP was modified under IDEA 1997 to emphasize the involvement of students with special needs in a general education classroom setting, with the services and modifications deemed necessary by the evaluation team.

The "Present Levels of Educational Performance" (PLEP) was changed to require a statement of how the child's disability affects his or her involvement and progress in the general curriculum. IDEA 1997 established that there must be a connection between the special education and general education curriculum. For this reason, the PLEP was required to include an explanation of the extent to which the student will *not* be participating with non-disabled children in the general education class, as well as in extracurricular and non-academic activities.

After this Public Law, the IEP now had an established connection to the general education setting. The IEP had to provide the needed test accommodations that would be provided on all state and district wide assessments of the student with special needs. IDEA 1997's emphasis on raising the standards of those in special education placed an additional requirement of definitive reasons why a standard general education assessment would not be deemed appropriate for a child, as well as how the child should then be assessed.

IDEA 1997 looked at how parents were receiving annual evaluations on their children's IEP goals and determined that this was not sufficient feedback for parents. It required schools to make reports to parents on the progress of their child at least as frequently as progress of their non-disabled peers.

The IEP was also modified to include a review of the student's transitional needs and services, specifically:

Beginning when a student is fourteen (this has recently been changed to age sixteen), and annually thereafter, the student's IEP must contain a statement of his or her transition service needs under the various components of that IEP that focus on the student's courses of study (e.g., vocational education or advanced placement); and

Beginning at least one year before the student reaches the age of majority under state law, the IEP must contain a statement that the student has been informed of the rights under the law that will transfer to him or her upon reaching the age of majority.

IDEA 1997 also broadened a school's right to take disciplinary action with children who have been classified as needing special education services when those students knowingly possess or use illegal drugs, or sell or solicit the sale of a controlled substance while at school or school functions.

Under IDEA 1997, suspensions and disciplinary consequences could result in an alternative educational placement. This possibility was to be weighed by a Manifest Determination Review, which is held by an IEP Team. Manifest Determination Reviews must occur no more than ten days after the disciplinary action. This review team has the sole responsibility of determining:

- Does the child's disability impair his or her understanding of the impact and consequences of the behavior under disciplinary action?
- Did the child's disability impair the ability of the child to control the behavior subject to discipline?
- Determination of a relationship of the student's disability and an inappropriate behavior could allow current placement to occur.

When no relationship between the "inappropriate" behavior is established, IDEA 1997 utilized FAPE to allow the relevant disciplinary procedures applicable to children without disabilities to be applied to the child in the same manner in which they would be applied to children with disabilities. Functional Behavioral Assessments (FBAs) and Behavior Intervention Plans (BIPs) became a requirement in many situations for schools to both modify and provide disciplinary consequences.

No Child Left Behind Act (NCLB) (2002): No Child Left Behind, Public Law 107-110, was signed on January 8, 2002. NCLB addresses accountability of school personnel for student achievement with the expectation that every child will demonstrate proficiency in reading, math, and science. The first full wave of accountability as scheduled to begin twelve years later, when children who first started to attend school under NCLB graduate; however, the process to meet that accountability began in 2002. In fact, as students progress through the school system, testing shows if an individual teacher has effectively met the needs of his or her students. Through testing, each student's adequate yearly progress or lack thereof is tracked.

NCLB affects regular and special education students, gifted students, slow learners, and children of every ethnicity, culture, and environment. NCLB is a document that encompasses every American educator and student.

Educators are affected in many ways. Elementary teachers (K-3) are responsible for teaching reading and using different, scientific-based approaches, as needed. Elementary teachers of upper grades teach reading, math, and science. Middle and high school teachers teach to new, higher standards. Sometimes, they have the task of playing catch up with students who did not have adequate education in earlier grades.

Special educators are responsible for teaching students to a level of comparable proficiency as their non-disabled peers. This will raise the bar of academic expectations throughout the grades. For some students with disabilities, the criteria for getting a diploma becomes more difficult. Although a small percentage of students with disabilities need alternate assessments, they still need to meet grade appropriate goals.

In order for special education teachers to meet the professional criteria of this act, they must be *highly qualified*—that is, certified or licensed in their area of special education—and show proof of a specific level of professional development in the core subjects that they teach. As special education teachers receive specific education in the core subjects they teach, they become better prepared to teach to the same level of learning standards as the general education teacher.

M.L. v. Federal Way School District, State of Washington (2004): The Ninth Circuit Court of Appeals ruled that absence of a regular education teacher on an IEP team was a serious procedural error.

Reauthorization of IDEA, (2004): Required all special education teachers on a secondary level to be no less qualified than other teachers of the subject areas. This second revision of IDEA occurred in 2004. IDEA was re-authorized as the Individuals with Disabilities Education Improvement Act of 2004 (IDEIA 2004), and is commonly referred to as IDEA 2004. IDEA 2004 was effective as of July 1, 2005.

It was the intention to improve IDEA by adding the philosophy/understanding that special education students need preparation for further study beyond the high school setting by teaching compensatory methods. Accordingly, IDEA 2004 provided a close tie to PL 89-10, the Elementary and Special Education Act of 1965, and stated that students with special needs should have maximum access to the general curriculum. This was defined as the amount of education necessary for an individual student to reach his or her fullest potential. Full inclusion was stated as not the only option by which to achieve this; it was specified that skills should be taught to compensate students later in life in cases where inclusion was not the best setting.

IDEA 2004 added a new requirement for special education teachers on the secondary level enforcing NCLB's "Highly Qualified" requirements in the subject area of their curriculum. The rewording in this part of IDEA states that they shall be "no less qualified" than teachers in the core areas.

Free and Appropriate Public Education (FAPE) was revised by mandating that students have maximum access to appropriate general education. Additionally, LRE placement for those students with disabilities must have the same school placement rights as those students who are not disabled. IDEA 2004 recognizes that due to the nature of some disabilities, appropriate education may vary in the amount of participation/placement in the general education setting. For some students, FAPE means a choice as to the type of educational institution they attend (e.g., public vs. private school), any of which must provide the special education services deemed necessary for the student through the IEP.

Skill 14.3 Demonstrating knowledge of current issues and trends in the field of special education (e.g., inclusion, standards-based reforms)

Present and Future Perspectives

What is the state of special education today? What can we anticipate as far as changes that might occur in the near future? It has been more than three decades since the passage of the initial Individuals with Disabilities Education Act as Public Law 93-142 in 1975. So far, mandates stand with funding intact.

The clients are still here, and in greater numbers (thanks to improved identification procedures and to medical advances that have left many who might have died in the past with conditions considered disabling). Among the disabling conditions afflicting the population with recently discovered lifesaving techniques are blindness, deafness, amputation, central nervous system or neurological impairments, brain dysfunction, and mental retardation from environmental, genetic, traumatic, infectious, and unknown etiologies.

Despite challenges to the principles underlying PL 94-142 in the early 1980s, total federal funding for the concept increased as new amendments were passed. These amendments expanded services to infants, preschoolers, and secondary students (Rothstein, 1995).

Following public hearings, Congress voted in 1990 not to include Attention Deficit Disorders (ADD) as a new exceptionality area. Determining factors included the alleged ambiguity of the definition and eligibility criteria for students with ADD, the large number of students who might be identified if it became a service delivery area, the subsequent cost of serving such a large population, and the fact that many of these students are already served in the exceptionality areas of learning disabilities and behavior disorders.

The revision of the original law, which we now call IDEA, included some other changes. These changes were primarily in language (terminology), procedures (especially transition), and the addition of new categories (autism and traumatic brain injury).

Thus, we can see that despite challenges to federal services and mandates in special education as an extension of the 14th Amendment since 1980, there has actually been growth in mandated categories and net funding. The Doctrine of Selective Incorporation is the name for one major set of challenges to this process. While the 1994 conservative turnover in the Congress might seem to undercut the force of PL 94-132, two decades of recent history show strong bi-partisan support for special education; consequently, IDEA, or a joint federal-state replacement, will most likely remain strong. Lobbyists and activists representing coalition and advocacy groups for those with disabilities combined with bi-partisan congressional support to avert the proposed changes, which would have meant drastic setbacks in services for persons with disabilities.

Nevertheless, there remain several philosophical controversies in special education. The need for labels for categories continues to be questioned. Many states are serving special needs students by severity level rather than by the exceptionality category.

Special educators are faced with possible changes in what is considered to be the least restrictive environment for educating students with special needs. Following upon the heels of the Regular Education Initiative, the concept of inclusion has come to the forefront. Both of these movements were, and are, an attempt to educate special needs students in the mainstream of the regular classroom. Both would eliminate pulling out students from regular classroom instructional activities, and both would incorporate the services of special education teachers in the regular classroom in collaboration with general classroom teachers.

Special education has changed significantly in recent decades. From separated, specialized classrooms for virtually every area of disability, special education has moved into the world of inclusion and undergone stricter accountability for general education learning standards.

According to IDEA 2004, special education students are to participate in general education programs to the fullest extent from which they can receive benefit. This often means accommodations and modifications in class work, employment of classroom assistants, and, in some cases, individual care aides. It also means there needs to be a closer working relationship between the special educator and general education teacher. Special education services are likely to be in the form of push-in services in the general education classroom, including team teaching or through consultation with the special educator. Fewer students are served in special education classrooms for the entire day, and resource services are used only as deemed absolutely necessary by the IEP team.

Special educators are accountable for meeting the same learning standards as general educators. No Child Left Behind (NCLB) stipulates that students are expected to read by grade three, requiring the use of a variety of reading methods (including phonics) to that end. In addition, all students are expected to show adequate yearly progress (AYP) as measured by the same standardized tests used in general education. In very few cases, when the disability is severe, the student may be given alternate assessment.

New and ever advancing technology has been beneficial to special education students, particularly those in the inclusion setting. Among commonly used technology are calculators, spell checking technology, augmentative communication devices, and computers (which are often effective for students to use for writing and revisions). In the area of education of the hearing impaired, fm auditory trainers allow students to focus on the teacher's voice while the environmental noise input from the classroom is minimized. Additionally, some deaf students have cochlear implants that allow them to hear speech and develop optimum speaking skills.

In some instances, person-centered planning is utilized to establish an educational program with the long-range personal goals of the individual with disabilities in mind. Like the traditional IEP team, the person-centered planning team includes family and school personnel. Additionally, friends may be included in the team. In contrast to traditional IEPs, which seek to find a placement within the existing system, the person-centered approach develops a program based on the student's strengths, weaknesses, and personal goals.

Skill 14.4 Demonstrating knowledge of definitions and issues in the identification of individuals with disabilities, including factors influencing the overrepresentation of students from culturally/linguistically diverse backgrounds in programs for students with disabilities

Please refer to http://rules.sos.state.ga.us/cgi-bin/page.cgi?d=1 for Georgia-specific information.

IDEA 2004 §300.8 defines a child with a disability as "having mental retardation, a hearing impairment (including deafness), a speech or language impairment, a visual impairment (including blindness), a serious emotional disturbance (referred to in this part as emotional disturbance), an orthopedic impairment, autism, traumatic brain injury, another health impairment, a specific learning disability, deaf-blindness, or multiple disabilities, and who, by reason thereof, needs special education and related services."

Eligibility for special education services is based on a student having one of the above disabilities (or a combination thereof) and a demonstration of educational need through professional evaluation. Simply having these conditions does not in itself qualify a child as having a disability under this law. The condition must prevent a child from being able to benefit from education.

The classification of exceptional student education is a categorical system. Within the categories are subdivisions which may be based on the severity or level of support services needed. Having a categorical system allows educators to differentiate and define types of disabilities, relate treatments to certain categories, and concentrate research and advocacy efforts. The disadvantage of the categorical system is the labeling of groups or individuals. Critics of labels say that labeling can place the emphasis on the label and not the individual needs of the child. The following table displays the current definitions of disabilities.

Definitions of Disabilities under IDEA 2004

Classification	Characteristics
Autism	A developmental disability significantly affecting verbal and nonverbal communication and social interaction, generally evident before age three, that adversely affects a child's educational performance. Other characteristics often associated with autism are engagement in repetitive activities and stereotyped movements, resistance to environmental change or change in daily routines, and unusual responses to sensory experiences. Autism does not apply if a child's educational performance is adversely affected primarily because the child has an emotional disturbance A child who manifests the characteristics of autism after age three could be identified as having autism if the above two indicators are present.
Deaf	A hearing impairment that is so severe that the child is impaired in processing linguistic information through hearing, with or without amplification, that adversely affects a child's educational performance.
Deaf-blind	The concomitant hearing and visual impairments, the combination of which causes such severe communication and other developmental and educational needs that they cannot be accommodated in special education programs solely for children with deafness or children with blindness.
Emotional Disturbance	Schizophrenia, and conditions in which 1 or more of these characteristics is exhibited over a long period of time and to a marked degree: (a) inability to learn not explained by intellectual, sensory, or health factors, (b) inability to build or maintain satisfactory interpersonal relationships, (c) inappropriate types of behavior or feelings, (d) general pervasive unhappiness or depression, (e) tendency to develop physical symptoms or fears associated with personal or school problems.
Hearing Impairment	An impairment in hearing, whether permanent or fluctuating, that adversely affects a child's educational performance but that is not included under the definition of deafness in this section.
Mentally Retarded	A significantly subaverage general intellectual functioning, existing concurrently with deficits in adaptive behavior and manifested during the developmental period, that adversely affects a child's educational performance.

Multiple Disabilities	Concomitant impairments (such as mental retardation-blindness, mental retardation-orthopedic impairment, etc.), the combination of which causes such severe educational needs that they cannot be accommodated in special education programs solely for one of the impairments. The term does not include deaf-blindness.
Orthopedic Impairment	A severe orthopedic impairment that adversely affects a child's educational performance. The term includes impairments caused by a congenital anomaly (e.g., clubfoot, absence of some member, etc.), impairments caused by disease (e.g., poliomyelitis, bone tuberculosis, etc.), and impairments from other causes (e.g., cerebral palsy, amputations, and fractures or burns that cause contractures).

Other Health Impairment	Having limited strength, vitality, or alertness, including a heightened alertness to environmental stimuli, that results in limited alertness with respect to the educational environment, that: Is due to chronic or acute health problems such as asthma, attention deficit disorder or attention deficit hyperactivity disorder, diabetes, epilepsy, a heart condition, hemophilia, lead poisoning, leukemia, nephritis, rheumatic fever, sickle cell anemia, or Tourette's syndrome; and adversely affects a child's educational performance.
Specific Learning Disability	This term means a disorder in one or more of the basic psychological processes involved in understanding or in using language, spoken or written, that may manifest itself in an imperfect ability to listen, think, speak, read, write, spell, or do mathematical calculations, including conditions such as perceptual disabilities, brain injury, minimal brain dysfunction, dyslexia, and developmental aphasia. **Disorders not included**. The term does not include learning problems that are primarily the result of visual, hearing, or motor disabilities, of mental retardation, of emotional disturbance, or of environmental, cultural, or economic disadvantage.
Speech or Language Impairment	A communication disorder, such as stuttering, impaired articulation, a language impairment, or a voice impairment, that adversely affects a child's educational performance.

Traumatic Brain Injury	An acquired injury to the brain caused by an external physical force resulting in total or partial functional disability or psychosocial impairment, or both, that adversely affects a child's educational performance. The term applies to open or closed head injuries resulting in impairments in one or more areas, such as cognition, language, memory, attention, reasoning, abstract thinking, judgment, problem-solving, sensory, perceptual, and motor abilities, psychosocial behavior, physical functions, information processing, and speech. The term does not apply to brain injuries that are congenital or degenerative or to brain injuries induced by birth trauma.
Visual Impairment including Blindness	An impairment in vision that, even with correction, adversely affects a child's educational performance. The term includes both partial sight and blindness.

It should be noted that there is no classification for gifted children under IDEA. Funding and services for gifted programs are left up to the individual states and school districts. Therefore, the number of districts providing services and the scope of gifted programs varies among states and school districts.

Seldom does a student with a disability fall into only one of the characteristics listed in IDEA 2004. For example, a student with a hearing impairment may also have a specific learning disability, or a student on the autism spectrum may also demonstrate a language impairment. In fact, language impairment is inherent in autism. Sometimes, the eligibility is defined as multiple disabilities (with one listed as a primary eligibility on the IEP, and the others listed as secondary). Sometimes there are overlapping needs that are not necessarily listed as a secondary disability.

Prevalence
The table below shows disability prevalence among children in the United States according to the 1988 National Educational Longitudinal Study (NELS).

Disability	Prevalence/Incidence
Mental retardation	0.1
Specific learning problem	6.1
Emotional problem	2.8
Speech problem	1.6
Hearing problem	2.2
Deafness	0.4
Visual handicap (not correctable with glasses)	1.6
Orthopedic problem	0.9
Other physical disability	1.1
Any other health problem	3.7

People with disabilities from diverse cultures are considerably disadvantaged in attaining complete participation in all areas of society. This is based on a wide range of barriers to the full benefits of civil and human rights. The obstacles that people from diverse cultures have to withstand include a lack of culturally appropriate outreach, language and communication barriers, attitudinal barriers, and the lack of individuals from diverse cultures in the disability services profession.

People with disabilities from diverse cultures have a harder time receiving services. The Individuals with Disabilities Education Act (IDEA) is a legislative act guaranteeing rights to individuals with disabilities to a full inclusive education, but IDEA has not fully reached people with disabilities from underserved populations. Individuals from diverse backgrounds are at a disadvantage when it comes to receiving services related to their disability and even being diagnosed with a disability. This is compounded by not having a significant number of teachers and other professional from diverse cultures, meaning that the communication barriers continue to exist.

Overrepresentation of Students from Diverse Backgrounds

Skill 5.2 outlined Salvia and Ysseldyke's (1995), description of three aspects of fairness in assessment of students from diverse backgrounds, and these factors are particularly relevant to screening and diagnosis of disabilities for placement in special education programs. The earlier objective pointed out that errors in these three aspects of test design made test *unfair* to students from diverse backgrounds. However, it is also true that these errors result in a disproportionate number of children from minority or diverse backgrounds being diagnosed with a disability that they, in fact, do not have.

Representation: Salvia and Ysseldyke pointed out that people from diverse backgrounds need to be represented in assessment materials. If the screening and placement tests used to determine whether a child has a disability do not have this balanced representation, then minority children will be taking tests that are far more *unfamiliar* to them than children from mainstream American culture, and they may not do as well on the tests, resulting in disproportionate numbers of minority children being diagnosed with disabilities.

Acculturation: They also pointed out the importance of the fact that norm-referenced tests are normed on American students who share certain commonalities in background and experience. This may make them somewhat questionable for screening and diagnosing special needs of children from *other* backgrounds. Children in American culture will have experience with certain nursery rhymes, historical figures, even television shows and fictional characters.

Students from other cultures may not share these experiences and may be confused by offhand references to them by teachers and in literature. For example, one child from a background that did not contain the Santa Claus figure was very confused by a holiday story that involved hanging stockings by the fire and finding them filled with candy the next morning. The only reason this child could imagine for hanging a stocking by the fire was to dry it out because it had gotten wet. The child, therefore, felt that the Santa figure was mean to put candy in a dirty, wet sock where it would get all mushy. Naturally enough, this child "failed" to identify the "main idea" in the story.

Strictly speaking, norm-referenced tests can only be used to assess students from the same cultural group as those upon whom the test was normed. Such tests are NOT valid for assessing students from diverse backgrounds. The inherent cultural bias on many screening and placement assessments accounts for much of the disproportionate representation of students from diverse background in special education.

Language: Children who are not tested in their native language, or who speak nonstandard dialects of English will be more likely to be diagnosed with a disability regardless of whether they actually have one or not. It is important to remember that an inability to understand English is not a disability requiring special education services. It may well require English as a Second Language services, but it is not a disability under IDEA regulations.

Educational Background

In addition to factors outlined above, and regardless of the culture or language involved, a child's previous access to education may affect the validity of many of the tests used to diagnose special education needs. Kirk, et al (2003) discuss research showing that children with school experience simply *think differently* than children with little or no school experience. They report that at least some school experience is needed before most students learn to categorize objects or reason logically and make inferences. Children without any school experience tend to rely on individual experience instead of using and manipulating information independently. Since these skills are typically tested on so-called IQ tests that are at the heart of many special needs screening batteries, children from backgrounds that involve little or no formal schooling may also be inappropriately diagnosed with disabilities and overrepresented in the special education population.

Skill 14.5 Demonstrating knowledge of the rights and responsibilities of all stakeholders (e.g., students, parents/guardians, teachers, schools) related to the education of students with disabilities

For teachers and school personnel see Objectives 7.all, Skills 13.2,13.4, 13.5, 13.7.

For student parental rights and responsibilities, see Objectives 12(all parts) and 14.2, as well as Objective 10 (all parts).

Skill 14.6 Demonstrating knowledge of the laws, litigation, policies, and ethical principles related to referral, assessment, eligibility, and placement within a continuum of services for students with disabilities, including issues, assurances, and due process rights

Please see IDEA: PL 101-476 (1990) in OBJECTIVE 14.02 for laws related to IDEA.

OBJECTIVE 15 UNDERSTAND THE PROFESSIONAL, ETHICAL, AND LEGAL ROLES AND RESPONSIBILITIES OF THE SPECIAL EDUCATOR

Skill 15.1 Applying knowledge of how to uphold high standards for professional practice, including participating in professional activities and organizations that benefit students with disabilities, their families, and colleagues

Please refer to Skill 15.2 for more information about professional organizations.

The special education teacher comes to the job with past experiences as well as personal opinions and beliefs. It is vital that he or she not let those personal persuasions guide any area of professional conduct. Objective professional judgment is important in all areas of the teacher's role. Educational decisions must be based on research based methods and procedures, as well as federal, state, and local laws and policies, rather than personal opinions and beliefs.

Objective professional judgment should be exercised when considering the cultural, religious, and sexual orientations of the special educator's students and their respective families. An unbiased approach to communication maintains positive interaction and increased cooperation between home and school. The result is a better educational program that will meet the individual student's needs.

Objectivity should also be exercised when considering assessment of a possible disability. Educator preference for a particular assessment should be secondary to matching the needs of the child with a specific instrument. Assessment tools should be researched-based and determined to be appropriate for the needs of the specific student, as well as unbiased.

When establishing the special education program, the specific student's IEP must be followed. The teacher must remember that the IEP is a **legally binding** contract. If the special educator determines that the goals and objectives of the IEP no longer fit the child's needs, an IEP meeting should be called to review and possibly revise the document. Again, the revision of the IEP should be based on the needs of the child as determined objectively, not the personal preference of the teacher for a particular type of program or schedule. This objectivity should include: materials, scheduling, activities, and evaluation.

The student's IEP should also be focused on the learning standards established by the state. In particular, learning activities that provide *measurable* outcomes should be employed. Such data provide objective evaluations of student progress as well as the student's possible mastery of the targeted standards.

Professional objectivity is crucial in communication with administration for the representation of students' needs for placement, programming, materials, scheduling, and staffing. When documented, data-driven information is presented, optimum decisions are made for students with disabilities and for the school community in general.

Skill 15.2 Demonstrating knowledge of how to use resources (e.g., professional organizations and journals, online resources, conferences, workshops, mentors) to enhance one's own professional knowledge (e.g., current research-validated practices, information about the characteristics and needs of students with disabilities) and engage in lifelong professional growth and development

A selection of professional associations representing the spectrum of services for individuals with disabilities are listed in the table below. Some of these organizations date from the pioneer times of special education and are still in active service.

Organization	Members	Mission
Alexander Graham Bell Association for the Deaf and Hard of Hearing 3417 Volta Place, N.W. Washington, D.C. 20007 http://www.agbell.org	Teachers of the deaf, speech-language pathologists, audiologists, physicians, hearing aid dealers	To promote the teaching of speech, lip reading, and use of residual hearing to persons who are deaf; encourage research; and work to further better education of persons who are deaf.
Alliance for Technology Access 1304 Southpoint Blvd., Suite 240, Petaluma, CA 94954 Phone: (707) 778-3011 Fax: (707) 765-2080 TTY: (707) 778-3015 http://ww.Ataccess.org	People with disabilities, family members, and professionals in related fields, and organizations with work in their own communities and ways to support our mission.	To increase the use of technology by children and adults with disabilities and functional limitations.

Organization	Members	Mission
American Council of the Blind 1155 15th Street, NW, Suite 1004, Washington, DC 20005 Phone: (202) 467-5081 (800) 424-8666 FAX: (202) 467-5085 http://Acb.org		To improve the well-being of all blind and visually impaired people by: serving as a representative national organization of blind people and conducting a public education program to promote greater understanding of blindness and the capabilities of blind people.
American Council on Rural Special Education (ACRES) Utah State University 2865 Old Main Hill Logan, Utah 84322 Phone: (435) 797-3728 http://acres-sped.org	Open to anyone interested in supporting their mission	To provide leadership and support that will enhance services for individuals with exceptional needs, their families, and the professionals who work with them, and for the rural communities in which they live
American Psychological Association 750 First Street, NE, Washington, DC 20002-4242 Phone: (800) 374-2721 FAX: (202) 336-5500. TTY: (202) 336-6123 http://www.apa.org	Psychologists and Professors of Psychology	Scientific and professional society working to improve mental health services and to advocate for legislation and programs that will promote mental health; facilitate research and professional development.

Organization	Members	Mission
American Society for Deaf Children 3820 Hartzdale Drive, Camp Hill, PA 17011 Phone: (717) 703-0073 (866) 895-4206 FAX: (717) 909-5599 http://www.deafchildren.org	Open to all who support the mission of the association	To provide support, encouragement and information to families raising children who are deaf or hard of hearing.
American Speech-Language-Hearing Association 10801 Rockville Pike Rockville, MD 20852 http://www.asha.org	Specialists in speech-language pathology and audiology	To advocate for provision of speech-language and hearing services in school and clinic settings; advocate for legislation relative to the profession; and work to promote effective services and development of the profession.
The Arc of the United States 1010 Wayne Avenue Suite 650 Silver Springs, MD 20910 Phone: (301) 565-3842 FAX:(301) 565-3843 http://www.thearc.org	Parents, professionals, and others interested in individuals with mental retardation	Work on local, state, and national levels to promote treatment, research, public understanding, and legislation for persons with mental retardation; provide counseling for parents of students with mental retardation.

Organization	Members	Mission
Asperger Syndrome Education Network (ASPEN) 9 Aspen Circle Edison, NJ 08820 Phone: (732) 321-0880 http://www.aspennj.org		Provides families and individuals whose lives are affected by Autism Spectrum Disorders and Nonverbal Learning Disabilities with education, support and advocacy.
Association for Children and Adults with Learning Disabilities 4156 Library Road Pittsburgh, PA 15234 http://www.acldonline.org	Parents of children with learning disabilities and interested professionals	Advance the education and general well-being of children with adequate intelligence who have learning disabilities arising from perceptual, conceptual, or subtle coordinative problems, sometimes accompanied by behavior difficulties.
Attention Deficit Disorder Association 15000 Commerce Pkwy, Suite C Mount Laurel, NJ 08054 Phone: (856) 439-9099 FAX: (856) 439-0525 http://www.add.org	Open to all who support the mission of ADDA	Provide information, resources and networking to adults with AD/HD and to the professionals who work with them.

Organization	Members	Mission
Autism Society of America 7910 Woodmont Avenue, Suite 300 Bethesda, Maryland 20814 Phone: (800) 328-8476 http://www.autism-society.org	Open to all who support the mission of ASA	To increase public awareness about autism and the day-to-day issues faced by individuals with autism, their families and the professionals with whom they interact. The Society and its chapters share a common mission of providing information and education, and supporting research and advocating for programs and services for the autism community.
Brain Injury Association of America 8201 Greensboro Drive Suite 611 McLean, VA 22102 Phone: (703) 761-0750 http://www.biausa.org	Open to all	Provide information, education and support to assist the 5.3 million Americans currently living with traumatic brain injury and their families.
Child and Adolescent Bipolar Association (CABF) 1187 Wilmette Ave. P.M.B. #331 Wilmette, IL 60091 http://www.bpkids.org	Physicians, scientific researchers, and allied professionals (therapists, social workers, educators, attorneys, and others) who provide services to children and adolescents with bipolar disorder or do research on the topic	Educate families, professionals, and the public about pediatric bipolar disorder; connects families with resources and support; advocates for and empowers affected families; and supports research on pediatric bipolar disorder and its cure.

Organization	Members	Mission
Children and Adults with Attention Deficit/ Hyperactive Disorder (CHADD) 8181 Professional Place - Suite 150 Landover, MD 20785 Phone: (301) 306-7070 Fax: (301) 306-7090 http://www.chadd.org	Open to all	Provide resources and encouragement to parents, educators and professionals on a grassroots level through CHADD chapters.
Council for Exceptional Children (CEC) 1110 N. Glebe Road Suite 300 Arlington, VA 22201 Phone: (888) 232-7733 TTY: (866) 915-5000 FAX: (703) 264-9494 http://www.cec.sped.org	Teachers, administrators, teacher educators, and related service personnel	Advocate for services for individuals with disabilities and gifted individuals. A professional organization that addresses service, training, and research relative to exceptional persons.
Council for Children with Behavioral Disorders Two Ballston Plaza 1110 N. Glebe Road Arlington, VA 22201 Phone: (800) 224-6830 FAX: (703) 264-9494 http://www.ccbd.net	Members of the Council for Exceptional Children who teach children with behavior disorders or who train teachers to work with those children	Promote education and general welfare of children and youth with behavior disorders or serious emotional disturbances. Promote professional growth and research on students with behavior disorders and severe emotional disturbances.

Organization	Members	Mission
Council for Educational Diagnostic Services Two Ballston Plaza 1110 N. Glebe Road Arlington, VA 22201 http://www.unr.edu/educ/ceds	Members of the Council for Exceptional Children who are school psychologists, educational diagnosticians, [and] social workers who are involved in diagnosing educational difficulties	Promote the most appropriate education of children and youth through appraisal, diagnosis, educational intervention, implementation, and evaluation of a prescribed educational program. Work to facilitate the professional development of those who assess students. Work to further development of better diagnostic techniques and procedures.
Council of Administrators of Special Education Two Ballston Plaza 1110 N. Glebe Road Arlington, VA 22201 http://www.casecec.org	Members of the Council for Exceptional Children who are administrators, directors, coordinators, or supervisors of programs, schools, or classes for exceptional children; college faculty who train administrators	Promote professional leadership; provide opportunities for the study of problems common to its members; communicate through discussion and publications information that will facilitate improved services for children with exceptional needs.

Organization	Members	Mission
Division for Communicative Disabilities and Deafness Two Ballston Plaza 1110 N. Glebe Road Arlington, VA 22201 http://www.dcdd.us	Members of the Council for Exceptional Children who are speech-language pathologists, audiologists, teachers of children with communication disorders, or educators of professionals who plan to work with children who have communication disorders	Promote the education of children with communication disorders. Promote professional growth and research.
Division for Early Childhood Two Ballston Plaza 1110 N. Glebe Road Arlington, VA 22201 http://www.dec-sped.org	Members of the Council for Exceptional Children who teach preschool children and infants or educate teachers to work with young children	Promote effective education for young children and infants. Promote professional development of those who work with young children and infants. Promote legislation and research.
Division for Physical and Health Disabilities Two Ballston Plaza 1110 N. Glebe Road Arlington, VA 22201 http://web.utk.edu/~dphd	Members of the Council for Exceptional Children who work with individuals who have physical disabilities or educate professionals to work with those individuals	Promote closer relationships among educators of students who have physical impairments or are homebound. Facilitate research and encourage development of new ideas, practices, and techniques through professional meetings, workshops, and publications.

Organization	Members	Mission
Division on Visual Impairments Two Ballston Plaza 1110 N. Glebe Road Arlington, VA 22201 http://www.cecdvi.org	Members of the Council for Exceptional Children who work with individuals who have visual disabilities or educate professionals to work with those individuals	Work to advance the education and training of individuals with visual impairments. Work to bring about better understanding of educational, emotional, or other problems associated with visual impairment. Facilitate research and development of new techniques or ideas in education and training of individuals with visual problems.
Division on Career Development and Transition Two Ballston Plaza 1110 N. Glebe Road Arlington, VA 22201 http://www.dcdt.org	Members of the Council for Exceptional Children who teach or in other ways work toward career development and vocational education of exceptional children	Promote and encourage professional growth of all those concerned with career development and vocational education. Promote research, legislation, information dissemination, and technical assistance relevant to career development and vocational education.
Division on Developmental Disabilities Two Ballston Plaza 1110 N. Glebe Road Arlington, VA 22201 http://www.dddcec.org	Members of the Council for Exceptional Children who work with students with mental retardation or educate professionals to work with those students	Enhance the competence of persons who work with individuals with cognitive disabilities/mental retardation, autism, and related disabilities. Respond to and address emergent and critical issues in the field. Advocate on behalf of individuals with developmental disabilities.

Organization	Members	Mission
Epilepsy Foundation of America (EFA) 8301 Professional Place Landover, MD 20785 Phone: (800) 332-1000 http://www.epilepsyfoundation.org	A non-membership organization	Work to ensure that people with seizures are able to participate in all life experiences; and to prevent, control and cure epilepsy through research, education, advocacy and services.
Family Center on Technology and Disability (FCTD) 1825 Connecticut Avenue, NW 7th Floor Washington, DC 20009 Phone: (202) 884-8068 Fax: (202) 884-8441 http://www.fctd.info	Non member association	Designed to support organizations and programs that work with families of children and youth with disabilities.
Hands and Voices P.O. Box 371926 Denver CO 80237 Phone: (866) 422-0422 http://www.handsandvoices.org	Families, professionals, other organizations, pre-service students, and deaf and hard of hearing adults who are all working towards ensuring successful outcomes for children who are deaf and hard of hearing.	Support families and their children who are deaf or hard of hearing, as well as the professionals who serve them.

Organization	Members	Mission
The International Dyslexia Association Chester Building, Suite 382 8600 LaSalle Road Baltimore, Maryland 21286 Phone: (410) 296-0232 Fax: (410) 321-5069 http://www.interdys.org	Anyone interested in IDA and its mission can become a member	Provide information and referral services, research, advocacy and direct services to professionals in the field of learning disabilities.
Learning Disabilities Association of America (LDA) 4156 Library Road Pittsburgh, PA 15234 Phone: (412) 341-1515 Fax: (412) 344-0224 http://www.ldanatl.org	Anyone interested in LDA and its mission can become a member	Provide cutting edge information on learning disabilities, practical solutions, and a comprehensive network of resources. Provides support to people with learning disabilities, their families, teachers and other professionals.
National Association of the Deaf (NAD) 8630 Fenton Street, Suite 820, Silver Spring, MD Phone: (209) 210-3819 TTY: (301) 587-1789, , FAX: (301) 587-1791 http://nad.org	Anyone interested in NAD and its mission can become a member	Promote, protect, and preserve the rights and quality of life of deaf and hard of hearing individuals in the United States of America.

Organization	Members	Mission
National Mental Health Information Center P.O. Box 42557 Washington, DC 20015 Phone: (800) 789-2647 http://www.mentalhealth.samhsa.gov	Government Agency	Developed for users of mental health services and their families, the general public, policy makers, providers, and the media.
National Dissemination Center for Children with Disabilities (NIHCY) P.O. Box 1492 Washington, DC 20013 Phone: (800) 695-0285 Fax: (202) 884-8441 http://www.mentalhealth.samhsa.gov	Government Agency	A central source of information on: disabilities in infants, toddlers, children, and youth; IDEA, which is the law authorizing special education; No Child Left Behind (as it relates to children with disabilities); and research-based information on effective educational practices.
TASH (Formerly The Association for Persons with Severe Handicaps) 29 W. Susquehanna Ave., Suite 210 Baltimore, MD 21204 Phone: (410) 828-8274 Fax: (410) 828-6706 http:// www.tash.org	Anyone interested in TASH and its mission can become a member	Create change and build capacity so that all people, no matter their perceived level of disability, are included in all aspects of society.

Organization	Members	Mission
US Department of Education Office of Special Education and Rehabilitative Services http://www.ed.gov/about/offices/list/osers/index.html	Government Resource	Committed to improving results and outcomes for people with disabilities of all ages.
Wrights Law http://wrightslaw.com	Non-membership organization	Provide parent advocacy training and updates on the law throughout the country.
National Association for the Education of Young Children 1313 L St. N.W. Suite 500, Washington DC 20005 Phone: (800) 424-2460 http://www.naeyc.org		Promote service and action on behalf of the needs and rights of young children, with emphasis on provision of educational services and resources.
The ARC of the United States 5101 Washington Ave., N.W. Washington, D.C 20005 http://www.thearc.org	Open to anyone interested in the mission of the ARC	Work to promote the general welfare of persons with mental retardation; facilitate research and information dissemination relative to causes, treatment, and prevention of mental retardation.

Organization	Members	Mission
National Easter Seal Society 230 West Monroe Street, Suite 1800 Chicago, IL 60606 Phone: (800) 221-6827 TTY: (312) 726-1494 http://www.easterseals.com	State units (49) and local societies (951); no individual members	Establish and run programs for individuals with physical impairments, usually including diagnostic services, speech therapy, preschool services, physical therapy, and occupational therapy.
The National Association of Special Education Teachers 1201 Pennsylvania Avenue, N.W., Suite 300Washington D.C. 20004 Phone: 800-754-4421 Fax: 800-424-0371 http://www.naset.org	Special Education Teachers	Render all possible support and assistance to professionals who teach children with special needs. Promote standards of excellence and innovation in special education research, practice, and policy in order to foster exceptional teaching for exceptional children.

Various divisional organizations of the Council for Exceptional Children publish professional journals in their areas of exceptionality. These journals and their corresponding organizations are listed, along with addresses from which journals may be ordered. Other journals are published by related fields such as rehabilitation, mental health, and occupational guidance.

Behavioral Disorders
Council for Children with Behavioral Disorders (CCBD)
1920 Association Drive
Reston, VA 22091-1589

Career Development for Exceptional Individuals
Division on Career Development (DCD)
1920 Association Drive
Reston, VA 22091-1589

Diagnostique
Council for Educational Diagnostic Services (CEDS)
1920 Association Drive
Reston, VA 22091-1589

Education and Training of the Mentally Retarded
Division on Mental Retardation (CEC-MR)
1920 Association Drive
Reston, VA 22091-1589

Journal of Childhood Communication Disorders
Division for Children with Communication Disorders (DCCD)
1920 Association Drive
Reston, VA 22091-1589

Journal of the Division for Early Childhood
Division for Early Childhood (DEC)
1920 Association Drive
Reston, VA 22091-1589

Journal for the Education of the Gifted
The Association for the Gifted (TAG)
JEG, Wayne State University Press
5959 Woodward Avenue
Detroit, MI 48202

Journal of Special Education Technology
Technology and Media Division (TAM)
JSET, UMC 68
Utah State University
Logan, UT 84322

Learning Disabilities Focus
Learning Disabilities Research
Division for Learning Disabilities
1920 Association Drive
Reston, VA 22091-1589

Teacher Education and Special Education
Teacher Education Division (TED)
Special Press
P.O. Box 2524, Dept. CEC
Columbus, OH 43216

Exceptional Children
1920 Association Drive
Reston, VA 22091-1589

Teaching Exceptional Children
1920 Association Drive
Reston, VA 22091-1589

Exceptional Child Education Resources
1920 Association Drive
Reston, VA 22091-1589

Canadian Journal for Exceptional Children
Publication Services
4-116 Education North
The University of Alberta
Edmonton, Alberta, Canada T6G 2G5

Skill 15.3 Applying knowledge of the Council for Exceptional Children (CEC) Code of Ethics and the Georgia Professional Standards Commission Code of Ethics for Educators

In 1922, the Council for Exceptional Children (first called the International Council for Exceptional Children) was founded. During the 1920s, many comprehensive statewide programs were initiated.

CEC Code of Ethics for Educators of Persons with Exceptionalities
We declare the following principles to be the Code of Ethics for educators of persons with exceptionalities. Members of the special education profession are responsible for upholding and advancing these principles. Members of The Council for Exceptional Children agree to judge and be judged by them in accordance with the spirit and provisions of this Code.

Special education professionals are committed to developing the highest educational and quality of life potential of individuals with exceptionalities. Special education professionals promote and maintain a high level of competence and integrity in practicing their profession.

Special education professionals engage in professional activities which benefit individuals with exceptionalities, their families, other colleagues, students, or research subjects.

Special education professionals exercise objective professional judgment in the practice of their profession.

Special education professionals strive to advance their knowledge and skills regarding the education of individuals with exceptionalities.
Special education professionals work within the standards and policies of their profession.

Special education professionals seek to uphold and improve where necessary the laws, regulations, and policies governing the delivery of special education and related services and the practice of their profession.

Special education professionals do not condone or participate in unethical or illegal acts, nor violate professional standards adopted by the Delegate Assembly of CEC.

The Council for Exceptional Children. (1993). CEC Policy Manual, Section Three, part 2 (p. 4). Reston, VA: Author.

Originally adopted by the Delegate Assembly of The Council for Exceptional Children in April 1983.

Georgia Professional Standards Commissions Code of Ethics
The Georgia Professional Standards Commissions Code of Ethics defines the professional behavior of educators in the state of Georgia and acts as a reference point for ethical conduct. The Professional Standards Commission has adopted standards that represent the conduct generally accepted by the education profession. The code protects the health, safety, and general welfare of students and educators, guarantees the citizens of Georgia a degree of accountability within the education profession, and defines unethical conduct warranting disciplinary sanction.

There are ten standards outlined in the GA PSC Code of Ethics. The standards are outlined below.

Standard 1: Criminal Acts - An educator should follow federal, state, and local laws and regulations. Unethical conduct includes but is not limited to the commission or conviction of a felony or of any crime involving moral turpitude.

Standard 2: Abuse of Students - An educator should uphold a professional relationship with all students, both in school and outside the school setting.

Standard 3: Alcohol or Drugs - An educator should abstain from the utilization of alcohol or illegal or unauthorized drugs during the course of professional practice.

Standard 4: Misrepresentation or Falsification - An educator should embody truthfulness and uprightness in the course of his or her professional duties.

Standard 5: Public Funds and Property - An educator entrusted with public funds and property should respect that trust with a high degree of truthfulness, correctness, and accountability.

Standard 6: Improper Remunerative Conduct - An educator should preserve his or her integrity with students, colleagues, parents, patrons, or businesses when accepting donations, gifts, favors, and additional compensation.

Standard 7: Confidential Information - An educator should follow state and federal laws and local school board/governing board policies involving the confidentiality of student and personnel records, standardized test documents, and other information covered by confidentiality agreements.

Standard 8: Abandonment of Contract - An educator should satisfy all of the terms and obligations detailed in the contract with the local board of education or education agency for the length of the contract.

Standard 9: Failure to Make a Required Report – An educator should submit reports describing a violation of any of the standards in the Code of Ethics, child abuse, or any other required report.

Standard 10: Professional Conduct – An educator should exemplify the highest standards of professional conduct.

For additional information on the standards, please visit the GA PSC website at www.gapsc.com or http://www.gapsc.com/Professionalpractices/NEthics.asp

Address:

Georgia Professional Standards Commission
Two Peachtree Street
Suite 6000
Atlanta, GA 30303

(404) 232-2500
ethics@gapsc.com
FAX: 404-232-2720

Skill 15.4 Demonstrating knowledge of laws, policies, and ethical principles related to behavior management, the provision of specialized health care in the educational setting and mandated reporting.

Please refer to http://rules.sos.state.ga.us/cgi-bin/page.cgi?d=1 for Georgia-specific information.

Please refer to Objective 10 (all subsets) for details on laws and policies regarding behavior management.

Please refer to Skill 2.2 for information on medical conditions such as asthma and tube feeding, Skill 2.4 for specialized medicines, and Skill 3.2 for disabling physical conditions in school.

Several laws and court cases have had direct impact on handling medical conditions in the school setting, so these cases are mentioned again here, though they can be found earlier in this guide:

School Board of Nassau County v. Arline, 1987: This case established that contagious diseases are a disability under Section 504 of the Rehabilitation Act and that people with them are protected from discrimination if otherwise qualified (actual risk to health and safety to others make persons unqualified).

Irving Independent School District v. Tatro 1984: IDEA lists health services as one of the "related services" that schools are mandated to provide to exceptional students. Amber Tatro, who had spina bifida, required the insertion of a catheter on a regular schedule in order to empty her bladder. The issue was specifically over the classification of clean, intermittent catheterization (CIC) as a medical service (not covered under IDEA) or a "related health service," which would be covered. In this instance, the catheterization was not declared a medical service, but a "related service" necessary for the student to have in order to benefit from special education. The school district was obliged to provide the service. The Tatro case has implications for students with other medical impairments who may need services to allow them to attend classes at the school.

Americans with Disabilities Act (ADA) 1990: Bars discrimination in employment, transportation, public accommodations, and telecommunications in all aspects of life, not just those receiving federal funding. Title II and Title III are applicable to special education because they cover the private sector (such as private schools) and require access to public accommodations. New and remodeled public buildings, transportation vehicles, and telephone systems now must be accessible to persons with disabilities. ADA also protects individuals with contagious diseases, such as AIDS, from discrimination.

In 2004, the reauthorization of IDEA IDEA reauthorization 2004 changed the definition of *assistive technology devices* to exclude devices that are surgically implanted (i.e., cochlear implants) and clarified that students with assistive technology devices shall not be prevented from having special education services. Assistive technology devices may need to be *monitored* by school personnel, but schools are not responsible for the *surgical implantation* or replacement of such devices.

Mandated Reporters

According to the laws of Georgia (O.C.G.A. 19-7-5), ALL school personnel are *mandated reporters*. The law specifically lists the following as mandated reporters:

- School teachers;
- School administrators;
- School guidance counselors, visiting teachers, school social workers or school psychologists certified pursuant to
- Registered professional nurses or licensed practical nurses licensed pursuant to;
- Professional counselors, social workers or marriage and family therapists licensed pursuant

Specifically, this means that school personnel have "the responsibility to report suspected cases of child abuse and neglect and that, in making a report regarding child abuse or neglect, they are immune from any civil or criminal liability that otherwise might be imposed, provided the report is made in good faith (an honest belief that a child's health/welfare may be in jeopardy)."

Skill 15.5 Applying knowledge of how to uphold high standards of competence, good judgment, and integrity when conducting instructional and other professional activities, including complying with all applicable laws, policies, and procedures (e.g., local, state, and federal monitoring and evaluation requirements).

Please refer to Skills 15.2, 15.3, and

http://rules.sos.state.ga.us/cgi-bin/page.cgi?d=1.

Skill 15.6 Recognizing effective strategies for engaging in reflection and self-assessment activities for the purposes of identifying one's own personal cultural biases, improving instruction, and guiding professional growth.

The role of the special education teacher is to advocate for the most appropriate education for students and to guide them in discovering new knowledge and developing new skills to the best of their potential. According to IDEA 2004, teachers are to prepare students for future, purposeful work in society with the possibility of post-secondary education or training.

Although each special educator is also a person with a set of experiences, opinions, and beliefs, it is important to remain unbiased and positive in the professional role with students, parents, administration, and the community. Differences in culture, religion, gender, or sexual orientation should not influence the teacher's approach to instruction, student goals, student expectations, or advocacy.

In order to remain unbiased, the special educator should avail him or herself of opportunities to learn about various cultures, religions, genders, and sexual orientations. This can be accomplished through reading, appropriate classroom awareness activities, and teacher in-service.

Reading to increase awareness and acceptance of cultural differences may be done through professional, adult literature as well as through books to be read with the class.

Cultural activities in the classroom are especially well-received; foods, dress, and games are easily added to curriculum and often address learning standards. The special educator is charged with academic, social, communicative, and independent skills instruction. Education or influence in other areas is not appropriate.

When the special educator remains unbiased, he or she is better able to meet the needs of students and to not react to additional factors. The students and their families are also more open to school-related suggestions.

The teacher's reaction to differences with students and their families models the commonly taught character education trait of respect. When the teacher demonstrates respect for all individuals in his or her program, it is likely that respect will also be practiced by students, parents, and administration.

Skill 15.7 Demonstrating knowledge of how to advocate effectively for individual students with disabilities, their families, and the special education program in general

Because of the unique needs of each student with disabilities, special education teachers are frequently advocates for their students and the special education program in general.

In order to be an effective advocate, the teacher must be knowledgeable in a number of areas. First, the special educator must understand the general education program that is the counterpart to his or her program. Factors such as student expectations (learning standards), materials used, and teacher training and inservice provide a starting point. If the special educator is familiar with the goals and overall programs for all students at his or her grade level, the educator will have a clear picture of the direction he or she should be moving with students with disabilities.

The special educator should also have a clear understanding of each student's strengths and needs. He or she must consider how each student can participate in the general education curriculum to the extent that it is beneficial for that student (IDEA 2004). For example, when should services and instruction take place outside of the general education classroom?

In addition, special educators should have an understanding of alternate materials that would be useful or necessary for the students, as well as what resources for materials are available.

Knowledge of the Individual's with Disabilities Education Act (IDEA 2004) and NCLB (No Child Left Behind) provides an outline of legislative mandates for special education. A clear understanding of the nature of the laws and court cases relevant to a student's right to special education, to a free appropriate education, can give the teacher power and leverage in advocating for the student's needs. These laws are intended to protect students, but knowledge of the laws is essential in order for that protection to be realized.

A clear understanding of the above points will allow the special educator to most effectively advocate for the most appropriate placement, programming, and materials for each student. He or she will be able to advocate for research-based methods with measurable outcomes.

Advocacy often happens between general and special education teachers. A special educator may see modification or accommodation possibilities that could take place in the general education classroom. It is his or her responsibility to advocate those practices. The special education teacher may also offer to make supplementary materials or to work with a group of students in the general education setting to achieve that goal. When students with disabilities are in an inclusion classroom, give and take on the part of both teachers as a team is crucial.

The special education teacher may also need to be an advocate for his or her program (or the needs of an individual student) with the administration. Although success for all students is important to administration, it is often up to the teacher to explain the need for comparable materials written at the different reading level, the need for assistance in the classroom, or the need for offering specific classes or therapies.

Skill 15.8 Recognizing appropriate procedures for creating and maintaining records regarding students with disabilities, including following legal and ethical guidelines for maintaining confidentiality

The Family Educational Rights and Privacy Act (1974), also known as the Buckley Amendment, assures confidentiality of student records. Parents are afforded the right to examine, review, and request changes in information deemed inaccurate and stipulate persons who might access their child's records. This means that written permission from parents or legal guardians is absolutely required before any printed or verbal information is shared with anyone outside the classroom or team (e.g., outside counselors, etc.).

"Due process is a set of procedures designed to ensure the fairness of educational decisions and the accountability of both professionals and parents in making these decisions" (Kirk and Gallagher, 1986, p. 24). These procedures serve as a mechanism by which the child and his or her family can voice opinions, concerns, and dissents. Due process safeguards exist in all matters pertaining to identification, evaluation, and educational placement.

Due process occurs in two realms: substantive and procedural. Substantive due process is the content of the law (e.g., appropriate placement for special education students). Procedural due process is the form through which substantive due process is carried out (e.g., parental permission for testing). Public Law 101-476 contains many items of both substantive and procedural due process.

A due process hearing may be initiated by parents or the LEA as an impartial forum for challenging decisions about identification, evaluation, or placement. Either party may present evidence, cross-examine witnesses, obtain a record of the hearing, and be advised by counsel or by individuals having expertise in the education of individuals with disabilities. Findings may be appealed to the state education agency (SEA), and, if still dissatisfied, either party may bring civil action in a state of federal district court. Hearing timelines are set by legislation.

Parents may obtain an independent evaluation if there is disagreement about the education evaluation performed by the LEA. The results of such an evaluation: (1) must be considered in any decision made with respect to the provision of a free, appropriate public education for the child; and (2) may be presented as evidence at a hearing. Further, the parents may request this evaluation at public expense: (1) if a hearing officer requests an independent educational evaluation; or (2) if the decision from a due process hearing is that the LEA's evaluation was inappropriate. If the final decision holds that the evaluation performed is appropriate, the parent still has the right to an independent educational evaluation, but not at public expense.

Written notice must be provided to parents prior to a proposal or refusal to initiate or make a change in the child's identification, evaluation, or educational placement. This notice includes:

- A listing of parental due process safeguards.
- A description and a rationale for the chosen action.
- A detailed listing of components (e.g., tests, records, reports) that were the basis for the decision.
- Assurance that the language and content of notices were understood by the parents

Parental consent must be obtained before evaluation procedures can occur, unless there is a state law specifying otherwise.
Sometimes, parents or guardians cannot be identified to function in the due process role. When this occurs, a suitable person must be assigned to act as a surrogate. This is done by the LEA in full accordance with legislation.

One of the most important professional practices a teacher must maintain is student confidentiality. This extends far beyond paper records and goes into the realm of oral discussions. Teachers are expected to refrain from mentioning the names of students and often the specifics of their character in conversations with those who are not directly involved with them, both inside and outside of school.

In the school environment, teacher recordkeeping comes in three main formats, each with specific confidentiality rules. All of the records stated below should be kept in a locked place within the classroom or an office within the school:

A teacher's personal notes on a student.

When a teacher takes notes on a student's actions, including behaviors and/or grade performances that are not intended to be placed in a school recorded format, the teacher may keep this information private and confidential to his/her own files. Teachers may elect to share this information or not.

Daily recorded grades and attendance of the student.

A teacher's grade books and attendance records are to be open to the parent/guardian of that child when he or she wishes. Only that child's information may be shared—not that of others.

Teacher notations on records that appear in the student cumulative file.

There are specific rules regarding the sharing of the cumulative records of students.

Cumulative files will follow a student who transfers from school to school within the school district.

All information placed in a cumulative file may be examined by a parent at any time it is requested. If a parent shows up to review his or her child's cumulative file, the file should be shown as it is in its current state (this includes IEPs).

When information from a cumulative file is requested by another person/entity other than the parent/guardian, the information may not be released without the express written consent of the parent/guardian. The parental consent must specify which records may be shared with the other party of interest.

A school in which a student may intend to enroll may receive the student's educational record without parental consent. However, the school sending that information must make a reasonable attempt to notify the parent/guardian of the request. (FERPA)

Today's world is quickly becoming a digital environment. Teachers now communicate with email and are keeping records in digital formats, often within a district mandated program. Teachers should keep in mind that emails and other electronic formats can be forwarded and are as “indelible” as permanent ink. They should maintain a professional decorum just as when they are writing their own records.

REFERENCES

Ager, C. L. & Cole, C. L. (1991). A review of cognitive-behavioral interventions for children and adolescents with behavioral disorders. *Behavioral Disorders,* 16, 260-275.

Aiken, L. R. (1985). *Psychological testing and assessment* (5th ed.). Boston: Allyn and Bacon.

Alberto, P. A. & Trouthman, A. C. (1990). *Applied behavior analysis for teachers: influencing student performance*. Columbus, Ohio: Charles E. Merrill.

Algozzine, B. (1990). *Behavior problem management: Educator's resource service*. Gaithersburg, MD: Aspen Publishers.

Algozzine, B., Ruhl, K., & Ramsey, R. (1991). *Behaviorally disordered: assessment for identification and instruction: CED mini-library*. Renson, VA: The Council for Exceptional Children.

Ambron, S. R. (1981). *Child development* (3rd ed.). New York: Holt, Rinehart and Winston.

Anders, P. L., & Bos, C. S. (1986). Semantic feature analysis: An interactive strategy for vocabulary development and text comprehension. *Journal of Reading,* 29, 610-16.

Anerson, V., & Black, L. (Eds.). (1987, Winter). National news: US Department of Education releases special report (editorial). *GLRS Journal* [Georgia Learning Resources System].

Anguili, R. (1987, Winter). The 1986 amendment to the Education of the Handicapped Act. *Confederation* [Georgia Federation Council for Exceptional Children].

Ashlock, R. B. (1976). *Error patterns in computation: A semi-programmed approach* (2nd ed.). Columbus, Ohio: Charles E. Merrill.

Association of Retarded Citizens of Georgia (1987). *1986-87 Government report*. College Park, GA: Author.

Ausubel, D. P. & Sullivan, E. V. (1970). *Theory and problems of child development*. New York: Grune & Stratton.

Banks, J. A., & McGee Banks, C. A. (1993). *Multicultural education* (2nd ed.). Boston: Allyn and Bacon.

Baratta-Lorton, M. (1978). *Mathematics their way: An activity-centered mathematics program for early childhood education*. Menlo Park, CA: Addison-Wesley.

Barrett, T. C. (1985). The relationship between measures of prereading visual discrimination and first grade reading achievement: A review of the literature. *Reading Research Quarterly,* 1, 51-76.

Barrett, T. C. (ed.) (1967). *The evaluation of children's reading achievement in perspectives in reading, No. 8*. Newark, Delaware: International Reading Association.

Bartoli, J. S. (1989). An ecological response to Cole's interactivity alternative. *Journal of Learning Disabilities*, 22, 292-297.

Bauer, A. M., & Shea, T. M. (1989). *Teaching exceptional students in your classroom*. Boston: Allyn and Bacon.

Bentley, E. L. (1980). *Questioning skills* (Videocassette & Manual Series). Northbrook, IL: Hubbard Scientific Company. (Project STRETCH [Strategies to Train Regular Educators to Teach Children with Handicaps], Module 1.

Berdine, W. H., & Blackhurst, A. E. (1985). *An introduction to special education*. (2nd ed.) Boston: Little, Brown and Company.

Bialo, E., & Sivin, J. (1990). *Report on the effectiveness of microcomputers in schools*. Washington, DC: Software Publishers Association.

Biemiller, A. (2003). Oral comprehension sets the ceiling on reading comprehension. *American Educator,* 27, 23-44.

Blake, K. (1976). *The mentally retarded: An educational psychology*. Englewood Cliff, NJ: Prentice-Hall.

Blevins, W. (1997). *Phonemic awareness activities for early reading success: Easy, playful activities that prepare children for phonics instruction*. New York: Scholastic.

Bley, N. S., Thornton, C. A., & Bley, N. S. (2001). *Teaching mathematics to students with learning disabilities.* Austin, Tex: Pro-Ed.

Bloom, B. S. (1956). *Taxonomy of educational objectives, handbook I: The cognitive domain.* New York: David McKay Co.

Bohline, D. S. (1985). Intellectual and affective characteristics of attention deficit disordered children. *Journal of Learning Disabilities*, 18, 604-608.

Boone, R. (1983). Legislation and litigation. In R. E. Schmid, & L. Negata (Eds.). *Contemporary Issues in Special Education*. New York: McGraw Hill.

Brantlinger, E. A., & Guskin, S. L. (1988). Implications of Social and Cultural Differences for Special Education. In Meten, E. L. Vergason, G. A., & Whelan, R. J. *Effective instructional strategies for exceptional children*. Denver, CO: Love Publishing.

Brolin, D. E. (Ed). (1989). *Life centered career education: A competency based approach*. Reston, VA: The Council for Exceptional Children.

Brolin, D. E., & Kokaska, C. J. (1979). *Career education for handicapped children and youth*. Renton, VA: The Council for Exceptional Children.

Brown, J. W., Lewis, R. B., & Harcleroad, F. F. (1983). *AV instruction: technology, media, and methods* (6th ed.). New York: McGraw-Hill.

Bryan, T. H., & Bryan, J. H. (1986). *Understanding learning disabilities* (3rd ed.). Palo Alto, CA: Mayfield.

Bryen, D. N. (1982). *Inquiries into child language*. Boston: Allyn & Bacon.

Bucher, B. D. (1987). *Winning them over*. New York: Times Books.

Burns, P. C., Roe, B. D., & Smith, S. H. (2002). *Teaching reading in today's elementary schools*. (8th ed.). Boston: Houghton Mifflin.

Bush, W. L., & Waugh, K. W. (1982). *Diagnosing learning problems* (3rd ed.). Columbus, OH: Charles E. Merrill.

Carbo, M., & Dunn, K. (1986). *teaching students to read through their individual learning styles*. Englewood Cliffs, NJ: Prentice Hall.

Carlyon, W. D. (1997). Attribution retraining: implications for its integration into prescriptive social skills training. *School Psychology Review*. 26 (1), 61.

Cartwright, G. P., & Cartwright, C. A., & Ward, M. E. (1984). *Educating special learners* (2nd ed.). Belmont, CA: Wadsworth.

Cejka, J. M., & Needham, F. (1976). *Approaches to mainstreaming*. (Filmstrip and cassette kit, units 1 & 2). Boston: Teaching Resources Corporation.

Chalfant, J. C. (1985). Identifying learning disabled students: A summary of the National Task Force Report. *Learning Disabilities Focus,* 1, 9-20.

Chaney, C. (1994). Language development, metalinguistic awareness, and emergent literacy skills of 3-year-old children in relation to social class. *Applied Psycholinguistics,* 15, 371.

Chard, D. J., & Osborn, J. 1999. Phonics and word recognition instruction in early reading programs: Guidelines for accessibility". *Learning Disabilities Research and Practice,* 14, 107-17.

Charles, C. M. (1976). *Individualizing instruction*. St Louis: The C. V. Mosby Company.

Chrispeels, J. H. (1991). District leadership in parent involvement: Policies and actions in San Diego. *Phi Delta Kappan,* 71, 367-371.

Clarizio, H. F. & McCoy, G. F. (1983). *Behavior disorders in children* (3rd ed.). New York: Harper & Row.

Clay, M. M. (1967). The reading behavior of five-year-old children. *New Zealand Journal of Educational Studies,* 2, 11-31.

Coles, G. S. (1989). Excerpts from the learning mystique: A critical look at disabilities. *Journal of Learning Disabilities*, 22, 267-278.

Collins, E. (1980). *Grouping and special students*. (Videocassette & manual series). Northbrook, IL: Hubbard Scientific Company. (Project STRETCH [Strategies to Train Regular Educators to Teach Children with Handicaps], Module 17.

Compton, C., (1984). *A guide to 75 tests for special education.* Belmont, CA., Pitman Learning.

Cooper, J. D., & Kiger, N. D. (2009). *Literacy: Helping students construct meaning*. Boston: Houghton Mifflin.

Council for Exceptional Children (1983). *Council for exceptional children code of ethics* (Adopted April 1983). Reston, VA: Author.

Council for Exceptional Children. (1976). *Introducing P. L. 94-142.* [Filmstrip-cassette kit manual]. Reston, VA: Author.

Council for Exceptional Children. (1987). *The council for exceptional children's fall 1987 catalog of products and services.* Renton, VA: Author.

Craig, E., & Craig, L. (1990). *Reading in the content areas*. (Videocassette & manual series). Northbrook, IL: Hubbard Scientific Company. (Project STRETCH [Strategies to Train Regular Educators to Teach Children with Handicaps], Module 13.

Czajka, J. L. (1984). *Digest of data on persons with disabilities* (Mathematics Policy Research, Inc.). Washington, D. C.: U. S. Government Printing Office.

Dell, H. D. (1972). *Individualizing instruction: Materials and classroom procedures.* Chicago: Science Research Associates.

Demonbreun, C., & Morris, J. *Classroom management* [Videocassette & Manual series]. Northbrook, IL: Hubbard Scientific Company. Project STRETCH (Strategies to Train Regular Educators to Teach Children with Handicaps]. Module 5.

Department of Health, Education, and Welfare, Office of Education. (1977, August 23). Education of handicapped children. *Federal Register,* 42, 163.

Digangi, S. A., Perryman, P., & Rutherford, R. B., Jr. (1990). Juvenile offenders in the 90's: A descriptive analysis. *Perceptions*, 25, 5-8.

Division of Educational Services, Special Education Programs (1986). *Fifteenth annual report to congress on implementation of the Education of the Handicapped Act.* Washington, D.C.: U.S. Government Printing Office.

Doyle, B. A. (1978). Math readiness skills. Paper presented at National Association of School Psychologists, New York. In Dunn, R. S. and Dunn, K. J. (1978). *Teaching students through their individual learning styles*. Reston, Va.: Reston Publishing.

Duke, N. K, Bennett-Armistead, V.S., & Roberts, E. M. (2003). Filling the nonfiction void. *American Educator,* 27, 30.

Dunn, R. S., & Dunn, K. J. (1978). *Teaching students through their individual learning styles: A practical approach.* Reston, VA: Reston Publishing.

Ekwall, E. E., & Shanker, J. L. 1983). *Diagnosis and remediation of the disabled reader* (2nd ed.) Boston: Allyn and Bacon.

Epstein, M. H., Patton, J. R., Polloway, E. A., & Foley, R. (1989). Mild retardation: student characteristics and services. *Education and Training of the Mentally Retarded*, 24, 7-16.

Ezell, H. K., & Justice, L. M. (2000). Increasing the print focus of adult-child shared book reading through observational learning". *American Journal of Speech Language Pathology,* 9, 36-47.

Firth, E. E. & Reynolds, I. (1983). Slide tape shows: A creative activity for the gifted students. *Teaching Exceptional Children,* 15, 151-153.

Flippo, R. F. (2002). *Reading assessment and instruction: A qualitative approach to diagnosis.* Portsmouth, NH: Heinemann.

Flippo, R. F. (2003). *Assessing readers: Qualitative diagnosis and instruction.* Portsmouth, NH: Heinemann.

Frith, U. (1985). Beneath the surface of developmental dyslexia. In Patterson, K., Marshall, J. C., & Coltheart, M. *Surface dyslexia: Neuropsychological and cognitive studies of phonological reading*. London: L. Erlbaum Associates, 1985.

Frymier, J., & Gansneder, B. (1989). The Phi Delta Kappa study of students at risk. *Phi Delta Kappan,* 71, 142-146.

Fuchs, D., & Deno, S. L. 1992). Effects of curriculum within curriculum-based measurement. *Exceptional Children,* 58, 232-42.

Fuchs, D., & Fuchs, L. S. (1989). Effects of examiner familiarity on Black, Caucasian, and Hispanic Children: A meta-analysis. *Exceptional Children,* 55, 303-308.

Fuchs, L. S., & Shinn, M. R. (1989). Writing CBM IEP Objectives. In M. R. Shinn, *Curriculum-based measurement: assessing special students*. New York: Guilford Press.

Gage, N. L. (1990). Dealing with the dropout problems? *Phi Delta Kappan,* 72, 280-85.

Gallagher, P. A. (1988). *Teaching students with behavior disorders: Techniques and activities for classroom instruction* (2nd ed.). Denver, CO: Love Publishing.

Gearheart, B. R. & Weishahn, M. W. (1986). *The handicapped student in the regular classroom* (2nd ed.). St Louis, MO: The C. V. Mosby Company.

Gearheart, B. R. (1980). *Special education for the 80s.* St. Louis, MO: The C. V. Mosby Company.

Gearheart, B. R. (1985). *Learning disabilities: Educational strategies* (4th ed.). St. Louis: C. V. Mosby Company.

Georgia Department of Education. Program for Exceptional Children (1986). *Mild mentally handicapped* (Vol. II), Atlanta, GA: Office of Instructional Services, Division of Special Programs, and Program for Exceptional Children. Resource Manuals for Program for Exceptional Children.

Geren, K. (1979). *Complete special education handbook.* West Nyack, NY: Parker.

Gillet, P. K. (1988). Career development. In Robinson, G. A., Patton, J. R., Polloway, E. A., & Sargent, L. R. (eds.). *Best practices in mild mental disabilities.* Reston, VA: The Division on Mental Retardation of the Council for Exceptional Children.

Gillingham, A., & Stillman, B. W. (1997). *The Gillingham manual: Remedial training for students with specific disability in reading, spelling, and penmanship.* Cambridge, MA: Educators Pub. Service.

Glass, G. G. (1967). The strange world of syllabication. *Elementary School Journal,* 67, 403-05.

Gleason, J. B. (1993). *The development of language* (3rd ed.). New York: Macmillan Publishing.

Good, T. L., & Brophy, J. E. (1978). *Looking into classrooms* (2nd Ed.). New York: Harper & Row.

Goodman, K. S. (1985). Growing into Literacy. *Prospects: Quarterly Review of Education,* 15, 57-65.

Gresham, F. (1995). Best practices in social skills training. In Thomas & Grimes (eds.) *Best practices in school psychology* (pp. 1021-1030). Washington, DC: National Association of School Psychologists.

Hall, M. A. (1979). Language-centered reading: Premises and recommendations. *Language Arts,* 56, 664-670.

Hallahan, D. P. & Kauffman, J. M. (1994). *Exceptional children: Introduction to special education* (6th ed.). Boston: Allyn and Bacon.

Halllahan, D. P. & Kauffman, J. M. (1988). *Exceptional children: Introduction to special education.* (4th ed.). Englewood Cliffs, NJ; Prentice-Hall.

Hamill, D. D., & Brown, L. & Bryant, B. (1989) *A consumer's guide to tests in print.* Austin, TX: Pro-Ed.

Hammill, D. D., & Bartel, N. R. (1982). *Teaching children with learning and behavior problems* (3rd ed.). Boston: Allyn and Bacon.

Hammill, D. D., & Bartel, N. R. (1986). *Teaching students with learning and behavior problems* (4th ed.). Boston and Bacon.

Haney, J. B. & Ullmer, E. J. (1970). *Educational media and the teacher.* Dubuque, IA: Wm. C. Brown Company.

Hardman, M. L., Drew, C. J., Egan, M. W., & Wolf, B. (1984). *Human exceptionality: Society, school, and family.* Boston: Allyn and Bacon.

Hardman, M. L., Drew, C. J., Egan, M. W., & Worlf, B. (1990). *Human exceptionality* (3rd ed.). Boston: Allyn and Bacon.

Hargrove, L. J., & Poteet, J. A. (1984). *Assessment in special education.* Englewood Cliffs, NJ: Prentice-Hall.

Haring, N. G., & Bateman, B. (1977). *Teaching the learning disabled child.* Englewood Cliffs, NJ: Prentice-Hall.

Harris, K. R., & Pressley, M. (1991). The nature of cognitive strategy instruction: Interactive strategy instruction. *Exceptional Children*, 57, 392-401.

Hart, T., & Cadora, M. J. (1980). The exceptional child: Label the behavior. [Videocassette & manual series], Northbrook, IL: Hubbard Scientific Company. (Project STRETCH [Strategies to Train Regular Educators to Teach Children with Handicaps], Module 12.

Hart, V. (1981) *Mainstreaming children with special needs.* New York: Longman.

Hatfield, M. M., Edwards, N. T., Bitter, G. G., & Morrow, J. (2005). *Mathematics methods for elementary and middle school teachers*. (5th ed.). New York: Wiley.

Henley, M., Ramsey, R. S., & Algozzine, B. (1993). *Characteristics of and strategies for teaching students with mild disabilities.* Boston: Allyn and Bacon.

Henry, F., Reed, V. & McAllister, L. (1995). Adolescents' perceptions of the relative importance of selected communications skills in their positive peer relationships. *Language, speech, and hearing services in schools.* 26, 263-272.

Hewett, F. M., & Forness, S. R. (1984). *Education of exceptional learners.* (3rd ed.). Boston: Allyn and Bacon.

Hoban, T. (1987) *26 letters and 99 cents*. New York: Greenwillow Books.

Hook, P., & Jones, S. (2002). The importance of automaticity and fluency for efficient reading comprehension. *Perspectives: The International Dyslexia Association,* 28, 9-14.

Howe, C. E. (1981) *Administration of special education.* Denver: Love.

Human Services Research Institute (1985). *Summary of data on handicapped children and youth.* Washington, D.C.: U.S. Government Printing Office.

International Reading Association. (1981). *Resolution on misuse of grade equivalents.* Newark, DE: Author.

International Reading Association. (1997). *The role of phonics in reading instruction: A position statement of the International Reading Association.* Newark, Del: International Reading Association.

Johnson, D. D., & Pearson, P. D. (1984). *Teaching reading vocabulary*. New York: Holt, Rinehart and Winston.

Johnson, D. W. (1972) *Reaching out: Interpersonal effectiveness and self-actualization*. Englewood Cliffs, NJ: Prentice-Hall.

Johnson, D. W. (1978) *Human relations and your career: A guide to interpersonal skills.* Englewood Cliffs, NJ: Prentice-Hall.

Johnson, D. W., & Johnson, F. P. (1975). *Joining together*. Englewood Cliffs, N.J.: Prentice-Hall, 1975.

Johnson, D. W., & Johnson, R. T. (1990). Social skills for successful group work. *Educational Leadership,* 47, 29-33.

Johnson, S. W., & Morasky, R. L. (1977). *Learning disabilities.* Boston: Allyn and Bacon.

Johnson, S. W., & Morasky, R. L. (1980). *Learning disabilities* (2nd ed.) Boston: Allyn and Bacon.

Jones, F. H. (1987). *Positive classroom discipline.* New York: McGraw-Hill Book Company.

Jones, V. F. & Jones, L. S. (1981). *Responsible classroom discipline: Creating positive learning environments and solving problems.* Boston: Allyn and Bacon.

Jones, V. F., & Jones, L. S. (1986). *Comprehensive classroom management: Creating positive learning environments.* (2nd ed.). Boston: Allyn and Bacon.

Justice, L. M., & Ezell, H. K. (2000). "Enhancing children's print and word awareness through home-based parent intervention". *American Journal of Speech Language Pathology,* 9, 257-269.

Justice, L., & Ezell, H. (2001). Written language awareness in preschool children from low-income households." *Communication Disorders Quarterly,* 22, 123-134.

Kauffman, J. M. (1981) *Characteristics of children's behavior disorders.* (2nd ed.). Columbus, OH: Charles E. Merrill.

Kauffman, J. M. (1989). *Characteristics of behavior disorders of children and youth.* (4th ed.). Columbus, OH: Merrill Publishing.

Kem, M., & Nelson, M. (1983). *Strategies for managing behavior problems in the classroom.* Columbus, OH: Charles E. Merrill.

Kerr, M. M., & Nelson, M. (1983) *Strategies for managing behavior problems in the classroom.* Columbus, OH: Charles E. Merrill.

Kirk, S. A., & Gallagher, J. J. (1986). *Educating exceptional children* (5th ed.). Boston: Houghton Mifflin.

Kohfeldt, J. (1976). Blueprints for Construction. *Focus on Exceptional Children,* 8, 1-14.

Kokaska, C. J., & Brolin, D. E. (1985). *Career education for handicapped individuals* (2nd ed.). Columbus, OH: Charles E. Merrill.

Lambie, R. A. (1980). A systematic approach for changing materials, instruction, and assignments to meet individual needs. *Focus on Exceptional Children,* 13, 1-12.

Landau, S. & Moore, L. (1991). Social skills deficits in children with attention-deficit hyperactivity disorder. *School Psychology Review* 20, 235-251.

Larson, S. C., & Poplin, M. S. (1980). *Methods for educating the handicapped: An individualized education program approach.* Boston: Allyn and Bacon.

Lerner, J. (1976) *Children with learning disabilities.* (2nd ed.). Boston: Houghton Mifflin.

Lerner, J. (1989). *Learning disabilities,: Theories, diagnosis and teaching strategies* (3rd ed.). Boston: Houghton Mifflin.

Levenkron, S. (1991). *Obsessive-compulsive disorders.* New York: Warner Books.

Lewis, R. B., & Doorlag, D. H. (1991). *Teaching special students in the mainstream.* (3rd ed.). New York: Merrill.

Lindberg, L., & Swedlow, R. (1985). *Young children exploring and learning.* Boston: Allyn and Bacon.

Lindsley, O. R. (1990). Precision teaching: By teachers for children. *Teaching Exceptional Children,* 22, 10-15.

Long, N. J., Morse, W. C., & Newman, R. G. (1980). *Conflict in the classroom: The education of emotionally disturbed children.* Belmont, CA: Wadsworth.

Lonigan, C. J., Bloomfield, B. G., Anthony, J. L. & Bacon, K. D. (1999). Relations among emergent literacy skills, behavior problems, and social competence in preschool children from low- and middle-income backgrounds. *Topics in Early Childhood Special Education,* 19, 40.

Losen, S. M., & Losen, J. G. (1985). *The special education team.* Boston: Allyn and Bacon.

Lovitt, T. C. (1989). *Introduction to learning disabilities.* Boston: Allyn and Bacon.

Lund, N. J., & Duchan, J. F. (1988) *Assessing children's language in naturalist contexts.* Englewood Cliffs, NJ: Prentice Hall

Male, M. (1994) *Technology for inclusion: Meeting the special needs of all children.* (2nd ed.). Boston: Allyn and Bacon.

Mandelbaum, L. H. (1989). Reading. In G. A. Robinson, J. R., Patton, E. A., Polloway, & L. R. Sargent (eds.). *Best practices in mild mental retardation.* Reston, VA: The Division of Mental Retardation, Council for Exceptional Children.

Mannix. D. (1993). *Social skills for special children.* West Nyack, NY: The Center for Applied Research in Education.

Marshall, E. K., Kurtz, P. D., & Associates. *Interpersonal helping skills.* San Francisco, CA: Jossey-Bass Publications.

Marshall, et al. vs. Georgia. U.S. District Court for the Southern District of Georgia. C.V. 482-233. June 28, 1984.

Marston, D. B. (1989) A Curriculum-based measurement approach to assessing academic performance: What it is and why do it. In M. Shinn (Ed.). *Curriculum-based measurement: Assessing special children*. New York: Guilford Press.

Mastropieri, M. A., Leinart, A., & Scruggs, T. E. (1999). Strategies to increase reading fluency. *Intervention in School and Clinic,* 34, 278-83, 92.

McDowell, R. L., Adamson, G. W., & Wood, F. H. (1982). *Teaching emotionally disturbed children.* Boston: Little, Brown and Company.

McGinnis, E., Goldstein, A. P. (1990). *Skill streaming in early childhood: teaching prosocial skills to the preschool and kindergarten child.* Champaign, IL: Research Press.

McLoughlin, J. A., & Lewis, R. B. (1986). *Assessing special students* (3rd ed.). Columbus, OH: Charles E. Merrill.

Mercer, C. D. (1987). *Students with learning disabilities.* (3rd. ed.). Merrill Publishing.

Mercer, C. D., & Mercer, A. R. (1985). *Teaching children with learning problems* (2nd ed.). Columbus, OH: Charles E. Merrill.

Meyen, E. L., Vergason, G. A., & Whelan, R. J. (Eds.). (1988). *Effective instructional strategies for exceptional children.* Denver, CO: Love Publishing.

Miller, L. K. (1980). *Principles of everyday behavior analysis* (2nd ed.). Monterey, CA: Brooks/Cole Publishing Company.

Mills v. Board of Education of the District of Columbia. 348 F. Supp. 866 (D.C. 1972).

Montierth, J. (2009). The C-V-C game. Retrieved from http://edweb.sdsu.edu/Courses/EDTEC670/Cardboard/Card/C/c-v-c_game.html]

Mopsik, S. L. & Agard, J. A. (Eds.) (1980). *An education handbook for parents of handicapped children.* Cambridge, MA: Abt Books.

Morris, C. G. (1985). *Psychology: An introduction* (5th ed.). Englewood Cliffs, NJ: Prentice-Hall.

Morris, J. & Demonbreun, C. (1980). *Learning styles* [Videocassettes & Manual series]. Northbrook, IL: Hubbard Scientific Company. (Project STRETCH [Strategies to Train Regular Educators to Teach Children with Handicaps], Module 15.

Morris, J. (1980). *Behavior modification*. [Videocassette and manual series]. Northbrook, IL: Hubbard Scientific Company. (Project STRETCH [Strategies to Train Regular Educators to Teach Children with Handicaps,] Module 16, Metropolitan Cooperative Educational Service Agency.).

Morris, R. J. (1985). *Behavior modification with exceptional children: Principles and practices.* Glenview, IL: Scott, Foresman and Company.

Morsink, C. V. (1984). *Teaching Special needs students in regular classrooms.* Boston: Little, Brown and Company.

Morsink, C. V., Thomas, C. C., & Correa, V. L. (1991). *Interactive teaming, consultation and collaboration in special programs.* New York: MacMillan Publishing.

Musselwhite, C. R. (1986). *Adaptive play for special needs children: strategies to enhance communication and learning.* San Diego: College Hill Press.

National Council of Teachers of Mathematics. (2000). *Principles and standards for school mathematics*. Reston, VA: National Council of Teachers of Mathematics.

National Reading Panel (2000). *Teaching children to read: An evidence-based assessment of the scientific research literature on reading and its implications for reading instruction : Reports of the subgroups.* Washington, D.C.: National Institute of Child Health and Human Development, National Institutes of Health.

North Central Georgia Learning Resources System/Child Serve. (1985). *Strategies handbook for classroom teachers.* Ellijay, GA.

Patton, J. R., Cronin, M. E., Polloway, E. A., Hutchinson, D., & Robinson, G. A. (1988). Curricular Considerations: A Life Skills Orientation. In Robinson, G. A., Patton, J. R., Polloway, E. A., & Sargent, L. R. (Eds.). *Best practices in mental disabilities.* Des Moines, IA: Iowa Department of Education, Bureau of Special Education.

Patton, J. R., Kauggman, J. M., Blackbourn, J. M., & Brown, B. G. (1991). *Exceptional children in focus* (5th ed.). New York: Macmillan.

Paul, J. L. & Epanchin, B. C. (1991). *Educating emotionally disturbed children and youth: Theories and practices for teachers.* (2nd ed.). New York: MacMillan.

Paul, J. L. (Ed.). (1981). *Understanding and working with parents of children with special needs.* New York: Holt, Rinehart and Winston.

Pellegrini, L. & Rooney Moreau, M. (1995). Pragmatics: The social uses of language. Professional development presentation, June 27, 1995.

Pennsylvania Association for Retarded Children v. Commonwealth of Pennsylvania, 343 F. Supp. 279 (E.D. Pa., 1972).

Phillips, V., & McCullough, L. (1990). Consultation based programming: Instituting the collaborative work ethic. *Exceptional Children,* 56, 291-304.

Pierangelo, R., & Giuliani, G. A. (2007). *EDM: The educator's diagnostic manual of disabilities and disorders.* San Francisco, CA: Jossey-Bass.

Podemski, R. S., Price, B. K., Smith, T. E. C., & Marsh, G. E., IL (1984). *Comprehensive administration of special education.* Rockville, MD: Aspen Systems Corporation.

Polloway, E. A., & Patton, J. R. (1989). *Strategies for teaching learners with special needs.* (5th ed.). New York: Merrill.

Polloway, E. A., Patton, J. R., Payne, J. S., & Payne, R. A. 1989). *Strategies for teaching learners with special needs* (4th ed.). Columbus, OH: Merrill Publishing.

Pugach, M. C., & Johnson, L. J. (1989a). The challenge of implementing collaboration between general and special education. *Exceptional children,* 56, 232-235.

Pugach, M. C., & Johnson, L. J. (1989b). Pre-referral interventions: Progress, problems, and challenges. *Exceptional Children,* 56, 217-226.

Radabaugh, M. T., & Yukish, J. F. (1982). *Curriculum and methods for the mildly handicapped.* Boston: Allyn and Bacon.

Ramsey R. W., & Ramsey, R. S. (1978). Educating the emotionally handicapped child in the public school setting. *Journal of Adolescence,* 13, 537-541.

Ramsey, R. S. (1981). Perceptions of disturbed and disturbing behavioral characteristics by school personnel. (Doctoral Dissertation, University of Florida) Dissertation Abstracts International, 42 (49), DA8203709.

Ramsey, R. S. (1986). Taking the practicum beyond the public school door. *Journal of Adolescence,* 21, 547-552.

Ramsey, R. S., (1988). *Preparatory guide for special education teacher competency tests.* Boston: Allyn and Bacon, Inc.

Ramsey, R. S., Dixon, M. J., & Smith, G. G.B. (1986) *Eyes on the special education: Professional knowledge teacher competency test.* Albany, GA: Southwest Georgia Learning Resources System Center.

Reinert, H. R. (1980). *Children in conflict: Educational strategies for the emotionally disturbed and behaviorally disordered.* (2nd ed.). St Louis, MO: The C. V. Mosby Company.

Robinson, F. P. (1961). *Effective study.* New York: Harper.

Robinson, G. A., Patton, J. R., Polloway, E. A., & Sargent, L. R. (Eds.) (1989a). *Best practices in mental disabilities.* Des Moines, IA: Iowa Department of Education, Bureau of Special Education.

Robinson, G. A., Patton, J. R., Polloway, E. A., & Sargent, L. R. (Eds.) (1989b). *Best practices in mental disabilities.* Renton, VA: The Division on Mental Retardation of the Council for Exceptional Children.

Rothstein, L. F. (1995). *Special education law* (2nd ed.). New York: Longman Publishers.

Sabatino, D. A., Sabatino, A. C., & Mann, L. (1983). *Discipline and behavioral management: A handbook of tactics, strategies, and programs.* Aspen Systems Corporation.

Salvia J., & Ysseldyke, J. E. (1991). *Assessment* (5th ed.). Boston: Houghton Mifflin.

Salvia, J. & Ysseldyke, J. E. (1995) *Assessment* (6th ed.). Boston: Houghton Mifflin.

Salvia, J., & Ysseldyke, J. E. (1985). *Assessment in special education (*3rd. ed.). Boston: Houghton Mifflin.

Sattler, J. M. (1982). *Assessment of children's intelligence and special abilities* (2nd ed.). Boston: Allyn and Bacon.

Schloss, P. J., & Sedlak, R. A.(1986). *Instructional methods for students with learning and behavior problems.* Boston: Allyn and Bacon.

Schloss, P. J., Harriman, N., & Pfiefer, K. (1985). Application of a sequential prompt reduction technique to the independent composition performance of behaviorally disordered youth. *Behavioral Disorders,* 11, 17-23.

Schmuck, R. A., & Schmuck, P. A. (1971). *Group processes in the classroom.* Dubuque, IA: William C. Brown Company.

Schubert, D. G. (1978). Your teaching - the tape recorder. *Reading improvement,* 15, 78-80.

Schulz, J. B., Carpenter, C. D., & Turnbull, A. P. (1991). *Mainstreaming exceptional students: A guide for classroom teachers.* Boston: Allyn and Bacon.

Semmel, M. I., Abernathy, T. V., Butera G., & Lesar, S. (1991). Teacher perception of the regular education initiative. *Exceptional Children,* 58, 3-23.

Shea, T. M., & Bauer, A. M. (1985). *Parents and teachers of exceptional students: A handbook for involvement.* Boston: Allyn and Bacon.

Simeonsson, R. J. (1986). *Psychological and development assessment of special children.* Boston: Allyn and Bacon.

Smith, C. R. (1991). *Learning disabilities: The interaction of learner, task, and setting.* Boston: Little, Brown, and Company.

Smith, D. D., & Luckasson, R. (1992). *Introduction to special education: Teaching in an age of challenge.* Boston: Allyn and Bacon.

Smith, J. E., & Patton, J. M. (1989). *A resource module on adverse causes of mild mental retardation.*

Smith, T. E.C., Finn, D. M., & Dowdy, C. A. (1993). *Teaching students with mild disabilities.* Fort Worth, TX: Harcourt Brace Jovanovich College Publishers.

Smith-Davis, J. (1989). *A national perspective on special education.* Keynote presentation at the GLRS/College/University Forum, Macon, GA.

Spafford, C., & Grosser, G. (1993). The social misperception syndrome in children with learning disabilities. *Journal of Learning Disabilities.* 26 (3), 178-189.

Stephens, T. M. (1976). *directive teaching of children with learning and behavioral disorders.* Columbus, OH Charles E. Merrill.

Sternberg, R. J. (1990). Thinking styles: Key to understanding Performance. *Phi Delta Kappan,* 71, 366-371.

Strickland, D. S., & Riley, S. (2006). *Early literacy: Policy and practice in the preschool years.* NIEER policy brief. New Brunswick, NJ: National Institute for Early Education Research.

Sulzer, B., & Mayer, G. R. (1972). *Behavior modification procedures for school personnel.* Hinsdale, IL: Dryden.

Swanson, H. L., & Malone, S. (1992). Social skills and learning disabilities: A meta-analysis of the literature. *School Psychology Review.* 21, 427.

Taberski, S. (2000). *On solid ground: Strategies for teaching reading K-3.* Portsmouth, NH: Heinemann.

Tateyama-Sniezek, K. M. (1990.) Cooperative Learning: Does it improve the academic achievement of students with handicaps? *Exceptional Children,* 57, 426-427.

Thiagarajan, S. (1976). Designing instructional games for handicapped learners. *Focus on Exceptional Children,* 7, 1-11.

Thomas, O. (1980). *Individualized instruction* [Videocassette & manual series]. Northbrook, IL: Hubbard Scientific Company. (Project STRETCH [Strategies to Train Regular Educators to Teach Children with Handicaps]. Module 14.

Thomas, O. (1980). *Spelling* [Videocassette & manual series]. (Project STRETCH [Strategies to Train Regular Educators to Teach Children with Handicaps]. Module 10.

Thornton, C. A., Tucker, B. F., Dossey, J. A., & Bazik, E. F. (1983). *Teaching mathematics to children with special needs.* Menlo Park, CA: Addison-Wesley.

Turkel, S. R., & Podel, D. M. (1984). Computer-assisted learning for mildly handicapped students. *Teaching Exceptional Children,* 16, 258-262.

Turnbull, A. P., Strickland, B. B., & Brantley, J. C. (1978). *Developing individualized education programs.* Columbus, OH: Charles E. Merrill.

U.S. Department of Education. (1993). *To assure the free appropriate public education of all children with disabilities: Fifteenth annual report to Congress on the implementation of the Individuals with Disabilities Education Act.* Washington, D. C.: U.S. Government Printing Office.

Walker, J. E., & Shea, T. M. (1991). *Behavior management: A practical approach for educators.* New York: Macmillan.

Wallace, G., & Kauffman, J. M. (1978). *Teaching children with learning problems.* Columbus, OH: Charles E. Merrill.

Wehman, P., & Mclaughlin, P. J. (1981). *Program development in special education.* New York: McGraw-Hill.

Wesson, C. L. (1991). Curriculum-based measurement and two models of follow-up consultation. *Exceptional Children,* 57, 246-256.

West, R. P., Young, K. R., & Spooner, F. (1990). Precision Teaching: An Introduction. *Teaching Exceptional Children,* 22, 4-9.

Wheeler, J. (1987). *Transitioning persons with moderate and severe disabilities from school to adulthood: What makes it work?* Materials Development Center, School of Education, and Human Services. University of Wisconsin-Stout.

Whiting, J., & Aultman, L. (1990). *Workshop for parents.* (Workshop materials). Albany, GA: Southwest Georgia Learning Resources System Center.

Wiederholt, J. L., Hammill, D. D., & Brown, V. L. (1983). *The resource room teacher: A guide to effective practices* (2nd ed.). Boston: Allyn and Bacon.

Wiig, E. H., & Semel, E. M. (1984). *Language assessment and intervention for the learning disabled.* (2nd ed.). Columbus, OH: Charles E. Merrill.

Willis, J. (2008). "Building a bridge from neuroscience to the classroom". *Phi Delta Kappan,* 89, 424-427.

Wolfgang, C. H., & Glickman, C. D.(1986). *Solving discipline problems: Strategies for classroom teachers* (2nd ed.). Boston: Allyn and Bacon.

Yssedlyke, J. E., Thurlow, M. L., Wotruba, J. W., Nania, Pa. A (1990). Instructional arrangements: Perceptions from general education. *Teaching Exceptional Children,* 22, 4-8.

Ysseldyke, J. E., Algozzine, B., & Thurlow, M. L. (1992). *Critical issues in special education* (2nd ed.). Boston: Houghton Mifflin Company.

Ysselkyke, J. E., Algozzine, B., (1990). *Introduction to special education* (2nd ed.). Boston: Houghton Mifflin.

Zargona, N., Vaughn, S., & Mcintosh, R. (1991). Social skills interventions and children with behavior problems: A review. *Behavior Disorders,* 16, 260-275.

Zigmond, N., & Baker, J. (1990). Mainstream experiences for learning disabled students (Project Meld): Preliminary report. *Exceptional Children, 57*, 176-185.

Zirpoli, T. J., & Melloy, K. J. (1993). *Behavior management.* New York: Merrill.

SAMPLE TEST

1. **Which of the following best describes how different areas of development impact each other? (Skill 1.1)**

   A. Development in other areas cannot occur until cognitive development is complete.
   B. Areas of development are interrelated and impact each other.
   C. Development in each area is independent of development in other areas.
   D. Development in one area leads to a decline in other areas.

2. **Poor moral development, lack of empathy, and behavioral excesses (such as aggression) are the most obvious characteristics of which behavioral disorder? (Skill 1.2)**

   A. Autism
   B. ADD-H
   C. Conduct disorder
   D. Pervasive developmental disorder

3. **A developmental delay may be indicated by : (Skill 1.3)**

   A. Second grader having difficulty buttoning clothing
   B. Stuttered response
   C. Kindergartner not having complete bladder control
   D. Withdrawn behavior

4. **Which of the following best explains why emotional upset and emotional abuse can reduce a child's classroom performance? (Skill 1.4)**

   A. They reduce the energy that students put towards schoolwork.
   B. They can result in the development of behavioral problems.
   C. They contribute to learning disorders such as dyslexia.
   D. Both A and B.

5. **Mark is a 6th grader. The teacher has noticed that he doesn't respond to simple requests like the other students in the class. If asked to erase the board, he may look, shake his head, and say no, but then he will clean the board. When the children gather together for recess, he joins them. Yet, the teacher observes that it takes him much longer to understand the rules to a game. Mark retains what he reads. Mark most likely has: (Skill 1.1)**

   A. Autism
   B. Tourette's syndrome
   C. Mental retardation
   D. A pragmatic language disability

6. A student on medication may have his or her dosage adjusted as the body grows. Parents may call and ask questions about their child's adjustment to the medication during the school day. During this time, you should: (Skill 2.2)

A. Observe the student for changes in behavior.
B. Watch for a progression of changed behavior.
C. Communicate concerns about sleepiness, etc., with the parent.
D. All of the above

7. Janice is a new student in your self-contained class. She is extremely quiet and makes little, if any, eye contact. Yesterday, she started to "parrot" what another student said. Today, the teacher became concerned when she did not follow directions and seemed not to even recognize his presence. Her cumulative file arrived today; when the teacher reviews the health section, it most likely will state that she is diagnosed with: (Skill 1.2 and 2.1)

A. Autism
B. Central processing disorder
C. Traumatic brain injury
D. Mental retardation

8. One common factor for students with all types of disabilities is that they are also likely to demonstrate difficulty with: (Skill 2.1)

A. Social skills
B. Cognitive skills
C. Problem-solving skills
D. Decision-making skills

9. In which of the following exceptionality categories may a student be considered for inclusion if his IQ score falls more than two standard deviations below the mean? (Skill 3.3)

A. Mental Retardation
B. Specific Learning Disabilities
C. Emotionally/Behaviorally Disordered
D. Gifted

10. Why is it of critical importance for teachers to ensure that students from different economic backgrounds have access to the resources they need to acquire the academic skills being taught? (Skill 3.4)

A. All students must work together on set tasks.
B. All students must achieve the same results in performance tasks.
C. All students must have equal opportunity for academic success.
D. All students must be fully included in classroom activities.

11. In the Grammatic Closure subtest of the Illinois Test of Psycholinguistic Abilities, the child is presented with a picture representing statements, such as: "Here is one die; here are two ____." This test is essentially a test of: (Skill 1.1)

A. Phonology
B. Syntax
C. Morphology
D. Semantics

12. A best practice for evaluating student performance and progress on IEPs is: (Skill 4.1 and 4.3)

A. Standardized assessment
B. Criterion referenced assessment
C. Rating scales
D. Norm-referenced evaluation

13. In exceptional student education, assessment is used to make decisions about all of the following EXCEPT: (Skill 4.2)

A. Screening and initial identification of children who may need services
B. Selection and evaluation of teaching strategies and programs
C. Determining the desired attendance rate of a student
D. Development of goals, objectives, and evaluation for the IEP

14. The Key Math Diagnostic Arithmetic Test is an individually administered test of math skills. It is comprised of fourteen subtests that are classified into the major math areas of content, operations, and applications for which subtest scores are reported. The test manual describes the population sample on which the test was normed, and reports data pertaining to reliability and validity. In addition, for each item in the test, a behavioral objective is presented. From the description, it can be determined that this achievement test is: (Skill 4.1)

A. Individually administered
B. Criterion-referenced
C. Diagnostic
D. All of the above

15. According to IDEA 2004, students with disabilities are to do what? (Skill 14.2)

A. Participate in the general education program to the fullest extent that is beneficial for them
B. Participate in a vocational training within the general education setting
C. Participate in a general education setting for physical education
D. Participate in a modified program that meets his or her needs

16. Which of the following is NOT one of the three aspects of the issue of fair assessment of individuals from minority groups that Slavia and Ysseldyke (1995) describe as particularly relevant to the assessment of students? (Skill 14.4)

A. Representation
B. Diversity
C. Acculturation
D. Language

17. Safeguards against bias and discrimination in the assessment of children include: (Skill 14.4)

A. The testing of a child in Standard English
B. The requirement to use one standardized test
C. The use of evaluative materials in the child's native language or other mode of communication
D. All testing administered by a certified, licensed psychologist

18. Children who write poorly might be given tests that allow oral responses unless the purpose for the test is to: (Skill 5.2)

A. Assess handwriting skills
B. Test for organization of thoughts
C. Answer questions pertaining to math reasoning
D. Assess rote memory

19. Which would NOT be an advantage of using a criterion-referenced test? (Skill 4.1)

A. Information about an individual's ability level is too specific for the purposes of the assessment.
B. It can pinpoint exact areas of weaknesses and strengths.
C. You can design them yourself.
D. You do not get comparative information.

20. Which is NOT an example of a standard score? (Skill 6.1)

A. T Score
B. Z Score
C. Standard Deviation
D. Stanine

21. Marisol has been included in a ninth grade language arts class. Although her behavior is satisfactory, and she likes the class, Marisol's reading level is about two years below grade level. The class has been assigned to read *Great Expectations* by Charles Dickens and write a report. What intervention would be LEAST successful in helping Marisol complete this assignment? (Skill 11.1 and 11.2)

A. Having Marisol listen to a taped recording while following the story in the regular text
B. Giving her a modified version of the story
C. Telling her to choose a different book that she can read
D. Showing a film to the entire class and comparing and contrasting it with the book

22. Which of the following is NOT an appropriate assessment modification or accommodation for a student with a learning disability? (Skill 5.2)

A. Having the test read orally to the student
B. Writing down the student's dictated answers
C. Allowing the student to take the assessment home to complete
D. Extending the time for the student to take the assessment

23. An emphasis on instructional remediation and individualized instruction in problem areas, with the student receiving instruction in a separate classroom, are characteristics of which model of service delivery? (Skill 12.1 and 12.2)

A. Regular classroom
B. Consultant teacher
C. Itinerant teacher
D. Resource room

24. Parent contact should first begin when: (Skill 7.3)

A. You are informed the child will be your student
B. The student fails a test
C. The student exceeds others on a task
D. A team meeting is coming and you have had no previous replies to letters

25. For which of the following uses are standardized individual tests MOST appropriate? (Skill 4.3 and 5.1)

A. Screening students to determine possible need for special education services
B. Evaluation of special education curricula
C. Tracking of gifted students
D. Evaluation of a student for eligibility and placement, or individualized program planning, in special education

26. To facilitate learning instructional objectives: (Skill 7.5)

A. They should be taken from a grade-level spelling list
B. They should be written and shared
C. They should be arranged in order of similarity
D. They should be taken from a scope and sequence

27. Which of the following words describes appropriate IEP objectives? (Skill 7.7)

A. Specific
B. Observable
C. Measurable
D. All of the above

28. Scott is in middle school but still makes statements like, "I gotted new high-tops yesterday," and "I saw three mans in the front office." Language interventions for Scott would target: (Skill 1.1)

A. Morphology
B. Syntax
C. Pragmatics
D. Semantics

29. Which of the following is NOT a feature of effective classroom rules? (Skill 8.2)

A. They are about four to six in number
B. They are negatively stated
C. Consequences are consistent and immediate
D. They can be tailored to individual teaching goals and teaching styles

30. Jonathan has Attention Deficit Hyperactivity Disorder (ADHD). He is in a regular classroom and appears to be doing okay. However, his teacher does not want John in her class because he will not obey her when she asks him to stop doing a repetitive action such as tapping his foot. The teacher sees this as distracting during tests. John needs: (Skill 7.1)

A. An IEP
B. A substantially separate classroom
C. A 504 Plan for the regular classroom
D. A one on one aide in the classroom

31. The transition activities that have to be addressed, unless the IEP team finds it uncalled for, include all of the following EXCEPT: (Skill 8.4)

A. Instruction
B. Volunteer opportunities
C. Community experiences
D. Development of objectives related to employment and other post-school areas

32. When a student begins to use assistive technology, it is important for the teacher to have a clear outline as to when and how the equipment should be used. Why? (Skill 8.5)

A. To establish a level of accountability with the student.
B. To establish that the teacher has responsibility for the equipment that is in use in his or her room.
C. To establish that the teacher is responsible for the usage of the assistive technology.
D. To establish a guideline for evaluation.

33. Changes in requirements for an IEP's Current Levels of performance require: (Skill 7.4)

A. Parent/Guardian must attend either by phone conference or in person.
B. CSE chair must tell parents when child has unrealistic goals
C. Student voice in each Present Level of Performance
D. Teachers must write post adult outcomes assigning a student to a specific field

34. Effective management transition involves all of the following EXCEPT: (Skill 9.3)

A. Keeping students informed of the sequencing of instructional activities
B. Using group fragmentation
C. Changing the schedule frequently to maintain student interest
D. Using academic transition signals

35. Which of the following are critical to the success for the exceptional student placed in a general education classroom? (Skill 9.4)

A. Access to appropriate accommodations and modifications
B. Support from the special education teacher
C. The general education teacher's belief that the student will profit from the placement
D. All of the above

36. Which of the following should be avoided when writing objectives for social behavior? (Skill 10.1)

A. Non-specific adverbs
B. Behaviors stated as verbs
C. Criteria for acceptable performance
D. Conditions where the behavior is expected to be performed

37. Criteria for choosing behaviors that are most in need of change involve all EXCEPT the following: (Skill 10.2)

A. Observations across settings to rule out certain interventions
B. Pinpointing the behavior that is the poorest fit with the child's environment
C. The teacher's concern about what is the most important behavior to target
D. Analysis of the environmental reinforcers

38. A BIP (Behavior Intervention Plan) is written to teach positive behavior. Which element listed below is NOT a standard feature of the plan? (Skill 10.3)

A. Identification of behavior to be modified
B. Strategies to implement the replacement behavior
C. Statement of distribution
D. Team creation of BIP

39. Teacher feedback, task completion, and a sense of pride over mastery or accomplishment of a skill are examples of: (Skill 10.7)

A. Extrinsic reinforcers
B. Behavior modifiers
C. Intrinsic reinforcers
D. Positive feedback

40. Crisis intervention methods are above all concerned with: (Skill 10.6)

A. Safety and well-being of the staff and students
B. Stopping the inappropriate behavior
C. Preventing the behavior from occurring again
D. The student learning that outbursts are inappropriate

41. Justin, a second grader, is reinforced if he is on task at the end of each ten-minute block of time that the teacher observes him. This is an example of what type of schedule? (Skill 10.7)

A. Continuous
B. Fixed interval
C. Fixed ratio
D. Variable ratio

42. A money bingo game was designed by Ms. Johnson for use with her middle grade students. Cards were constructed with different combinations of coins pasted on each of the nine spaces. Ms. Johnson called out various amounts of change (e.g., 30 cents), and students were instructed to cover the coin combinations on their cards that equaled the amount of change (e.g., two dimes and two nickels, three dimes, and so on). The student who had the first bingo was required to add the coins in each of the spaces covered and tell the amounts before being declared the winner. Five of Ms. Johnson's sixth graders played the game during the ten minutes of free activity time following math the first day the game was constructed. Which of the following attributes are present in this game in this situation? (Skill 11.2)

A. Accompanied by simple, uncomplicated rules
B. Of brief duration, permitting replay
C. Age appropriateness
D. All of the above

43. Transfer of learning occurs when:
(Skill 11.3)

A. Experience with one task influences performance on another task
B. Content can be explained orally
C. Student experiences the "I got it!" syndrome
D. Curricular objective is exceeded

44. Taiquan's parents are divorced and have joint custody. They both have requested to be present at the IEP meeting. You call to make sure that they received the letter informing them of the coming IEP meeting. Taiquan's father did not receive the notification and is upset. You should:
(Skill 12.1)

A. Tell him that you could review the meeting with him later
B. Ask him if he can adjust his schedule
C. Tell him you can reschedule the meeting
D. Ask him to coordinate a time for the IEP meeting to meet with his ex-wife

45. Which of these would not be considered a valid attempt to contact a parent for an IEP meeting?
(Skill 12.2)

A. Telephone call
B. Copy of correspondence
C. Message left on answering machine
D. Record of home visits

46. Otumba is a 16 year old in your class who recently came from Nigeria. The girls in your class have come to you to complain about the way he treats them in a sexist manner. When they complain, you reflect that this is also the way he treats adult females. You have talked to Otumba before about appropriate behavior. What should you do first?
(Skill 12.3)

A. Complain to the principal
B. Ask for a parent-teacher conference
C. Check to see if this is a cultural norm in his country
D. Create a behavior contract for him to follow

47. The integrated approach to learning utilizes all available resources to address student needs. What are the resources? (Skill 13.1)

A. The student, his or her parents, and the teacher.
B. The teacher, the parents, and the special education team.
C. The teacher, the student, and an administrator to perform needed interventions
D. The student, his or her parents, the teacher, and community resources.

48. According to IDEA law, a student cannot be removed from school for disciplinary reasons if: (Skill 10.3)

A. The student's behavior represents a danger to himself or others
B. The student's misbehavior is a manifestation of the student's disability
C. The student is under age 14
D. The school does not have parent permission

49. The ability to supply specific instructional materials, programs, and methods, as well as the ability to influence environmental learning variables, are advantages of which service model for exceptional students? (Skill 13.3)

A. Regular classroom
B. Consultant teacher
C. Itinerant teacher
D. Resource room

50. Knowledge of evaluation strategies, program interventions, and types of data are examples of which variable for a successful consultation program? (Skill 13.4)

A. People
B. Process
C. Procedural implementation
D. Academic preparation

51. Janice requires occupational therapy and speech therapy services. What must her teacher do to ensure her needs are met? (Skill 13.5)

A. Watch the services being rendered
B. Schedule collaboratively
C. Ask for services to be given in a push-in model
D. Ask to be trained to give the service him or herself

52. Which of these is the best resource a teacher can have to reach a student? (Skill 13.6)

A. Contact with the parents/guardians
B. A successful behavior modification exam
C. A listening ear
D. Gathered scaffold approach to teaching

53. The early 19th century is considered a period of great importance in the field of special education because principles presently used in working with exceptional students were formulated by Itard. These principles included: (Skill 14.1)

A. Individualized instruction
B. Sequence of tasks
C. Functional life-like skills curriculum
D. All of the above

54. How was the training of special education teachers changed by the No Child Left Behind Act of 2002? (Skill 14.2)

A. It required all special education teachers to be certified in reading and math
B. It required all special education teachers to take the same coursework as general education teachers
C. If a special education teacher is teaching a core subject, he or she must meet the standard of a highly qualified teacher in that subject
D. All of the above

55. NCLB (No Child Left Behind Act), was signed on January 8, 2002. What does NCLB address? (Skill 14.2)

A. Accessibility of curriculum to the student
B. Administrative incentives for school improvements
C. A national standard for standards and learning proficiency
D. Accountability of school personnel for student achievement

56. What legislation started FAPE? (Skill 14.2)

A. Section 504
B. EHCA
C. IDEA
D. Education Amendment 1974

57. Satisfaction of the LRE requirement means: (Skill 14.2)

A. The school is providing the best services it can offer
B. The school is providing the best services the district has to offer
C. The student is being educated with the fewest special education services necessary
D. The student is being educated in the least restrictive setting that meets his or her needs

58. Which law specifically states that "Full Inclusion is not the only way for a student to reach his/her highest potential?" (Skill 14.2)

A. IDEA
B. IDEA 97
C. IDEA 2004
D. Part 200

59. Teachers have a professional obligation to do all of the following EXCEPT: (Skill 15.1)

A. Join a professional organization such as CEC or LDA
B. Attend in-services or seminars related to your position
C. Stay after school to help students
D. Advise school clubs

60. One of the most important goals of the special education teacher is to foster and create with the student: (Skill 8.3)

A. Handwriting skills
B. Self-advocacy
C. An increased level of reading
D. Logical reasoning

61. Teachers must keep meticulous records. They are required to share all of them with the student's parent/guardian EXCEPT: (Skill 15.8)

A. Daily attendance records
B. Grade reports
C. Teacher's personal notes
D. Discipline notice placed in cumulative record

SAMPLE ESSAY QUESTIONS

TEST I: ELEMENTARY EDUCATION

Question 1: Recent research has highlighted the importance of reading fluency in improving overall reading comprehension. Describe the nature of reading fluency, its relationship to reading comprehension, and methods you would use to promote it in an early elementary class.

SAMPLE ANSWER:

In its report on teaching children to read (2000), the National Reading Panel defined fluency; the ability to read with speed, accuracy and proper expression without conscious attention and to handle both word recognition and comprehension simultaneously. A fluent reader reads accurately at a speed appropriate to the text, and with expression and phrasing that show an understanding of what is being read. Readers who are not fluent read slowly, often one word at a time or sounding out individual words haltingly, without expression or comprehension. They often leave out words or substitute other words for what is in the text. Measures of fluency typically include accuracy, speed, and prosody, or expression. Running records are frequently used to assess fluency.

Fluency is an important skill when learning to read because it helps readers to progress from the word recognition stage to one where they can understand what they read. When readers don't have to spend time focusing on reading individual words, they can group words together to form ideas, which leads to comprehension. Not only can they grasp the main idea of the text, but they can also make connections between the text and their prior knowledge and events in their own lives.

In order to improve reading fluency, students need practice reading connected text that has been chosen to be consistent with their reading level. I would give students repeated opportunities to read aloud to the teacher, to aides, and to one another. Arranging for the class to read to students at a lower grade level (say, reading to Kindergarten buddies, etc) can provide fun practice of this sort. I would provide ample adult modeling of appropriate oral reading. I would first describe the skills they should practice in a short mini-lesson. I would read a passage inappropriately, demonstrating common mistakes as well as appropriate prosody, etc. I would be sure to read aloud to students frequently. Other techniques I might use would include:

Arranging for students to listen to stories on tape or CD, then having them read the same story to a teacher

Holding whole class or small group choral reading—choral reading provides struggling readers with lots of external cues to help them read fluently.

I would arrange reader's theatre activities with stories like *Anansi and the Talking Melon*, a story with lots of dialogue. Students enjoy theatre and will be practicing their oral fluency skills every time they read.

I would arrange for a "radio" time when children could practice reading text like a news or weather announcer, anything to let them practice reading aloud.

Question #2: You are an elementary teacher of math. Other teachers notice that your students are not spending much time at their desks writing down problems. They are playing with all sorts of blocks, chips, and objects, arranging and rearranging them, talking about them and it's all actually rather noisy. They ask why your kids spend so much time playing. How do you justify the way you run your math class?

SAMPLE ANSWER:

I would point out that the NCTM standards state that children should spend lots of time actively exploring math concepts and *doing* math things. There should be lots of hands-on math at the first stage of math learning, the *concept stage.* At this level, children need lots of interaction with manipulatives. They need to interact intensively with a variety of objects, to see patterns, combinations and relationships among the objects before they can internalize concepts. When introducing new concepts, this is the level at which the child will spend the most time. I know that it is not enough for the teacher to use the objects to demonstrate concepts; the child needs to *discover* concepts and relationships. My role is to ask questions that trigger higher order thinking and learning from the child.

I would point out that all this "playing" IS actually learning math. Not only are they internalizing math concepts, but they are learning how to solve problems together. I have some groups looking for patterns and others making patterns for them to find. I have some groups counting objects into cups that will only hold a specified number, then transferring them all to another level of cup when they reach a certain amount as they explore different base number systems. They work together to find out how to get 45 chips can be put into 8 cups, and how many will be left over, etc.

I would point out that I try to keep the math activities as close to the real uses for which they will need math as possible. Once they are confident in the concrete concepts, I will introduce connections to the more symbolic math that is familiar to adults. We will begin by drawing pictures or using symbols with the objects present (the *connecting level* of instruction). They will begin to write down problems and solutions, design ways to draw and explain what they are doing in symbols and words.

This foundation in concrete manipulation of concepts followed by an increasing use of symbols will provide a strong foundation for later math concepts and work.

TEST II SPECIAL EDUCATION SAMPLE ESSAY QUESTIONS:

Question #3: You are a special education teacher in an elementary school. One of your students, who has autism, is receiving academic instruction in a general education class. The general education teacher approaches you for information regarding strategies for working with this student.

Identify at least two characteristics of autism. Identify strategies to address those characteristics of autism within the general classroom setting.

Sample Response:

Characteristics of Autism:

- Apparent sensory deficit
- Severe affect isolation
- Self-stimulation
- Tantrums and self-injurious behavior
- Echolalia
- Severe deficits in behavior and self-care skills

In working with a student with autism within the general education classroom, the teacher must be aware of the student's sensory deficits and often the need for sensory stimulation. Strategies such as allowing for movement are helpful. Some teachers allow the student to be out of his/her seat or to sit on the floor, or define a specific "space" for the student. Students might be allowed to use "squeeze balls" or other items.

Teachers should also be aware that many students with autism are highly sensitive to sound. Loud noises, such as the fire alarm can be particularly stressful. If possible, warn the student ahead of time. If a warning is not possible, provide reassurance and explanation about what is happening. For general classroom noises, some students are allowed to wear headphones to "tune out" noises.

Students with autism need structure. A classroom schedule, preferably a picture schedule works well and an individual schedule for the student is ideal. If the teacher must deviate from the regular schedule for an assembly or special event, warn the student with autism about the schedule change. It can be helpful to have a visual signal to use when transitions are necessary.

For the higher functioning student with autism, it is important to establish clear rules and expectations for behavior. The teacher needs to provide the student with a means of "escape" if he/she senses that he/she is experiencing stress or sensory overload. This could mean a trip to the restroom or to get a drink or water or a visit to the counselor if the student feels the need.

Many students with autism are highly visual. Use pictures or actual objects as much as possible.

Question #4: Lamar is an eighth grade student who has been identified as having ADD. He has been having behavioral difficulties in school. The IEP team has conducted a Functional Behavioral Assessment (FBA) and has targeted these behaviors: Blurts out in class, talks without permission

The team determines that the antecedents to these behaviors are:

- Independent work
- Teacher directive
- Teacher correction
- During unstructured time.

The behaviors occur on an average of 15 to 20 times a day throughout the school day.

Develop a Behavior Intervention Plan for this student, following this format:

I. Target Behaviors and Definitions
II. Functional Behavioral Assessment and Identified Function of the Target Behavior
III. Intervention Strategies (Positive Behavioral Supports)
   A. Modifications to the Identified Antecedents
   B. Alternative Behaviors (meet the same function as the target behavior)
IV. Reinforcers and Consequences
   A. Reinforcers
   B. Consequences
V. Action Plan for Data Collection and Monitoring of BIP

Sample Response:

I. Target Behavior and Definitions: Lamar talks out in class without permission.

II. Identified Function of the Behavior: gain attention, gain power & control

III. Intervention Strategies: Staff will remind Lamar to raise his hand before speaking. Staff will only acknowledge Lamar when he raises his hand. Staff will reinforce class rules. Staff will praise or reward Lamar for following the steps.

   A. Modifications to the Identified Antecedents: Lamar will raise his hand to talk to the teacher or class. He will start assignments immediately after they are given. He will ignore other things going on around him.
   B. Alternative Behaviors: Lamar will raise his hand and wait to be acknowledged before speaking. He will write things down that he would normally shout out in class. He can tell the teacher later and does not need to worry about forgetting to say whatever it is he needs to say.

IV. Reinforcers and Consequences:

   A. Reinforcers: Reminders, positive reinforcement, positive attention when on task, reward chart to be submitted for game time on computer
   B. Consequences: Redirection, reminders, private conference with student, loss of computer game time, call parents, office referral.

V. Action Plan: Data will be collected by each teacher on a daily basis using an interval time checklist. Special education teacher will compile weekly report.

ANSWER KEY

1. B
2. C
3. A
4. D
5. D
6. D
7. A
8. A
8. A
10. C
11. C
12. B
13. C
14. D
15. A
16. B
17. C
18. A
19. D
20. C
21. C
22. C
23. D
24. A
25. D
26. C
27. D
28. A
29. B
30. C
31. B
32. A
33. C
34. C
35. D
36. A
37. C
38. C
39. C
40. A
41. B
42. D
43. A
44. C
45. C
46. C
47. D
48. B
49. B
50. B
51. B
52. A
53. D
54. C
55. D
56. A
57 D
58. C
59. D
60. B
61. C

SAMPLE TEST WITH RATIONALES

1. Which of the following best describes how different areas of development impact each other?
(Skill 1.1)

A. Development in other areas cannot occur until cognitive development is complete.
B. Areas of development are interrelated and impact each other.
C. Development in each area is independent of development in other areas.
D. Development in one area leads to a decline in other areas.

Answer B: Areas of development are interrelated and impact each other.

Child development does not occur in a vacuum. Each element of development impacts other elements of development. For example, as cognitive development progresses, social development often follows. The reason for this is that all areas of development are fairly interrelated.

2. Poor moral development, lack of empathy, and behavioral excesses (such as aggression) are the most obvious characteristics of which behavioral disorder?
(Skill 1.2)

A. Autism
B. ADD-H
C. Conduct disorder
D. Pervasive developmental disorder

Answer C: Conduct disorder

A student with conduct disorder or social maladjustment displays behaviors and/or values that are in conflict with the school, home, or community. The characteristics listed are all behavioral/social.

3. A developmental delay may be indicated by :
(Skill 1.3)

A. Second grader having difficulty buttoning clothing
B. Stuttered response
C. Kindergartner not having complete bladder control
D. Withdrawn behavior

Answer A: Second grader having difficulty buttoning clothing

Buttoning clothing is generally mastered by the age of four. While many children have full bladder control by age four, it is not unusual for "embarrassing accidents" to occur.

4. Which of the following best explains why emotional upset and emotional abuse can reduce a child's classroom performance?
(Skill 1.4)

A. They reduce the energy that students put towards schoolwork.
B. They can result in the development of behavioral problems.
C. They contribute to learning disorders such as dyslexia.
D. Both A and B.

Answer D: Both A and B

Although cognitive ability is not lost due to abuse, neglect, emotional upset, or lack of verbal interaction, the child will most likely not be able to provide as much intellectual energy as the child would if none of these things were present. In addition, prolonged abuse or neglect can result in behavioral problems that also interfere with school performance. Learning disorders such as Dyslexia are not the result of abuse or neglect.

5. **Mark is a 6th grader. The teacher has noticed that he doesn't respond to simple requests like the other students in the class. If asked to erase the board, he may look, shake his head, and say no, but then he will clean the board. When the children gather together for recess, he joins them. Yet, the teacher observes that it takes him much longer to understand the rules to a game. Mark retains what he reads. Mark most likely has:**
(Skill 1.1)

A. Autism
B. Tourette's syndrome
C. Mental retardation
D. A pragmatic language disability

Answer D: A pragmatic language disability

Pragmatics is the basic understanding of a communicator's intent, particularly when nonverbal cues and body language are involved. The issue here is Mark's ability to respond correctly to another person.

6. **A student on medication may have his or her dosage adjusted as the body grows. Parents may call and ask questions about their child's adjustment to the medication during the school day. During this time, you should:**
(Skill 2.2)

A. Observe the student for changes in behavior.
B. Watch for a progression of changed behavior.
C. Communicate concerns about sleepiness, etc., with the parent.
D. All of the above

Answer D: All of the above.

If you have students on medication, it is important to communicate with the parents about any changes in behavior, as the students' bodies are constantly growing. Being informed about the medication(s) your students are on allows you to assist the students and the parents as an objective observer.

7. Janice is a new student in your self-contained class. She is extremely quiet and makes little, if any, eye contact. Yesterday, she started to "parrot" what another student said. Today, the teacher became concerned when she did not follow directions and seemed not to even recognize his presence. Her cumulative file arrived today; when the teacher reviews the health section, it most likely will state that she is diagnosed with:
(Skill 1.2 and 2.1)

A. Autism
B. Central processing disorder
C. Traumatic brain injury
D. Mental retardation

Answer A: Autism

Janice is exhibiting three symptoms of autism. While a child may demonstrate some of these behaviors if he or she is diagnosed with traumatic brain injury or mental retardation, the combination of these symptoms is more likely to indicate autism.

8. One common factor for students with all types of disabilities is that they are also likely to demonstrate difficulty with:
(Skill 2.1)

A. Social skills
B. Cognitive skills
C. Problem-solving skills
D. Decision-making skills

Answer A: Social skills

Students with disabilities (in all areas) may demonstrate difficulty in social skills. For a student with a hearing impairment, social skills may be difficult because of not hearing social language. However, the emotionally disturbed student may have difficulty because of a special type of psychological disturbance. An autistic student, as a third example, would be unaware of the social cues given with voice, facial expression, and body language. Each of these students would need a different type of social skills instruction.

9. In which of the following exceptionality categories may a student be considered for inclusion if his IQ score falls more than two standard deviations below the mean? (Skill 3.3)

A. Mental Retardation
B. Specific Learning Disabilities
C. Emotionally/Behaviorally Disordered
D. Gifted

Answer A: Mental Retardation

Only about 1 to 1.5% of the population fit the AAMD's definition of mental retardation. They fall outside the two standard deviations limit for special learning disabilities and emotionally/behaviorally disordered.

10. Why is it of critical importance for teachers to ensure that students from different economic backgrounds have access to the resources they need to acquire the academic skills being taught? (Skill 3.4)

A. All students must work together on set tasks.
B. All students must achieve the same results in performance tasks.
C. All students must have equal opportunity for academic success.
D. All students must be fully included in classroom activities.

Answer C: All students must have equal opportunity for academic success.

The economic backgrounds of students can impact the resources they have. Regardless of the positive or negative impacts on the students' education from outside sources, it is the teacher's responsibility to ensure that all students in the classroom have an equal opportunity for academic success. This includes ensuring that all students have equal access to the resources needed to acquire the skills being taught.

11. In the Grammatic Closure subtest of the Illinois Test of Psycholinguistic Abilities, the child is presented with a picture representing statements, such as: "Here is one die; here are two ____." This test is essentially a test of:
(Skill 1.1)

A. Phonology
B. Syntax
C. Morphology
D. Semantics

Answer C: Morphology

Morphology refers to the rules governing the structure of words and how to put morphemes together to make words. "Dice" is the irregular plural form of "Die." Changing the ending to 'ce' is using a morphological structure. Syntax is a system of rules for sentence formation, not word formation.

- Phonology: the study of significant units of speech sounds
- Syntax: a system of rules for making grammatically correct sentences
- Semantics: the study of the relationships between words and grammatical forms in a language, as well as the underlying meaning

12. A best practice for evaluating student performance and progress on IEPs is:
(Skill 4.1and 4.3)

A. Standardized assessment
B. Criterion referenced assessment
C. Rating scales
D. Norm-referenced evaluation

Answer B: Criterion Referenced assessment

Evaluating progress on an IEP requires criterion-based assessment because one is evaluating the extent to which the student has met certain criteria (the goals and objectives in the IEP). Such criterion based assessment can be formal or informal, commercial or teacher designed, as long as it assesses the relevant criteria. Standardized assessments may or may not be criterion based ("standardized" refers to the manner in which the test is administered, not its content). Norm referenced assessments are designed to compare the student to grade or age peers, not whether the student has met certain learning goals. Rating scales are assessments of behavioral or emotional variables, not learning goals.

13. In exceptional student education, assessment is used to make decisions about all of the following EXCEPT: (Skill 4.2)

A. Screening and initial identification of children who may need services
B. Selection and evaluation of teaching strategies and programs
C. Determining the desired attendance rate of a student
D. Development of goals, objectives, and evaluation for the IEP

Answer C: Determining the desired attendance rate of a student

School attendance is required, and assessment is not necessary to measure a child's attendance rate.

14. The Key Math Diagnostic Arithmetic Test is an individually administered test of math skills. It is comprised of fourteen subtests that are classified into the major math areas of content, operations, and applications for which subtest scores are reported. The test manual describes the population sample on which the test was normed, and reports data pertaining to reliability and validity. In addition, for each item in the test, a behavioral objective is presented. From the description, it can be determined that this achievement test is: (Skill 4.1)

A. Individually administered
B. Criterion-referenced
C. Diagnostic
D. All of the above

Answer D: All of the above

The test has a limited content designed to measure to what extent the student has mastered specific areas in math. The expressions "individually administered" and "diagnostic" appear in the description of the test.

15. According to IDEA 2004, students with disabilities are to do what? (Skill 14.2)

A. Participate in the general education program to the fullest extent that is beneficial for them
B. Participate in a vocational training within the general education setting
C. Participate in a general education setting for physical education
D. Participate in a modified program that meets his or her needs

Answer A: Participate in the general education program to the fullest extent that is beneficial for them

Answers B, C, and D are all possible settings related to participating in the general education setting to the fullest extent possible. This still can mean that a student's LRE may restrict him or her to a 12:1:1 for the entire school day.

16. Which of the following is NOT one of the three aspects of the issue of fair assessment of individuals from minority groups that Slavia and Ysseldyke (1995) describe as particularly relevant to the assessment of students? (Skill 14.4)

A. Representation
B. Diversity
C. Acculturation
D. Language

Answer B: Diversity

The issue of fair assessment for individuals from minority groups has a long history in law, philosophy, and education. Individuals from diverse backgrounds need to be represented in assessment materials. It is also important that individuals from different backgrounds receive opportunities to acquire the tested skills, information, and values. The language and concepts that comprise test items should be unbiased, and students should be familiar with terminology and references to which the language is being made when they are administered tests, especially when the results of the tests are going to be used for decision-making purposes.

17. Safeguards against bias and discrimination in the assessment of children include: (Skill 14.4)

A. The testing of a child in Standard English
B. The requirement to use one standardized test
C. The use of evaluative materials in the child's native language or other mode of communication
D. All testing administered by a certified, licensed psychologist

Answer C: The use of evaluative materials in the child's native language or other mode of communication

The law requires that the child be evaluated in his or her native language or mode of communication. Having a licensed psychologist evaluate the child does not meet the criteria if it is not done in the child's normal mode of communication.

18. Children who write poorly might be given tests that allow oral responses unless the purpose for the test is to: (Skill 5.2)

A. Assess handwriting skills
B. Test for organization of thoughts
C. Answer questions pertaining to math reasoning
D. Assess rote memory

Answer A: Assess handwriting skills

It is necessary to have the child write if a teacher is assessing his or her skill in that domain.

19. Which would NOT be an advantage of using a criterion-referenced test?
(Skill 4.1)

A. Information about an individual's ability level is too specific for the purposes of the assessment.
B. It can pinpoint exact areas of weaknesses and strengths.
C. You can design them yourself.
D. You do not get comparative information.

Answer D: You do not get comparative information

Rationale: Criterion-referenced tests measure mastery of content rather than performance compared to others. Test items are usually prepared from specific educational objectives and may be teacher-made or commercially prepared. Scores are measured by the percentage of correct items for a skill (e.g., adding and subtracting fractions with like denominators).

20. Which is NOT an example of a standard score?
(Skill 6.1)

A. T Score
B. Z Score
C. Standard Deviation
D. Stanine

Answer C: Standard Deviation

A, B, and D are all standardized scores. Stanines are whole number scores from 1 to 9, each representing a wide range of raw scores. Standard deviation is not a score. It measures how widely scores vary from the mean.

21. Marisol has been included in a ninth grade language arts class. Although her behavior is satisfactory, and she likes the class, Marisol's reading level is about two years below grade level. The class has been assigned to read *Great Expectations* by Charles Dickens and write a report. What intervention would be LEAST successful in helping Marisol complete this assignment? (Skill 11.1 and 11.2)

A. Having Marisol listen to a taped recording while following the story in the regular text
B. Giving her a modified version of the story
C. Telling her to choose a different book that she can read
D. Showing a film to the entire class and comparing and contrasting it with the book

Answer C: Telling her to choose a different book that she can read

A, B, and D are positive interventions. C is not a positive intervention. In addition, it effectively *removes her from the rest of the class,* and **denies** her **access** to the same curriculum the other students have. The other interventions constitute valid accommodations that allow her to access the same curriculum the students without disabilities have.

22. Which of the following is NOT an appropriate assessment modification or accommodation for a student with a learning disability? (Skill 5.2)

A. Having the test read orally to the student
B. Writing down the student's dictated answers
C. Allowing the student to take the assessment home to complete
D. Extending the time for the student to take the assessment

Answer: C: Allowing the student to take the assessment home to complete

Unless a student is homebound, the student should take assessments in class or in another classroom setting. All the other items listed are appropriate accommodations.

23. An emphasis on instructional remediation and individualized instruction in problem areas, with the student receiving instruction in a separate classroom, are characteristics of which model of service delivery?
(Skill 12.1 and 12.2)

A. Regular classroom
B. Consultant teacher
C. Itinerant teacher
D. Resource room

Answer D: Resource room

The resource room can serve as a bridge to inclusion.

24. Parent contact should first begin when:
(Skill 7.3)

A. You are informed the child will be your student
B. The student fails a test
C. The student exceeds others on a task
D. A team meeting is coming and you have had no previous replies to letters

Answer A: You are informed the child will be your student

Student contact should begin as a getting-to-know-you piece, which allows the teacher to begin on a non-judgmental platform. It also allows the parent to receive a view that you are a professional who is willing to work with them.

25. For which of the following uses are standardized individual tests MOST appropriate?
(Skill 4.3 and 5.1)

A. Screening students to determine possible need for special education services
B. Evaluation of special education curricula
C. Tracking of gifted students
D. Evaluation of a student for eligibility and placement, or individualized program planning, in special education

Answer D: Evaluation of a student for eligibility and placement, or individualized program planning, in special education

Standardized tests are useful for these decisions, because they are very objective and can provide a wide range of data, from comparison with grade peers (a norm-referenced test), to mastery of certain skills (criterion referenced test), to pinpointing specific areas of strength or weakness (intelligence tests or psychological tests).

26. To facilitate learning instructional objectives:
(Skill 7.5)

A. They should be taken from a grade-level spelling list
B. They should be written and shared
C. They should be arranged in order of similarity
D. They should be taken from a scope and sequence

Answer C: They should be arranged in order of similarity

To facilitate learning, instructional objectives should be arranged in order according to their patterns of similarity. Objectives involving similar responses should be closely sequenced; thus, the possibility for positive transfer is stressed. Likewise, learning objectives that involve different responses should be programmed within instructional procedures in the most appropriate way possible.

27. Which of the following words describes appropriate IEP objectives? (Skill 7.7)

A. Specific
B. Observable
C. Measurable
D. All of the above

Answer D: All of the above.

All objectives in an Individual Education Plan should be specific, observable, and measurable. If they are not observable and measurable, it will be impossible to determine whether they have been met. If they are vague and nonspecific the same difficulty applies.

28. Scott is in middle school but still makes statements like, "I gotted new high-tops yesterday," and "I saw three mans in the front office." Language interventions for Scott would target: (Skill 1.1)

A. Morphology
B. Syntax
C. Pragmatics
D. Semantics

Answer A: Morphology

Morphology is the process of combining phonemes into meaningful words. It includes inflections and affixes related to tense and number.

29. Which of the following is NOT a feature of effective classroom rules? (Skill 8.2)

A. They are about four to six in number
B. They are negatively stated
C. Consequences are consistent and immediate
D. They can be tailored to individual teaching goals and teaching styles

Answer B: They are negatively stated

Rules should be positively stated, and they should follow the other three features listed.

30. Jonathan has Attention Deficit Hyperactivity Disorder (ADHD). He is in a regular classroom and appears to be doing okay. However, his teacher does not want John in her class because he will not obey her when she asks him to stop doing a repetitive action such as tapping his foot. The teacher sees this as distracting during tests. John needs:
(7.1)

A. An IEP
B. A substantially separate classroom
C. A 504 Plan for the regular classroom
D. A one on one aide in the classroom

Answer C: A 504 Plan for the regular classroom

John is exhibiting normal grade level behavior with the exception of the ADHD behaviors, which may need some acceptance for his academic success. John has not shown any academic deficiencies. John needs a 504 Plan to provide small adaptations to meet his needs. These would be accommodations that would allow alternative behaviors that would meet his ADHD needs without distracting his classmates (e.g., wiggle seat, pillow or sponge to tap on, other "fiddle objects).

31. The transition activities that have to be addressed, unless the IEP team finds it uncalled for, include all of the following EXCEPT:
(Skill 8.4)

A. Instruction
B. Volunteer opportunities
C. Community experiences
D. Development of objectives related to employment and other post-school areas

Answer B: Volunteer opportunities

Volunteer opportunities, although worthwhile, are not listed as one of the three transition activities that have to be addressed on a student's IEP.

32. When a student begins to use assistive technology, it is important for the teacher to have a clear outline as to when and how the equipment should be used. Why?
(Skill 8.5)

A. To establish a level of accountability with the student.
B. To establish that the teacher has responsibility for the equipment that is in use in his or her room.
C. To establish that the teacher is responsible for the usage of the assistive technology.
D. To establish a guideline for evaluation.

Answer A: To establish a level of accountability with the student

Establishing clear parameters as to the usage of assistive technology in a classroom creates a level of accountability in the student. The student will know that the teacher understands the intended purpose and appropriate use of the device and expects the student to do so, as well.

33. Changes in requirements for an IEP's Current Levels of performance require: (Skill 7.4)

A. Parent/Guardian must attend either by phone conference or in person.
B. CSE chair must tell parents when child has unrealistic goals
C. Student voice in each Present Level of Performance
D. Teachers must write post adult outcomes assigning a student to a specific field

Answer: C. student voice in each Present Level of Performance

Idea's new Indicator 13 is changing the way IEPs are written. The federal government is requiring changes in IEPs to create an easier way to collect statistics on student success at reaching post school goals. While many of the requirements have been used for years, compliance is now being measured by the items listed below.

Present Levels of Performance: Student voice must be included in each Present Level of Performance. This means that Academic, Social, Physical, Management, etc. must include one student voice statement either in the strengths or needs or both. For example, "John reads fluently on a 3rd grade level. He is able to add and subtract two digit numbers. He has difficulty with grouping and multiplying. *John states that he would rather read than do math."*

Student voice can express either his/her strengths, preferences and/or interests. When the child begins to do vocational assessments, student voice should be related to transition to post-school activities of his/her choice. In addition, Present Levels of Performance must indicate why a student's post adult goals are realistic, or why they are not.

34. Effective management transition involves all of the following EXCEPT: (Skill 9.3)

A. Keeping students informed of the sequencing of instructional activities
B. Using group fragmentation
C. Changing the schedule frequently to maintain student interest
D. Using academic transition signals

Answer C: Changing the schedule frequently to maintain student interest

While you do want to use a variety of activities to maintain student interest, changing the schedule too frequently will result in loss of instructional time due to unorganized transitions. Effective teachers manage transitions from one activity to another in a systematically oriented way through efficient management of instructional matter, sequencing of instructional activities, movement of students in groups, and employment of academic transition signals. Through an efficient use of class time, achievement is increased, as students spend more class time engaged in on-task behavior.

35. Which of the following are critical to the success for the exceptional student placed in a general education classroom?: (Skill 9.4)

A. Access to appropriate accommodations and modifications
B. Support from the special education teacher
C. The general education teacher's belief that the student will profit from the placement
D. All of the above

Answer D: All of the above

In order for the exceptional student to be successful in the general education classroom, the needed curriculum and instructional accommodations and modifications must be made, and support from special education resources provided. Unfortunately, without the general education teacher's belief that the student can benefit, the necessary special accommodations will be provided. It should be noted that such failure to provide these accommodations violates the law.

36. Which of the following should be avoided when writing objectives for social behavior?
(Skill 10.1)

A. Non-specific adverbs
B. Behaviors stated as verbs
C. Criteria for acceptable performance
D. Conditions where the behavior is expected to be performed

Answer A: Non-specific adverbs

Behaviors should be specific. The more clearly the behavior is described, the less the chance for error.

37. Criteria for choosing behaviors that are most in need of change involve all EXCEPT the following:
(Skill 10.2)

A. Observations across settings to rule out certain interventions
B. Pinpointing the behavior that is the poorest fit with the child's environment
C. The teacher's concern about what is the most important behavior to target
D. Analysis of the environmental reinforcers

Answer C: The teacher's concern about what is the most important behavior to target

The teacher must take care of the criteria in A, B, and D. His or her concerns are of the least importance.

38. A BIP (Behavior Intervention Plan) is written to teach positive behavior. Which element listed below is NOT a standard feature of the plan?
(Skill 10.3)

A. Identification of behavior to be modified
B. Strategies to implement the replacement behavior
C. Statement of distribution
D. Team creation of BIP

Answer C: Statement of distribution

There is no statement on how or who shall receive the BIP on the student. Individual schools determine how the BIP is distributed and who requires a copy of the plan.

39. Teacher feedback, task completion, and a sense of pride over mastery or accomplishment of a skill are examples of:
(Skill 10.7)

A. Extrinsic reinforcers
B. Behavior modifiers
C. Intrinsic reinforcers
D. Positive feedback

Answer C: Intrinsic reinforcers

These are intangibles. Motivation may be achieved through intrinsic reinforcers or extrinsic reinforcers. Intrinsic reinforcers are usually intangible, and extrinsic reinforcers are usually tangible rewards from an external source.

40. Crisis intervention methods are above all concerned with:
(Skill 10.6)

A. Safety and well-being of the staff and students
B. Stopping the inappropriate behavior
C. Preventing the behavior from occurring again
D. The student learning that outbursts are inappropriate

Answer A: Safety and well-being of the staff and students

The safety and well being of students and staff are the primary concerns of crisis intervention plans. The other choices are all *elements* of maintaining everyone's safety.

41. Justin, a second grader, is reinforced if he is on task at the end of each ten-minute block of time that the teacher observes him. This is an example of what type of schedule?
(Skill 10.7)

A. Continuous
B. Fixed interval
C. Fixed ratio
D. Variable ratio

Answer B: Fixed interval

Ten minutes is a fixed interval of time.

42. A money bingo game was designed by Ms. Johnson for use with her middle grade students. Cards were constructed with different combinations of coins pasted on each of the nine spaces. Ms. Johnson called out various amounts of change (e.g., 30 cents), and students were instructed to cover the coin combinations on their cards that equaled the amount of change (e.g., two dimes and two nickels, three dimes, and so on). The student who had the first bingo was required to add the coins in each of the spaces covered and tell the amounts before being declared the winner. Five of Ms. Johnson's sixth graders played the game during the ten minutes of free activity time following math the first day the game was constructed. Which of the following attributes are present in this game in this situation? (Skill 11.2)

A. Accompanied by simple, uncomplicated rules
B. Of brief duration, permitting replay
C. Age appropriateness
D. All of the above

Answer D: All of the above

Games and puzzles should also be colorful and appealing, of relevance to individual students, and appropriate for learners at different skill levels in order to sustain interest and motivational value.

43. Transfer of learning occurs when: (Skill 11.3)

A. Experience with one task influences performance on another task
B. Content can be explained orally
C. Student experiences the "I got it!" syndrome
D. Curricular objective is exceeded

Answer A: Experience with one task influences performance on another task

Transfer of learning occurs when experience with one task influences performance on another task. Positive transfer occurs when the required responses and the stimuli are similar, and prior learning helps improve new learning. Negative transfer occurs when the stimuli remain similar, but the required responses change, so prior learning actually interferes with and retards new learning.

44. Taiquan's parents are divorced and have joint custody. They both have requested to be present at the IEP meeting. You call to make sure that they received the letter informing them of the coming IEP meeting. Taiquan's father did not receive the notification and is upset. You should:
(Skill 12.1)

A. Tell him that you could review the meeting with him later
B. Ask him if he can adjust his schedule
C. Tell him you can reschedule the meeting
D. Ask him to coordinate a time for the IEP meeting to meet with his ex-wife

Answer C: Tell him you can reschedule the meeting

A parent should be informed if he or she is divorced, has joint custody, and has expressed a desire to be present at the CSE. In this case, if the one of the parents wants to be at the meeting but is unable to attend, it should be rescheduled.

45. Which of these would not be considered a valid attempt to contact a parent for an IEP meeting?
(Skill 12.2)

A. Telephone call
B. Copy of correspondence
C. Message left on answering machine
D. Record of home visits

Answer C: Message left on answering machine

A message left on an answering machine is not direct contact. In addition, it may violate confidentiality regulations, since anyone might overhear the message when it is played back.

46. Otumba is a 16 year old in your class who recently came from Nigeria. The girls in your class have come to you to complain about the way he treats them in a sexist manner. When they complain, you reflect that this is also the way he treats adult females. You have talked to Otumba before about appropriate behavior. What should you do first? (Skill 12.3)

A. Complain to the principal
B. Ask for a parent-teacher conference
C. Check to see if this is a cultural norm in his country
D. Create a behavior contract for him to follow

Answer C: Check to see if this is a cultural norm in his country

While A, B, and D are good actions, it is important to remember that Otumba comes from a culture where women are treated differently than they are in America. Learning this information will enable the school as a whole to address this behavior.

47. The integrated approach to learning utilizes all available resources to address student needs. What are the resources? (Skill 13.1)

A. The student, his or her parents, and the teacher.
B. The teacher, the parents, and the special education team.
C. The teacher, the student, and an administrator to perform needed interventions
D. The student, his or her parents, the teacher, and community resources.

Answer D: The student, his or her parents, the teacher, and community resources

The integrated response encompasses all possible resources, including the resources in the community.

48. According to IDEA law, a student cannot be removed from school for disciplinary reasons if:
(Skill 10.3)

A. The student's behavior represents a danger to himself or others
B. The student's misbehavior is a manifestation of the student's disability
C. The student is under age 14
D. The school does not have parent permission

Answer B: The student's misbehavior is a manifestation of the student's disability.

According to IDEA a student with a disability can be removed from class as a disciplinary tactic for less than ten days in order to give the team time to implement an FBA and determine whether the behavior is due to the student's disability. If the student's behavior is assessed to be part of the student's disability, the student's placement cannot be modified as part of a disciplinary tactic. Of course, the IEP team may consult and decide that the student's behavior indicates that a modification of placement is required in order to provide in order for the student to have access to a free and appropriate education.

49. The ability to supply specific instructional materials, programs, and methods, as well as the ability to influence environmental learning variables, are advantages of which service model for exceptional students?
(Skill 13.3)

A. Regular classroom
B. Consultant teacher
C. Itinerant teacher
D. Resource room

Answer B: Consultant teacher

Consultation is usually done by specialists.

50. Knowledge of evaluation strategies, program interventions, and types of data are examples of which variable for a successful consultation program?
(Skill 13.4)

A. People
B. Process
C. Procedural implementation
D. Academic preparation

Answer B: Process

Consultation programs cannot be successful without knowledge of the process.

51. Janice requires occupational therapy and speech therapy services. What must her teacher do to ensure her needs are met?
(Skill 13.5)

A. Watch the services being rendered
B. Schedule collaboratively
C. Ask for services to be given in a push-in model
D. Ask to be trained to give the service him or herself

Answer B: Schedule collaboratively

Collaborative scheduling of students to receive services is the responsibility of both the teacher and the service provider. Scheduling together allows for the convenience of both. It also will provide the teacher with an opportunity to make sure the student does not miss important information.

52. Which of these is the best resource a teacher can have to reach a student?
(Skill 13.6)

A. Contact with the parents/guardians
B. A successful behavior modification exam
C. A listening ear
D. Gathered scaffold approach to teaching

Answer A: Contact with the parents/guardians

Parents are often the best source of information on their children. They generally know if a behavior management technique will be successful.

53. The early 19th century is considered a period of great importance in the field of special education because principles presently used in working with exceptional students were formulated by Itard. These principles included:
(Skill 14.1)

A. Individualized instruction
B. Sequence of tasks
C. Functional life-like skills curriculum
D. All of the above

Answer D: All of the above

A French Physician, Jean Marc Itard, found a boy abandoned in the woods of Aveyron, France. His attempts to civilize and educate the boy, Victor, established these principles, including developmental and multisensory approaches. At that time, students with mild intellectual sensory impairments, mild intellectual disabilities, and emotional disorders were referred to as "idiotic" or "insane."

54. How was the training of special education teachers changed by the No Child Left Behind Act of 2002?
(Skill 14.2)

A. It required all special education teachers to be certified in reading and math
B. It required all special education teachers to take the same coursework as general education teachers
C. If a special education teacher is teaching a core subject, he or she must meet the standard of a highly qualified teacher in that subject
D. All of the above

Answer C: If a special education teacher is teaching a core subject, he or she must meet the standard of a highly qualified teacher in that subject

In order for a special education teacher to be a student's sole teacher of a core subject, he or she must meet the professional criteria of NCLB. The teacher must be *highly qualified*—that is, certified or licensed in the appropriate area of special education—and show proof of a specific level of professional development in the core subjects that he or she teaches. As special education teachers receive specific education in the core subject they teach, they will be better prepared to teach to the same level of learning standards as the general education teacher.